RELIGION ACROSS BORDER

RELIGION ACROSS BORDER

Dr Rajeev Prasad

MD PUBLICATIONS PVT LTD
NEW DELHI
www.mdppl.com

Published by :

MD Publications Pvt Ltd
"MD House", 11, Darya Ganj,
New Delhi - 110 002
Phone : +91-11-41563325 (Customer Service)
+91-11-41562846 (Editorial)
E-mail (orders): order@mdppl.com
Website: www.mdppl.com

ISBN: 978-81-7533-240-9

Published and Printed by **Mr. Pranav Gupta** on behalf of MD Publications Pvt Ltd at Mohit Enterprises, New Delhi.

PREFACE

This religious perspective on life can also be empowering. People who occupy low-status and marginal positions in society can be reassured of their own self-worth and inspired to action. Religious experiences and visions can provide a critical perspective against which to judge the world and toward which to work for change. Religious traditions often provide alternative ways to look at the world and offer people the promise that God will help them. Even worship that appears to have little to say about this world may give important spiritual strength to the worshipers.

One of the most significant aspects of a congregation's life is simply its size. Larger congregations have more resources - of all sorts - than smaller ones. While most people are in moderate-to-large congregations, most congregations are quite small. In the country as a whole, half of all congregations have fewer than 75 regular participants. In rural areas, the average size is even smaller. The typical urban congregation has about 100 people on an average weekend. The typical rural congregation has less than 50. In other words, in all communities there are many small gatherings, alongside a few much larger, more visible ones. The larger ones, together, have most of the members, but the smaller ones are themselves more numerous.

While congregations are intimately involved in the good work that is done in every community, their primary task is not the delivery of social services or supporting cultural organizations. Their primary task is the spiritual well-being of their members. Across every tradition and in every region, congregations agree - their highest priority is providing opportunities for vital spiritual worship. That is where leaders put the most energy, and that is the first thing members look for when they are seeking a place to join. Congregations cooperate with other voluntary organizations in other important community activities, as well.

They contribute to programs of education and service provision that surround issues as diverse as AIDS, unwanted pregnancies, handicapped persons, adoption, and more. They support and refer parishioners to counseling centers of all sorts. And they cooperate with others in delivering spiritual care to people in hospitals, nursing homes, on college campuses, and even in police and fire departments. These needs are less basic than the food, clothing, and shelter provided by human service organizations, but they are no less essential to community life.

On-going efforts to build up the strength of a community are captured in our "community development" category. Most of these are all-purpose associations - block watch groups, neighborhood associations, civic clubs, and the like. They take on tasks as mundane as trash pickup and as complicated as policing issues. Some of them attempt to implement longer-term changes that are needed to make the community a better place to live. Providing permanent affordable housing is one of the most common activities in which these congregations are involved.

I am very grateful to Mr. Pranav Gupta, Director of MD Publications Pvt Ltd, New Delhi, for his kind cooperation and support for this book.

Dr Rajeev Prasad

Contents

1

Lessons from American Immigrant Congregations

When we think of the great masses of immigrants who came to the shores of America around the turn of the twentieth century, most of us envision vast steamships, overloaded with people, all peering up towards the towering Statue of Liberty at the port of New York. We imagine these travellers encountering Ellis Island, or its forerunner, Castle Gardens, the tedious processing they endured, and the excitement they must have felt when stepping out into the city for the first time. Not many people realize that Baltimore was the second largest port of entry for immigrants in America. Instead of the Statue of Liberty, these immigrants first saw the enormous American flag flying above the star-shaped stronghold, Fort McHenry. Instead of Ellis Island, they came through Locust Point at the mouth of Baltimore's Inner Harbor. Before the Civil War, most immigrants arrived in Baltimore via the wharves of Fell's Point, including both West European immigrants and slaves aboard ships from Africa.

Following the Civil War in 1868, the Baltimore & Ohio Railroad, partnered with the North German Lloyd Steamship Line to construct two terminals for steamship lines and railroads at Locust Point on the other side of the Inner Harbor. Many immigrants utilized Baltimore as a port to the West, following the B and O Railroad, while others found large, thriving immigrant communities and stayed here. In 1869, Mrs. Koether, herself a German immigrant, ran a boarding house at Pier 9 on Locust Point. She was paid by the steamship companies to feed and house new immigrants, earning $0.75 per person. She served her first meal to 350 newcomers of all backgrounds. For the next fifty years, she would receive as many as 40,000 newcomers per year. Locust Point did not regularly function as an inspection center in the same vein as Ellis Island or Castle Gardens. Rather, because Baltimore's Inner Harbor was so far inland, doctors and immigration officials often boarded the ships while they were still in the Chesapeake Bay.

An employee of one of the German steamship lines described the situation: The quarantine men boarded the boat on its way up the bay. Every immigrant went through a quick medical examination. Checking of the luggage by Customs was a quick and cursory affair. From that point, most of the immigrants who landed in Baltimore stepped aboard B & O trains and travelled on to Chicago, St. Louis, or Cincinnati. Similar to Ellis Island, each passenger was checked for diseases, including trachoma, a contagious eye disease. The Baltimore Sun, in 1904, described the examination process, "Quickly and skillfully the doctor lifted the eyelids of each [passenger], for it is here that disease usually manifests itself. A quick glance was given to the head also for traces of favus, a disease of the scalp, before the alien was passed along." Following their examination, the immigrants were directed into "pens" and grouped alphabetically at the terminal.

Their information was then verified, and they were redirected again. Immigrants remaining in Baltimore were led to another pen to wait for friends or relatives. Other immigrants went to the ticket counter and bought their tickets for trains heading west. The Baltimore Sun proclaimed Locust Point to be "far superior" to Ellis Island, as the landing facilities, examination area, and train terminal existed "not only in the same building, but on the same floor..." The number of immigrants entering Baltimore increased substantially during the 1800s. In 1820, only a few hundred came to Baltimore. When Locust Point opened in 1868, it welcomed more than ten thousand travellers, compared to fewer than four thousand the previous year. In 1907, Baltimore reached its peak, with 1,285,000 immigrants disembarking at Locust Point. In 1913, the federal government took over Mrs. Koether's boarding house and the B&O Railroad terminals, constructing three new large buildings. However, just as the buildings were finished, World War I broke out, effectively ending the surging wave of immigration.

After July 1914, no new immigrants entered Baltimore through Locust Point. Baltimore's Jewish Immigrant Community While the largest wave of immigrants into Baltimore came in the late 19th and early 20th centuries, the first waves of Jewish immigrants began coming to Baltimore fifty years earlier. Beginning in the mid-1800s, many Jews fled intolerance in Bavaria (southern part of present-day Germany) for America. Bavaria curtailed the rights of Jews, making it difficult for them to settle or marry, so as to limit the Jewish population living there. Furthermore, anti-Semitic riots plagued central Europe in 1819 and again in 1848. Not all Jews were escaping persecution however; many also came for the economic opportunities America presented. In 1820, only about 120 Jews lived in Baltimore.

By the onset of the Civil War, 7,000 Jewish German immigrants had made their new home in Baltimore. They primarily moved into East Baltimore, not far from the Inner Harbor. Many started off as itinerant (or "wandering") peddlers, offering goods, such as dishes or tools, door to door. Those who succeeded then opened shops, particularly along Lombard Street, the commercial center of East Baltimore. Most of the new immigrants were traditional

Jews who formed informal congregations. The first legally chartered congregation was Nidchei Yisroel (the Scattered of Israel), licensed in 1829. It still exists today as Baltimore Hebrew Congregation. In 1845, they opened the first synagogue in Maryland, the Lloyd Street Synagogue. Jewish schools, charitable societies, literary clubs, and other organizations soon followed, making Baltimore appealing to other Jewish immigrants. Beginning in the late 1870s and through the 1910s, many Russian and East European Jews travelled to America for its economic opportunities.

Furthermore, after 1877, many came to Baltimore in response to periodic violent riots known as pogroms. Like the earlier immigrants from Germany, the Russian and East European Jews moved into East Baltimore, peddling goods and working in the sweatshops. They too established newspapers, schools, social clubs, beneficial societies, and other organizations specifically designed for newcomers. At the same time as new Eastern European immigrants were arriving, many of the German Jews had become successful and moved northwest in the city, relocating their homes and synagogues to fashionable Eutaw Place. By 1903, all German Jewish synagogues had moved uptown. Furthermore, German Jewish religious practice had become more liberal over the generations, compared to the more traditional approach of the new arrivals from East Europe and Russia. During the early 20th century, the Jewish community was able to grow in numbers and advance economically. 23,000 Jews, about 70% of the community, worked in the clothing industry, a quarter of the overall garment labour force.

Having been in America for several generations, the German Jews now prospered. Several opened large factories and warehouses, employing large numbers of the newer Jewish immigrants. While the work was difficult and the conditions often deplorable, these jobs created incomes for new families. Both shop owners and workers, many making as little as twelve dollars a week, saved money and organized charitable organizations to support the burgeoning Jewish community.

Modern Day Immigration

Today, Baltimore's immigrant experience has changed remarkably. Instead of enormous ships serving as floating cities, most new immigrants come by airplane from overseas or by car from the Americas. According to the Maryland Office for New Americans (MONA), immigrants and refugees account for 10% of Maryland's 5.5 million residents. According to the Baltimore magazine, Urbanite, "Immigrants account for 5.5 percent of Baltimore residents, roughly half the national average, with Asians making up the largest proportion, and Mexicans the fastest-growing. African communities are on the rise, particularly among Nigerians.

West Indians, from Jamaica and Trinidad and Tobago, are arriving in growing numbers." Several organizations are dedicated to welcoming Baltimore's immigrant communities, including MONA, the Immigration Outreach Services Center at St. Matthew's Roman Catholi c Church and the Baltimore Resettlement Project. Today's Jewish immigrants come primarily from the former Soviet Union and Iran. Iranian Jewish immigrants left their homeland following the Iranian Revolution of 1978. Jews have also been arriving from Russia since the demise of communism and the collapse of the Soviet Union in 1991.

Within the Baltimore Jewish community, there are many organizations that assist new immigrants, including HIAS (Hebrew Immigrant Aid Society), J.O.I.N. (Jewish Outreach Intervention Network) for Russian-speaking teens and their families, JURI (Jewish Union of Russian Immigrants), JVS (Jewish Vocational Services) Immigrant Employment Services, and the Ezras Ameinu Immigrant Education Center.

Early Jewish Baltimore Timeline

1657: Maryland's first known Jewish colonist appears: Dr. Jacob Lumbrozo, who lives in Calvert County.

1729: Baltimore Town is chartered.

1768: Merchant Jacob Hart signs his name to a petition. He is the first known Jew to live in Baltimore.

1786: Around thirty Jews live in Baltimore. They maintain a burial ground on land owned by Charles Carroll and William McMechen (exact location unknown).

1814: Several Jews are among the American forces at the Battle of Fort McHenry.

1820: Baltimore's Jewish population reaches 120. A substantial migration of Jews from Bavaria and other German states begins in the 1820s and lasts for decades, peaking in the 1850s. Most of the new arrivals settle in East Baltimore.

1826: After heated debate, the "Jew Bill" is enacted by the Maryland legislature, modifying the state constitution's Christian oath requirement for public office. A few months later, Solomon Etting and Jacob Cohen are elected to the Baltimore City Council.

1829: Baltimore Hebrew Congregation becomes the first incorporated Jewish organization in Maryland. It meets in rented rooms over a grocery at Bond and Fleet streets.

1840: Rabbi Abraham Rice (1800-1862) arrives from Bavaria to serve the Baltimore Hebrew Congregation. He is the first ordained rabbi in America.

1842: Har Sinai Congregation starts meeting at Moses Hutzler's home in Fells Point as a Reform alternative to the traditionalist Baltimore Hebrew Congregation. Today it is the oldest Reform congre-gation in America in continuous operation.

1845: Baltimore Hebrew Congregation builds the Lloyd Street Synagogue, the first synagogue in Maryland

and, today, the third oldest surviving synagogue building in the U.S. A separate mikvah and schoolhouse are constructed behind the synagogue.

1849: Rabbi Rice resigns from Baltimore Hebrew Congregation, dismayed by his congregants' growing religious laxity. Traditionalists at Baltimore Hebrew nevertheless maintain control over the ritual life of the congregation. Two years later Rabbi Rice founds a small, strictly Orthodox congregation at his home, which will eventually grow into Congregation Shearith Israel.

1851: 150 students attend school at Lloyd Street Synagogue.

1852: Fewer students attend as a new school is built uptown.

1853: The Oheb Shalom congregation is founded by up-and-coming German immigrants as a midway alternative to Har Sinai's radical Reform and Baltimore Hebrew Congregation's continued (yet increasingly fractious) Orthodoxy.

1860: Schoolhouse demolished.

1861: The Civil War divides Baltimore Jewry, with most Jews trying to maintain a moderate position. Oheb Shalom's Rabbi David Einhorn's abolitionist newspaper, Sinai, is destroyed by a pro-slavery mob and Einhorn flees to Philadelphia. He does not return.

1867: The North German Lloyd Steamship Line joins with the B&O Railroad to boost shipping links between Baltimore and Bremen. The ships transport Maryland tobacco and lumber to Germany; on the reverse trip they bring immigrants. Other steamship lines also step up traffic, bringing an immediate rise in immigration to Baltimore from German port cities. Over coming decades, Baltimore's Jewish population will be swelled by the Central and East European Jews who stream into the steamship companies' docks at Locust Point.

1870: Traditionalists at Baltimore Hebrew Congregation who can no longer keep Reform at bay break off to form Chizuk Amuno, a traditional congregation. By century's end, Baltimore Hebrew and Oheb Shalom are counted as Reform, while Chizuk Amuno joins the Conservative movement.

1876: Chizuk Amuno builds the last great German Jewish synagogue in East Baltimore, on Lloyd Street just a few steps from its forerunner, Baltimore Hebrew. But the Germans soon begin their move uptown, and within twenty years the neo- Moorish building will become home to B'nai Israel, founded in 1873.

1881: A wave of pogroms in the Russian Empire helps spur the Great Migration of East European Jewry to America. The Jewish population of Baltimore grows from 10,000 in 1880 to 24,000 in 1890. Most of the new arrivals find work in the sweatshops and factories of the city's garment district. The East Europeans create a bustling culture in East Baltimore, with their own synagogues, communal institutions, and shops.

1890: With economic success enabling more and more German Jews to move "uptown," Baltimore Hebrew becomes the first congregation to leave East Baltimore. After selling the Lloyd Street Synagogue to a Lithuanian Catholic parish, it settles into the imposing Madison Avenue Temple in the fashionable northwest Baltimore neighborhood of Eutaw Place. All the established German Jewish congregations relocate uptown by 1903, constructing monumental temples.

1893: The Lithuanian Catholic parish, St. John the Baptist, constructs a bell tower on Lloyd Street Synagogue. 1904 Baltimore & Ohio Railroad builds an immigration pier at Locust Point to serve North German Lloyd Co. steamships.

1905: After 15 years as St. John the Baptist, the Lloyd Street Synagogue once again becomes home to a Jewish congregation, Shomrei Mishmeres Hakadosh. Its spiritual leader, Rabbi Avraham Schwartz, becomes known as the "chief rabbi" of the Orthodox East European Jewish community. Shomrei Mishmeres occupies the Synagogue until disbanding in the 1950s. They remove the bell tower and add a new bimah.

1907: Some 40,000 Jews live in Baltimore.

1914: The onset of World War I brings migration from Europe to a standstill. During the war, Baltimore Jewry raises funds to help suffering Jews in the wartorn Pale of Settlement.

1920s: Chandeliers salvaged from demolished Second Presbyterian Church installed. Second Presbyterian had been located around the corner from Lloyd Street Synagogue, on the corner of Baltimore and Lloyd Street.

1921-1924: New federal laws cut off immigration from Eastern and Southern Europe, ending the Great Migration of East European Jewry. Some 65,000 Jews live in Baltimore.

1933: Adolph Hitler comes to power in Germany and immediately initiates anti-Semitic actions. Jews begin to leave, though U.S. immigration restrictions hamper their efforts. Around 3,000 German Jewish refugees settle in Baltimore between 1933 and 1941, aided by individual Jewish Baltimoreans as well as the city's organized Jewish community.

1950s-1970s: A new generation of Baltimore Jewry continues the geographic move north and west, into upper Park Heights, Pikesville, Reisterstown, and beyond. Many synagogues locate along the upper Park Heights corridor. Block-busting by real estate speculators causes rapid racial turnover in West Baltimore, including Jewish areas such as Eutaw Place and lower Park Heights. East Baltimore suffers the effects of disinvestment, job loss, poverty, and misguided urban renewal.

1957: Baltimore's Jewish population is estimated at 80,000.

1958: With most of its membership base having moved from East Baltimore, the dwindling Shomrei Mishmeres Congregation contemplates selling the deteriorating Lloyd Street Synagogue to commercial buyers. Wilbur Hunter, director of the Peale Museum, learns of the potential sale and alerts the Baltimore Jewish community to the urgent need to save the building from possible destruction. The Baltimore Board of Rabbis appoints a committee to investigate how the historic landmark might be preserved.

1960: The Jewish Historical Society of Maryland is created, with the mission to acquire, renovate, and maintain the Lloyd Street Synagogue. Four years later the partially-restored Synagogue is dedicated and opened to the public.

1968: Baltimore is hit by riots after the death of Martin Luther King, Jr. Many of the remaining Jewish businesses in East Baltimore are damaged and never reopen. Today, the famed delicatessens of Corned Beef Row on Lombard Street persist as the only remnant of Jewish commercial life in East Baltimore.

1970s: The two latest waves of Jewish migration to Baltimore gather force. Iranian Jews arrive after the Iranian Revolution of 1978. Soviet Jews leave Russia in increasing numbers, a trend that has continued in the post-Communist era.

1975: Baltimore's Jewish population is estimated at 94,000, tenth largest in America.

1981: B'nai Israel Congregation deeds its Lloyd Street building to the Jewish Historical Society of Maryland. The Society restores the synagogue while leasing it back to B'nai Israel, which remains to this day the oldest continuously-operating Orthodox congregation in Baltimore.

1987: The Jewish Historical Society of Maryland opens a Jewish Heritage Center on the lot between the Lloyd Street Synagogue and the B'nai Israel Synagogue. In 1998 the Society and Heritage Center will become known as the Jewish Museum of Maryland.

1999: Baltimore's Jewish population is 91,400, according to the Associated's Jewish Community Study of Baltimore (2001). The study notes that Baltimore has the largest percentage of Orthodox households of any community in the U.S. The study also reports that Baltimore's Jewish community remains active and close- knit, with a high degree of Jewish cultural participation and ritual observance.

Colonial Foundations

One of the reasons given for USA have higher levels of interest in religion is that the USA was supposedly built on religious foundations. Some of its earliest immigrants went to America to find religious freedom. They were seeking the opportunity to develop new communities in which they could practice their faith as they thought it should be practiced. In contrast, Australian immigration began with convicts. In the earliest days of the colony, the churches were part of the penal structure in which the establishment sought to maintain control over the convicts. Convicts were forced to go to church. However, the contrast between religion in America and Australia is not as clear as that. A book published in 1992 by Roger Finke and Rodney Stark, The Churching of America, 1776-1990, has sought to rework the figures on growth and decline of churches in America. Their work raises real questions about the stereotypes that Australians, and many Americans, have about their origins, and about the factors which lead to growth and decline in churches. From a detailed analysis of historical data, Finke and Stark argue that from the very beginning, the Puritans only made up a small portion of the immigrants. In 1776, between 10 and 20 percent of Americans actually belonged to a church. The rates were lower in the southern colonies of Virginia, North and South Carolina and Georgia because slaves made up 42 percent of the population and most slaves did not have the option of going to church even if they had wanted to do so. Among white people, however, the rates were generally around 20 percent in most of the colonies.

Finke and Stark point to the factors which push and pull people to immigrate. The major factors which push people to move to a new land are:

1. Lack of opportunity in the old land
2. Weak attachments
3. Fear of punishment
4. Disgrace
5. Persecution.

The factors which pull people are:

1. Economic opportunity
2. Anonymity and escape
3. Greater freedom.

As these factors were present in the eighteenth century in America, some farmers, miners and merchants were encouraged to seek a better life, as did some religious minorities who had experienced persecution. However, many immigrants were 'scoundrels, misfits, and others of dubious past and character, who were fleeing their pasts or seeking opportunities to practice illegal or morally stigmatized activities'. To these were added 50,000 convicts from England and 16,000 from Ireland transported to America between 1718 and 1775. This was also true among clergy. The clergy who were willing to go to America were often people leaving to escape 'debts, wives, or onerous duties'. The first Methodist Bishop in America, Thomas Coke described them in 1793 as 'with few exceptions to the contrary, as bad a set of men as perhaps ever disgraced the Church of God'.

In the seventeenth century, the Episcopalians (Church of England) enjoyed legal establishment in New York, Virginia, Maryland, North and South Carolina and Georgia. The Congregationalists were established in New England. This meant that clergy were paid by the government from taxes and thus were not reliant on their congregations. As Adam Smith noted in 1776, clergy not reliant on the voluntary contributions of their congregations were less likely to approach the task of building their churches with zeal and industry. Between 1776 and 1850 the religious profile of America changed very considerably. The Congregationalists, Episcopalians, and, to a lesser extent, the Presbyterians, declined. The Baptists and Catholics grew, and the Methodist church experienced a meteoric rise, as shown in the graph opposite.

Different Styles of Leadership

Finke and Stark argue that a range of factors caused this change. The Baptist and Methodist churches, particularly on the frontiers, were often led by 'amateurs'. In the Methodist system, only the circuit-riders were full-time professionals. These 'amateurs' were often recommended by the small congregations, or emerged as leaders within them. With local control, these churches were able to respond to the specific needs of the local people. Most of these leaders had little formal education, but were often neighbours, friends or relatives of the members of their congregations, and shared their wants, needs and desires. In general, there was a good supply of such leaders. Many Baptist and Methodist clergy received little pay. Even the Methodist circuit riders received only $100 per year in 1834. In comparison, the annual income Presbyterian and Congregational clergy was between $400 and $1000 in small country towns and $1000 to $3000 in large towns.

The low overheads and use of unpaid clergy meant the Baptists and Methodists could sustain small congregations in isolated areas. The Congregationalists, on the other hand, opted for well-paid, highly-trained clergy, despite such people being in short supply. Their churches were often organised through town meetings and were supported by the town's religious taxes. However, churches were only established where there were sufficient resources to support the institution. Consequently, Congregationalists failed to establish many churches outside New England.

The very level of education of their clergy, often increased the social distance between the clergy and their actual or potential congregations. With many colleges, universities, seminaries, and other possibilities, these clergy also had a variety of 'career opportunities' to which they could move - apart from building local congregations. The Episcopalians were badly affected by the American Revolution and lost much of their support from England. The Presbyterians failed to expand as much as they might have done because of the energy put into the enforcement of national standards on polity and doctrine which tended to shatter the unity for which they worked so hard.

Different Styles in the Message

Another factor in the growth of the Baptists and Methodists, say Finke and Stark, was the nature of the message. The Episcopalian, Presbyterian and Congregational clergy preached literate and intellectual sermons, but they did not convey the same power as the direct, simple messages of the Methodists and Baptists. If the goal was to arouse faith, the carefully drafted, scholarly, and often dry sermons of the learned clergy were no match for the impromptu emotional pleas of the uneducated pre vance. Local clergy and laity were trained to work with people who made religious commitments.

While Finney and Whitefield held their meetings mainly in towns and cities, rural America developed its own evangelistic method: the camp meeting. These were very popular among the isolated farming communities. Many came, not only to renew their faith, but to meet old friends and make new acquaintances. For many farming communities, the camp meetings with their revival preaching were their annual holiday. The mainstream denominations would not take part in the camp meetings or the revival campaigns. They condemned the theology, the emotional dimensions, and the fact that women were allowed to pray with men. Such methods did not suit their educated, genteel styles. In that sense, says Finke and Stark, those mainstream denominations 'chose to lose'.

Models for Successful Churches

Behind the historical analysis of Finke and Stark lies a model of why religious groups grow and decline. That model has become known as the 'Rational Choice Model'. It is developed at length in Rodney Stark and William Sims Bainbridge, A Theory of Religion, first published in 1987. Finke, Bainbridge and Stark are arguing that religious groups which have the flexibility, freedom and desire to meet the situation of the 'religious market place' are most likely to succeed. Their theories will be explored further in other issues of Pointers this year. The well-being of every community depends on harnessing the contributions of its citizens. Sustaining viable communities requires places where people can gather, work together, and learn to trust one another – where we generate what Robert Putnam has called "social capital.

We depend on the neighborhood associations and political action groups, parent associations and leagues of civil rights activists, as well as the churches, synagogues, and mosques that provide places of concern, belonging and action. This is a report on the work being done by such religious organizations and their community partners in seven representative communities in the U.S. In 1997, the Hartford Institute for Religion Research launched the "Organizing Religious Work" project in an effort to document and better understand what people of faith are doing in their communities and which organizations enable them to accomplish their goals. You can find additional information about the study and about our Institute on this site. For this study, we selected seven research sites: Albuquerque, Nashville, Chicago, Hartford, rural counties in Alabama, rural counties in Missouri, and Seattle. Our work in each place was assisted by a research team from a local university.

These seven areas allowed us to catch a glimpse of the country as a whole (and our results have been statistically weighted to approximate known characteristics of the nation's congregations and their attenders). Across the country, we talked with representatives of 549 congregations and surveyed all the attenders in 32 of them. We also gathered information on nearly 6000 connections between congregations and other organizations, and we talked with nearly 200 representatives of those organizations. We compiled all the surveys, transcribed and analyzed all the interviews, and this is a report on what we have found.

Throughout the nation, more than 300,000 congregations provide a point of gathering, worship, and community engagement for the roughly half of Americans who participate on a regular basis in them. They range from small storefronts to huge mega-complexes, from traditional Protestants and Catholics to newer arrivals like Hindus and Muslims. The sheer pervasiveness of these organizations makes them impossible to ignore for anyone who is looking for ways to mobilize energy toward the good of communities. What we will see in the pages to follow is that they are already remarkably involved in serving both their own members and the larger community. But they do not do their work alone. It is by weaving together a network of money, volunteers, and other supports that service agencies and congregations together do good in their communities. We hope that this report will remind you of how important that is, highlight for you the key partners in your community, and inspire your own imagination in thinking about how you can be involved.

Congregational Connections in the U.S.

The nation's congregations are important links in the delivery of the services and activities that make their communities a better place in which to live.

A total of 6 community outreach organizations:

- On average, 2 of these provide direct services – food, clothing, and shelter — to people in need. Congregations connect to organizations like food pantries, soup kitchens, shelters for victims of domestic abuse, and hundreds of ministerial alliances that coordinate emergency relief.
- 1 connection may support long-term community development and/or makes possible political and social advocacy. This might be Habitat for Humanity, Urban League, a neighborhood association, Heifer Project, or Bread for the World.
- 2 connections help to provide activities that enhance the educational, health and cultural life of the community, such as day care centers, scout troops, blood banks, and theatre groups.
- Among the one quarter of congregations who engage in evangelistic and mission work (beyond what they do on their own or through their denomination), each congregation helps to support 2 organizations that do

evangelistic outreach, including such groups as Campus Crusade for Christ, Gideons, or Youth With a Mission.

- The remainder are connections to a variety of other civic and social causes, including many opportunities for personal growth and self-help.

And all of this is in addition to the work they do through their own individual congregation, through their denomination, or by way of the encouragement they give to their own members to be personally involved. Not all congregations are equally involved, and different congregations emphasize different kinds of activities or different sorts of organizational partners. But the overall level of connection between congregations and community organizations is considerable. Only forty-nine of the 549 congregations we interviewed reported that they did no work that connected them beyond their own internal or denominational organizations. In the sections that follow, we will look more closely at who these congregations are and what they do. Before we return to a more detailed look at their community connections, it is important to put them in perspective...

The Work of Congregations

While congregations are intimately involved in the good work that is done in every community, their primary task is not the delivery of social services or supporting cultural organizations. Their primary task is the spiritual well-being of their members. Across every tradition and in every region, congregations agree – their highest priority is providing opportunities for vital spiritual worship. That is where leaders put the most energy, and that is the first thing members look for when they are seeking a place to join. Some people might think that this spiritual activity is irrelevant to the larger community, that it is "otherworldly." It is certainly true that the effects of a worship service are less easily measured than the effects of a food pantry or job training program. But worship services can make a real difference, too. People we have interviewed tell us that worship is a time when they put their individual priorities in perspective, reminding themselves of what is really important in life. Participating in worship and religious ritual reminds people that they are not the center of the universe and that they should care for others. Congregations of all sorts are places that teach people to "do unto others" as they would wish others to do unto them. Even people who disagree about many other things, agree that this is at the heart of being a religiously-faithful person. And they agree that it is important for children to have a place that teaches them right from wrong. In a society that often seems at moral loose ends, congregations provide a community in which values are discussed and modeled for the good of children and adults alike.

The link between worship and everyday life was made by the pastor of a large Chicago African-American Baptist church. He said, "All of us are in the same boat. My main burden is to get us to see the need to move closer to the Lord, to exercise our gifts, to get out there and exercise our faith, to help somebody, to be real Christians, and to be committed to what we're about." The same message was voiced in a different way by the pastor of a mid-sized Seattle Episcopal parish:

"I think most people who come here have recognized that they need spiritual and ethical moorings in their lives. It's not just working and consuming and spending leisure time, there has to be a spiritual pursuit....We're not holding up a model of the church that says we live in another age and everything's black and white. We're saying, these questions have been around in different forms for a long time and there's a way in which one can journey through life without becoming totally unglued. I think that people are looking for a way to make a difference in the world. We're seeing a real interest in outreach here. People want to reach out and help others. People are also looking for something that's transcendent from their lives. They come to worship and want to have a spiritual experience."

The Rabbi of a large Hartford Conservative Jewish synagogue, describing a "Havurah" (prayer and study) group, said,

"When we get together, there's a great hunger for basics and for kind of a spiritual dimension, the poetry behind the concrete action. We try to provide that whenever possible."

And the pastor of a mid-sized Southern Baptist church in Seattle returned to the theme of helping members make connections between their spiritual lives and everyday situations. "In members' daily life, there is a lot of possibility for compromise. There's a lot of temptation to do a lot of things. And just that week-by-week encouragement, the focus on being connected with God, encountering God – we strive to do that."

This religious perspective on life can also be empowering. People who occupy low-status and marginal positions in society can be reassured of their own self-worth and inspired to action. Religious experiences and visions can provide a critical perspective against which to judge the world and toward which to work for change. Religious traditions often provide alternative ways to look at the world and offer people the promise that God will help them. Even worship that appears to have little to say about this world may give important spiritual strength to the worshipers.

The work congregations put second on their list – right behind worship and spiritual life – is "fellowship." They see themselves as a family, a community of people who care for each other and do things together. Again, there is very broad agreement about how important this work is. Across religious traditions, regions, class, and ethnicity people agree about what is most basic to congregational life. Leaders say they work hard at providing this family-like atmosphere, and members say they are looking for a warm, friendly community when they choose a congregation to join. Again, it would be easy to dismiss this inwardlooking emphasis as irrelevant, perhaps even harmful, to the larger community.

The danger that many see is that people may gather in congregations that are insular, basking in the warmth of people just like themselves, and perhaps despising those who are different. Such a barricade mentality is clearly unhealthy, and some congregations are guilty. But there are also good reasons to celebrate the "bonding" that is going on inside congregations. As Robert Putnam has recently argued, in his book Bowling Alone, every society needs the "social capital" that is generated when people gather in voluntary organizations, working and playing together.

- As we learn to communicate with each other and trust each other, we provide a vital network that helps to hold society together.
- As we work together, debating and organizing to get things done, we also provide valuable opportunities for people to learn the civic skills they need for participation in democracy.
- And as we care for each other through thick and thin, we pick up much of the first-line social service delivery that might otherwise have to be done by government agencies.

All of the work that congregations do at building up a caring, functioning internal community pays off for the larger community, even if indirectly. Even the insularity of some congregations is not all bad. When a group of people is disadvantaged in the larger society, the existence of an alternative community is critical. African Americans have long known that black churches were a vital refuge. What happened there on Sunday morning (and throughout the week) enabled community leadership development, celebrated and preserved a unique culture, created a space where the rules and authorities of the other culture were suspended, and provided a staging-ground for action. Today (as throughout our history), dozens of immigrant communities are discovering similar benefits. And in an American culture that is less committed to assimilation than it used to be, congregations of all sorts are places where the many unique cultures of this nation are nurtured and passed on. Earlier immigrant congregations typically disappeared after their members (or their children) learned English. But that may not happen with this newer generation. Both because discrimination persists and because they wish to preserve their particular cultural and religious heritage, children and grandchildren are maintaining the hundreds of Korean and Mexican and Chinese churches that have been founded in the last three decades. In our extraordinarily diverse society, congregations are a healthy way for us to express that diversity. Providing a gathering place, then, is part of the "work" congregations do for their communities. The next section of this report turns to the question of just what sorts of religious gathering places there are in Chicago and how they compare to the rest of the nation.

The Religious Scene

Size. One of the most significant aspects of a congregation's life is simply its size. Larger congregations have more resources – of all sorts – than smaller ones. While most people are in moderate-to-large congregations, most congregations are quite small. In the country as a whole, half of all congregations have fewer than 75 regular participants! In rural areas, the average size is even smaller. The typical urban congregation has about 100 people on an average weekend. The typical rural congregation has less than 50. In other words, in all communities there are many small gatherings, alongside a few much larger, more visible ones. The larger ones, together, have most of the members, but the smaller ones are themselves more numerous.

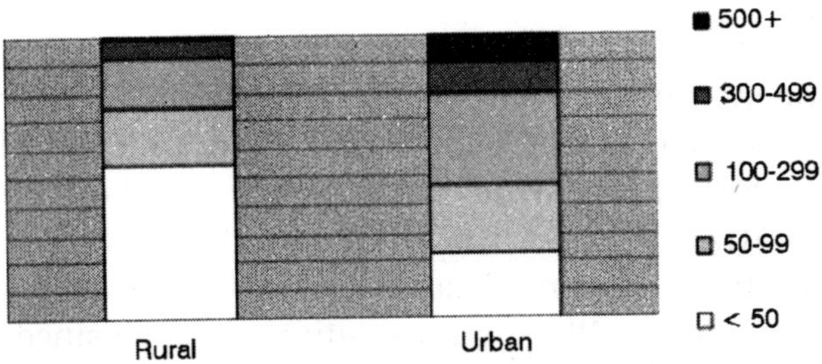

Fig. 1.1 Congregational Size (average weekly attendance)

Longevity. Not quite a quarter of today's congregations were founded before 1900. These oldest congregations are much more likely to be Mainline Protestant than to be from any other religious tradition. Another way to look at that fact is to note that half of today's Mainline Protestant congregations were founded before 1900. Another quarter of today's congregations were founded in the first half of the twentieth century. Notable during this period was the building boom among African American churches sparked by the Great Migration into northern cities.

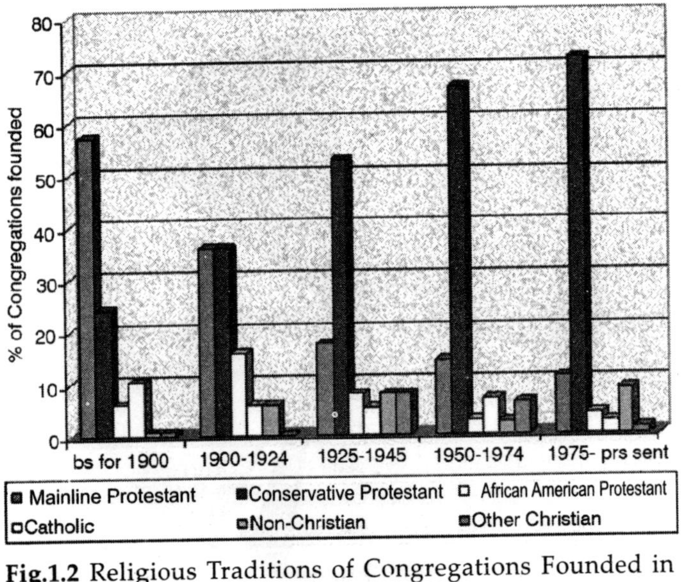

Fig.1.2 Religious Traditions of Congregations Founded in Different Eras

Slightly over half (54%) of today's U.S. congregations have been founded since 1950. There was a flurry of religious activity in the "baby boom" years after World War II, but that flurry was much more marked among conservative Protestants than among other groups. Conservatives – evangelicals, Pentecostals, independent churches, and the like – have continued apace since 1975, dominating the ranks of newly-founded congregations. Also noteworthy is the fact that groups outside the Christian tradition are almost as numerous among these new congregations as are Mainline Protestants.

Ethnicity. While a majority of congregations are more than 90% Euro-American, nearly as many are either significantly integrated or are congregations of Latino, Asian, and African American members. In fact, our sample probably under-represents those groups. For a variety of reasons, including language barriers, we were less likely to be able to complete interviews with Latino and Asian congregations.

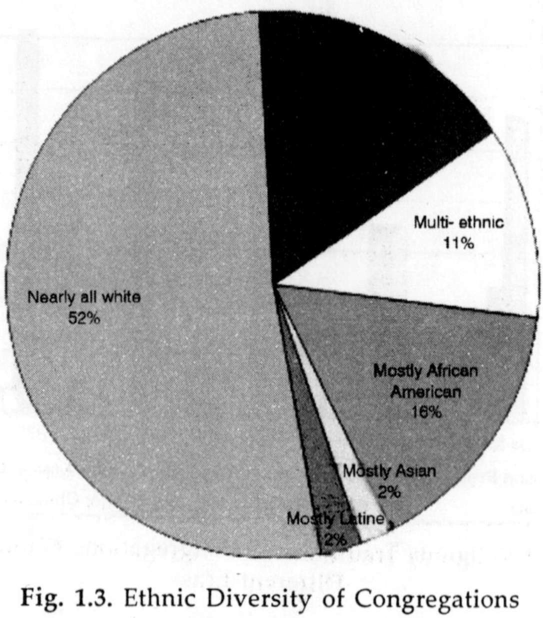

Fig. 1.3. Ethnic Diversity of Congregations

Note that, very few "nearly all" white congregations claimed that they were, in fact, all white. Nearly everyone claims at least minimal ethnic diversity in their congregations. Some, however, literally have no single ethnic group with a majority of more than 60%. Some of these have more than two ethnic groups; others balance nearly equal numbers of two groups. We need to know more about congregations than just their age and size and demographics. There are, of course, religious differences, as well. One way to take a measure of the religious traditions in the nation is to look at the particular denominations and faiths that are represented.

Christian groups can be seen as clustering around categories such as "Mainline" Protestant (groups like Presbyterians, Episcopalians, Methodists, and Lutherans, for instance), Conservative Protestant (like Pentecostals, independent churches, Southern Baptists, and Nazarenes), Roman Catholic or Eastern Orthodox groups, and the historic African American denominations (like the Church of God in Christ, the AME, or the National Baptists).

In addition, there are other Christian groups, like the Jehovah's Witnesses or Mormons. Beyond the Christian tradition, there are Jewish groups, and other non-Christian groups (like Muslims and Buddhists). In the nation as a whole, for instance, over half of all congregations are in the various conservative Protestant traditions, and only small (but growing) numbers are outside the Protestant/Catholic part of the circle.

It is important to note here that the percentage of congregations in a given group does not necessarily parallel the percentage of participants in that group. Catholic churches, for instance, are much larger than the average Protestant church, so fewer congregations does not mean fewer participants. These large parishes and congregations are relatively few in number, but claim relatively large portions of the population.

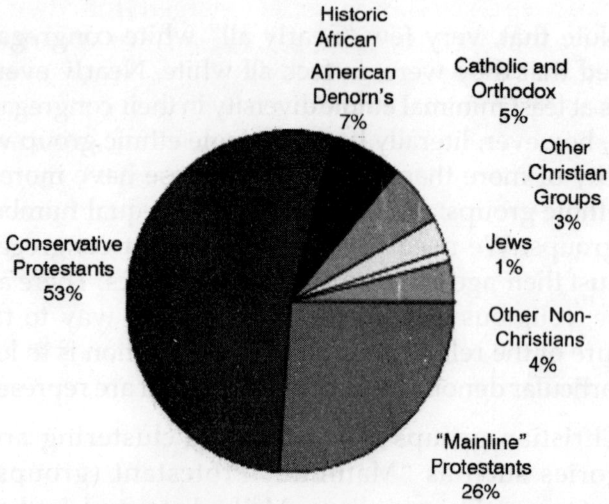

Fig. 1.4. Religious Traditions of Congregations

Another way to look at the religious landscape is to see how congregations think about what they ought to be doing in the world. We asked those we interviewed to tell us how important various activities and emphases were to their congregations.

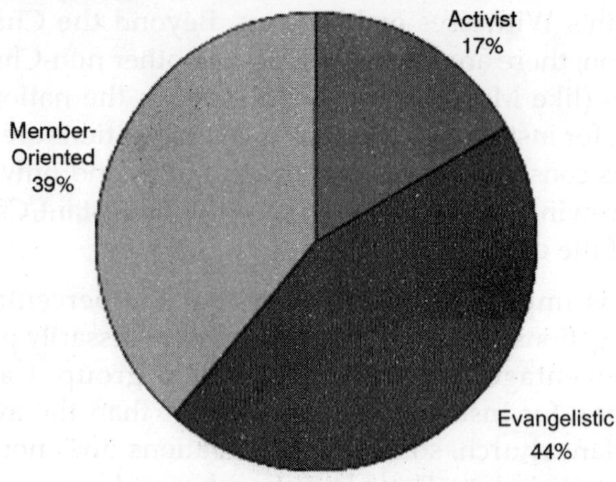

Fig. 1.5. Percent of Congregations Holding Various Mission Orientations

Three clusters of activities emerged from their answers. As we will see in a few pages, these "mission orientations" make a real difference in how congregations engage with the community. Note that while the term "evangelism" is a particularly Christian term, other kinds of congregations sometimes valued similar activities and ranked these statements highly.

Those we'll call "member-oriented" gave especially high ratings to:

- Providing fellowship activities for members
- Providing counseling and other services for members
- Fostering members' spiritual growth

Those we'll call "evangelistic" gave especially high ratings to:

- Maintaining an active evangelism and outreach program, encouraging members to share their faith
- Helping members to resist the temptations of this world and prepare for a world to come
- preserving the truths of the religious tradition

Those we call "activist" gave especially high ratings to:

- Promoting social change in this world by organizing and speaking out against injustice
- Serving the poor and needy

Congregations Reaching out to the Community

As we saw at the beginning, congregations are highly connected to the rest of their communities' voluntary and social service sector, reporting, on average more than 6 connections to groups that provide for the well-being of the community in a variety of ways. In addition to the work they do in providing for the spiritual well-being of their own members and the caring fellowship they provide for those members, congregations are important links in the delivery of the services and activities that make the country a better place in which to live.

These congregations come in all shapes and sizes and have many different religious ideas and traditions from which they draw. It's time now to take a closer look at the community work they do. As we looked at all the information we gathered on the work congregations were doing in partnership with other community organizations, we asked about what kinds of work was being done. While congregations understandably spend most of their energy taking care of the spiritual and social well-being of their members, when they turn their attention to the larger community, just what do they seek to accomplish?

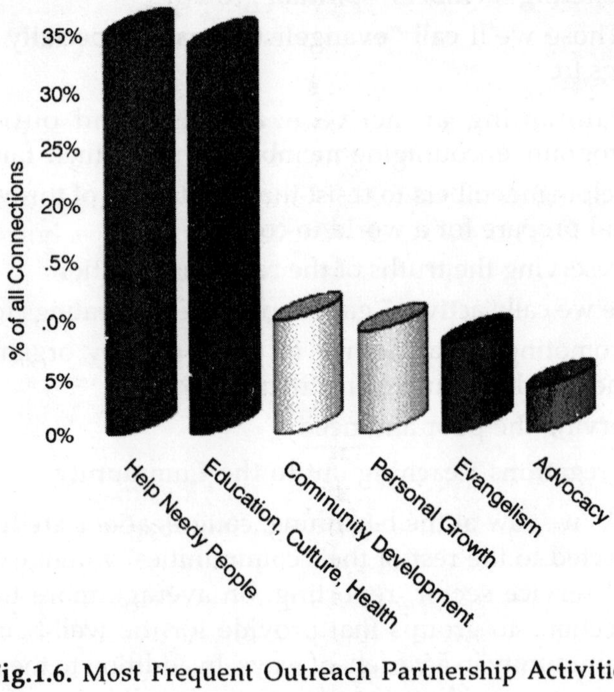

Fig.1.6. Most Frequent Outreach Partnership Activities

Throughout the country, the number-one activity that draws congregations into partnership with other community organizations is direct service to people in immediate need. Whether the need is for food or clothing, shelter or other emergency aid, congregations help to supply the resources that make this work possible. Among the organizations through which congregations most frequently work are:

- Homeless shelters
- Food pantries
- Domestic violence shelters
- Meal programs
- Clergy associations' emergency assistance funds
- Red Cross
- Salvation Army

These services take a variety of forms in communities around the country. Here are some of the voices we heard:

- In Chicago, a representative of Hesed House told us, "We feed, clothe and shelter very poor homeless people. And hopefully, try to give them reason to hope again."
- In Middletown, near Hartford, St. Vincent de Paul Place provides hot meals, clothing, and "supportive housing," a program aimed at helping homeless people get the services they need in order to stay off the street.
- In Nashville, Room in the Inn includes both shelter facilities and a "Guest House" unit for people who arrive too intoxicated to be admitted to the shelter. When they sober up, counseling and medical assistance is available.
- In Seattle, Northwest Harvest provides food and meals, but its major task is serving as the primary distribution system for other shelters and feeding programs around the state, buying truckloads of beans and cargo containers full of rice, in addition to receiving food donations from dozens of congregations and businesses. The director explained that the total "amounts to close to 15 million pounds of food a year. We distribute only through non-profit 501C3 organizations....They in turn give it to people who present themselves in need." In Albuquerque, the director of Storehouse rattled off

these numbers for yearly contributions to poor people in the community: "somewhere between 38,000 and 42,000 bags of clothing. We're projecting over 100,000 meals. We will help 250 families with furniture."

When people are in immediate need, congregations want to be part of the solution. People want to salve some of society's wounds, and most of them recognize that they cannot respond to all the need around them with only their own resources. They need to work with others, pooling money, person-power, and expertise that can go beyond a quick handout at the door.

Educational, Cultural and Health Activities

Congregations cooperate with other voluntary organizations in other important community activities, as well. The second most common activity nationwide, to support for various educational, cultural, or health-related activities. Everywhere you look among the congregations we interviewed, there are scout troops and nursery schools, senior centers and sports leagues – all existing independently of any single congregation, but often housed and supported by religious groups in cooperation with others in the community. In addition, there are arts organizations that use religious buildings for rehearsals, performances and lessons. Congregations support formal and informal programs of tutoring, after-school care, and literacy classes.

They contribute to programs of education and service provision that surround issues as diverse as AIDS, unwanted pregnancies, handicapped persons, adoption, and more. They support and refer parishioners to counseling centers of all sorts. And they cooperate with others in delivering spiritual care to people in hospitals, nursing homes, on college campuses, and even in police and fire departments. These needs are less basic than the food, clothing, and shelter provided by human service organizations, but they are no less essential to community life. They bring together persons from throughout a community who share a concern or interest, and they mobilize the resources of a diverse set of persons and organizations to respond to those needs. In helping to provide for the social, health, educational, and cultural needs of the community, congregations – working through affiliated organizations of all sorts — play an important role in enhancing community life.

Community Development Activities

On-going efforts to build up the strength of a community are captured in our "community development" category. Most of these are all-purpose associations – block watch groups, neighborhood associations, civic clubs, and the like. They take on tasks as mundane as trash pickup and as complicated as policing issues. Some of them attempt to implement longer-term changes that are needed to make the community a better place to live. About a quarter of conservative Protestant churches participate in such civic-minded activities, while around half of the mainline Protestant, African American, and Catholic parishes have at least some tie to a group working for community betterment.

Providing permanent affordable housing is one of the most common activities in which these congregations are involved. And the premier organization that has mobilized the energies of congregations and others in behalf of this cause is Habitat for Humanity. No other form of community economic development activity has anything like the presence of Habitat among congregations. Another organization with which congregations work is Heifer Project, an Arkansas-based ministry that provides livestock as a means toward economic self-sufficiency in communities around the world. Seattle-based World Vision is another development organization with a significant base of support among the congregations we surveyed.

Both World Vision and Heifer Project work primarily overseas; local economic development partnerships are considerably more rare. African American churches were more than three times as likely (22% v 6% in other traditions) to name a local economic development group as a partner. While the idea of "community development corporations" is getting a good deal of attention these days, it is the rare congregation that has taken on this sort of economic partnership.

Self-help and Personal Growth Groups

Much more specialized work is done by people who gather in small groups to help themselves and each other to deal with specific problems and interests. By far the best known and most widespread, of course, are the Alcoholics Anonymous and other 12-step groups for narcotics addicts, overeaters, and even "sex and love addicts." Congregations across the religious spectrum provide support for these groups, but mainline Protestant churches are especially likely to be involved. As numerous as AA groups are in the basements of American churches and synagogues, there are an equal number of other support and spirituality groups, as well. Here we are not counting groups run as part of the congregation's own internal programming.

Beyond their own Sunday School classes and men's and women's groups, about one in three congregations also hosts or provides resources to a support and growth group that encompasses persons from beyond its own membership. These include the usual religiously-focused groups like Bible study and prayer groups. But even more common are sports leagues and support groups for people encountering both mundane and extraordinary challenges in living. There are parenting groups for "Mothers of Preschoolers (MOPS)" and weight control groups, including Take Off Pounds Sensibly (TOPS) and Weight Watchers. There are groups dealing with birth defects and disability, as well as groups for people who have encountered less common difficulties – Turret syndrome, Lyme Disease, and incest, to name a few of those we found.

There are even groups for transvestites and for Christian motorcycle enthusiasts, for people recovering from divorce and people who are victims of violence. Small groups can be an effective means for sustaining social and emotional bonds and promoting mutual aid. When one or two people see a need, they often make their interest known through and beyond their own congregation.

They draw on the net-works of knowledge and communication that can be tapped there and often end up housing the resulting group in the parlor or fellowship hall. Again, the resources of congregations facilitate the creation of the sorts of social capital that sustain the common good by helping citizens to help each other.

Evangelistic Outreach Activities

Evangelism is another activity in which religious people encounter persons outside their own religious community in an effort to change the world for the better – one soul at a time. In supporting such efforts, the scope of the congregation's concern is often enlarged to include a public much wider than their immediate locale. It is this sort of evangelical activity, in fact, that most commonly involves congregations in connections beyond the local region. From Jamaica and Haiti to Mexico and Lebanon and Bosnia and Nigeria, many congregations are directly connected to missionaries they support, hearing from them about the cultures, challenges, and needs of those distant places, and often sending delegations to deliver goods and work along-side overseas missionaries.

Public Advocacy

In addition to these on-the-ground efforts to build up community well-being, a few congregations also make connections with organizations that allow them to give voice to public policy concerns. From the environment to health care and from civil rights to animal rights, congregations sometimes pursue the cause of justice in this world through advocacy organizations that include:

Amnesty International, The Audubon Society, Bread for the World, The Sierra Club, Earth Ministry, Children's Defense Fund, Fellowship of Reconciliation, Gay Pride parade and AIDS Walk, Interfaith Alliance, Physicians for Social Responsibility, Protestants for the Common Good, Union of Concerned Scientists, United Power for Action and Justice — as well as the March for Jesus and Life Chain.

In most cases, congregations participate with local chapters of large national groups, but the national and international scope of the issues being addressed draws congregations into a large public arena. African American churches were the only ones in our study to report alliances with specifically political or voter education organizations. Their members, in turn, were also the most likely to report that they participate in political activities in the community.

The largest proportion of congregational energy goes into providing relief for people in need, but nearly as much is directed at the education and self-improvement of others who may be less immediately needy. The kinds of things we often think about when we think about "activist" congregations are actually relatively rare. Few are involved in economic development or policy advocacy, and almost none in overtly political groups. Rather, congregations are working with other community organizations to provide more immediate enrichment and relief. By combining efforts with other organizations, aid and services are provided far beyond what any one congregation could do and with a far more diverse set of partners than would be possible if work were confined to denominational channels alone.

Just what kinds of commitment do such outreach partnerships entail? Rarely does a partnership involve a whole congregation on an on-going and intense basis. But rarely is it something about which they know or care little. We attempted to find out as much as we could about these connections, and in about half the cases we were able to discern some countable measures of what is being invested. Where our informant did not know the answers to our specific questions about volunteers, contributions, and other aspects of the connection, we have erred on the conservative side and counted as if no such contributions exist, so the numbers in this Table clearly underestimate the amount of contributions being made by congregations to their outreach partners.

Table: 1.1 Levels of Involvement with Outside Organizations

	Mainline Protestant	Conservative Protestant	African American Protestant	Cath-olic	Weig-hted Total
% With at least one community connection	93%	90%	84%	91%	87%
% of Churches that provide volunteers to at least one organization	86%	73%	65%	77%	74%
Average Number of Organizations to which the Church sends volunteers	3.71	2.54	2.21	2.91	2.80
% of Churches that provide space to at least one organization	72%	51%	66%	76%	57%
Average Number of Organizations to which the Church provides space	.06	1.30	1.35	2.33	1.76
% of Churches that donate material goods to at least one organization	49%	23%	28%	28%	30%
Average Number of Organizations to which Churches donate material goods	.85	.35	.30	.60	.48
% of Churches that donate money to at least one organization	67%	41%	27%	27%	45%
Average Number of Organizations to which Churches donate money	4.32	1.95	1.59	2.73	2.53
Average total contributions to non-denominational outreach organizations	$3404	$4199	$ 727	$487 8	$3538

Even with incomplete information, the numbers are substantial. Well over half of all congregations have at least one outside organization that uses space in their buildings (either donated outright or made available at minimal cost). On average, in fact, there are nearly two such organizations for every congregation. If nothing else, congregations are valuable to their communities because they provide meeting space and other facilities to support the work of organizations beyond their own membership. What congregations contribute is not just empty space; it is also person-power. Each congregation contributes, on average, volunteers to three organizations, and 74% report that they send volunteers to help in at least one group. For the groups to which they send volunteers, the median number of members who are involved is five, with a few reporting literally dozens of routine volunteers.

That, of course, does not begin to count the number of groups in which individual members work, not as official representatives of their congregations, but at least in part because their congregation encourages such activity. Fifty-nine percent of the individual members we surveyed claim that they participate in community service organizations at least a few times a year. In addition, seventy-nine percent claim that they at least occasionally provide informal service to people in need.

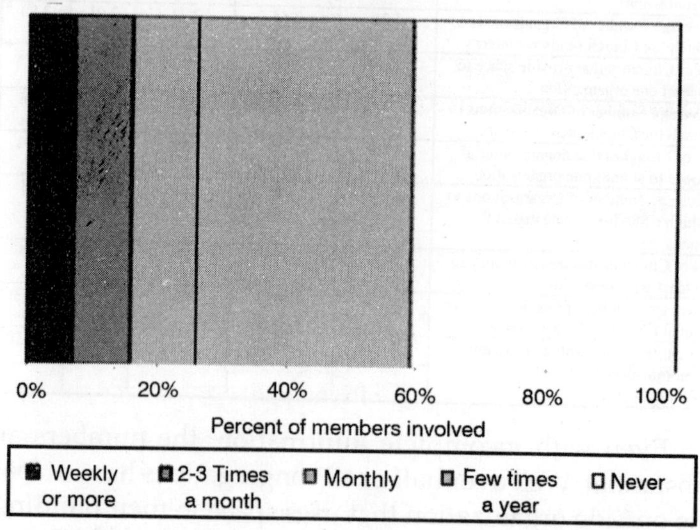

Fig. 1.7. Involvement of Members as Volunteers in Community Service Organizations

The connections go beyond volunteers and space. On average two or three organizations receive money from each congregation, amounting, on average, to nearly $1400 per organization per year. And about a third supplement their monetary contributions to at least one organization with other material goods –food, clothing, furniture, Christmas gifts, and the like – collected by the members.

Congregations also encourage their individual members to give to causes in the community. Only one in six of the participants we surveyed said that they gave nothing to secular causes. In fact, in mainline Protestant congregations, 11% claimed to contribute $1000 or more, compared to 5% of conservatives, 7.5% of Catholics, but 13% of respondents in African American churches who gave that generously.

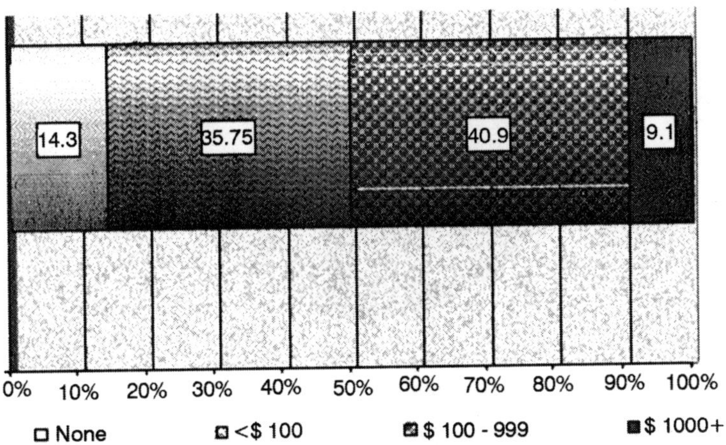

Fig. 1.8. Annual Giving to Secular Charity by Individual Religious Participants

This pattern of multi-faceted participation with outside organizations is present across the nation at roughly the same levels. Our research sites do not differ significantly from each other, but there are differences across religious traditions. Almost all religious traditions are at least minimally involved, but the level of activity in Jewish and mainline Protestant congregations tends to be higher than in conservative, African American, and Catholic churches. Mainline churches send volunteers to, provide space for, and give money and goods to roughly twice as many organizations.

Across all the traditions, the average number of volunteers per group is the same, so given that mainline churches support more groups, their total number of volunteers is therefore considerably larger than the total coming from other traditions. Monetary contributions, however, are different. Mainline Protestants spend a similar number of dollars, but spread them among more groups. Along with contributions from virtually all other religious groups, their resources help to sustain the community.

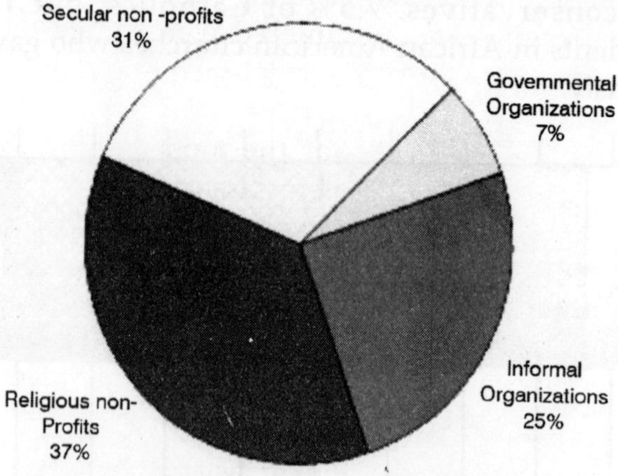

Fig. 1.9. Just what Sorts of Organizations do Congregations Work with?

How Congregations Organize. Our first discovery is that many of the "organizations" through which congregations do their work are not formal organizations at all. They are often simply informal partnerships among two or more congregations, partnerships that have no staff of their own and often not even a name. Many food pantries and clothes closets are run this way.

A group of congregations agrees informally that one will collect, store, and distribute furniture, while another will take care of the food, and a third will collect clothing. They may notify various social service agencies of the arrangement so that needy persons can be referred to the right place. This network of caring may never show up on anyone's annual report, but it is a critical link in the safety net in many communities. Equally informal are the groups who share a common interest or concern and form a self-help or support group. Rather than being part of a formal national network (like AA, for instance), many are simply community folk who decide to get together. We found Alzheimers and disability support groups and groups that gather to practice Aikido, Irish Step Dancing, or Zen meditation, for instance. Many (although not all) of the sports leagues we encountered were similarly informal. They have an on-going existence and a recognizable identity, but there is little if any financial or legal infrastructure. But by far the most important of these informal groups are the clergy associations that are present in nearly every community. They offer clergy an opportunity to share their burdens with others who understand, but often the prayer and fellowship of these groups is specifically directed at needs and concerns in the community, and the concerns expressed in prayer spill over into concrete actions the group may undertake.

Among the most common tasks of clergy associations is working out the sorts of informal social service arrangements we just mentioned. Churches and synagogues are obvious stopping points for people in need, but it is hard for a pastor or rabbi (or a secretary) to make a judgment about what is best when someone knocks on the door. By banding together, and often by enlisting the help of local merchants, congregations establish some semblance of rationality in a situation they find otherwise frustratingly ambiguous. If everyone cooperates, each has a sense that appropriate help is being delivered. Not surprisingly, the *religious nonprofit sector* is the largest block of organizations through which congregations do their work in the community.

Nearly half of the human service connections and over half of the links to community development groups are links to formal religious nonprofit organizations – Community Centers and shelters, food pantries and rescue missions, pastoral counseling centers and refugee resettle-ment programs, prison ministries and drug rehab programs, senior centers and AIDS ministries. It is important to note that these religious nonprofits bring together people from a wide variety of religious traditions (and often people of no tradition at all). Even an identifiably denominational group, such as Catholic Charities or Lutheran Social Services is very likely to have tangible support from persons and congregations outside that denomination. When they serve their communities, religious people rub shoulders with an often unlikely array of people from beyond their own traditions.

Secular nonprofits are also important players. While they may have some congregational donors and volunteers that come through religious channels, their work is defined primarily in secular terms. About one third of all the human service, community development, and culture/education/ health connections that congregations have are connections to explicitly secular organizations. Education and self help work is, in fact, more often accomplished through secular groups. From literacy programs to choirs and dance troops, secular community benefit organizations often receive space, volunteers, and monetary support from congregations. The other activity in which secular nonprofits are the dominant player is policy advocacy. As we saw above, congregations provide support to groups as diverse as Amnesty International, the Sierra Club, and Physicians for Social Responsibility.

Such secular groups are considerably more common than religiously based ones (such as Interfaith Alliance or Bread for the World) in the advocacy partnerships cited by congregations. Some may be surprised to learn that 29% of congregations are also involved in program partnerships with various governmental organizations. Most common are connections between congregations and schools, and most often those connections involve members in tutoring and other support programs. In addition, congregations are often partners in public projects that are run by parks departments, police departments, and chambers of commerce. In Chicago, for instance, a number of congregations participate in the CAPS (Chicago Alternative Policing Strategy) program. One church in Hartford provides resources for special activities at the public library.

And in both of our rural locations, churches have especially close working relationships with the county welfare office. Social workers know which churches to call when there are emergency needs. These partnerships all began long before the current discussion of "charitable choice." They are part of the long-standing pattern of more informal cooperation between religious groups and government. In none of these cases was a congregation receiving government funds to support any service activity. Rather, government programs were receiving volunteer, in-kind, and other support from congregations.

It is worth noting that mainline Protestant congregations are much more likely to make connections to secular nonprofits and governmental agencies than are conservative, African American, or even Catholic churches. Again, we see that the connections between congregations and their communities are both extensive and diverse. Some connections are very informal, some through formal organizations. Some are through other religious groups, while others link congregations with secular nonprofits and public agencies. And some of the connections are indirect, through the giving and volunteering that members undertake on their own.

Explanations for Congregational Involvement

Not every congregation is equally involved in providing services to the larger community through organizational partnerships beyond their own denomination. A variety of factors differentiate the most actively-connected from others. Demographics make surprisingly little difference. Some expect regions to be different from each other, but there are no real differences among regions – that is, net of the other factors (especially religious traditions) that make regions distinctive. Congregations in rural areas are less involved in outside partnerships than are urban ones, but the educational and racial composition of the congregation makes no difference, other things being equal. On the other hand, resources are a significant part of the story.

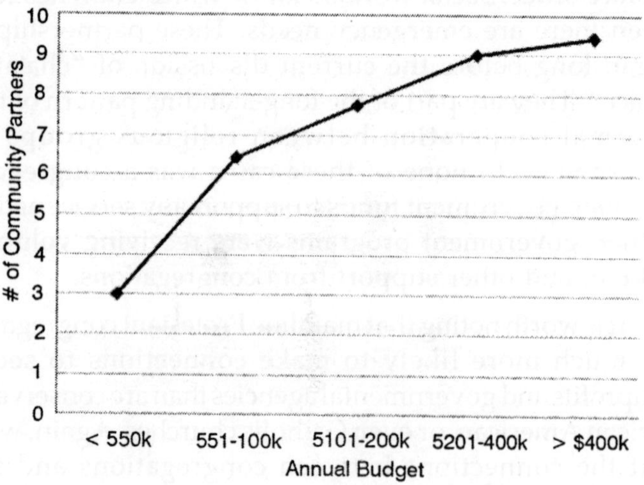

Fig. 1.10. Effect of Budget Size on Community Involvement

The more money a congregation has in its budget, the more connections it is likely to form, and the more high-income parishioners it has—over and above the size of the budget—the more connections it can sustain. It is money, in fact, not sheer size, that makes a difference.

The differences we have seen, then, are partly a matter of money and context — bigger congregations with bigger budgets do more — but more than that there are real differences based on a congregation's situatedness within a particular religious tradition.

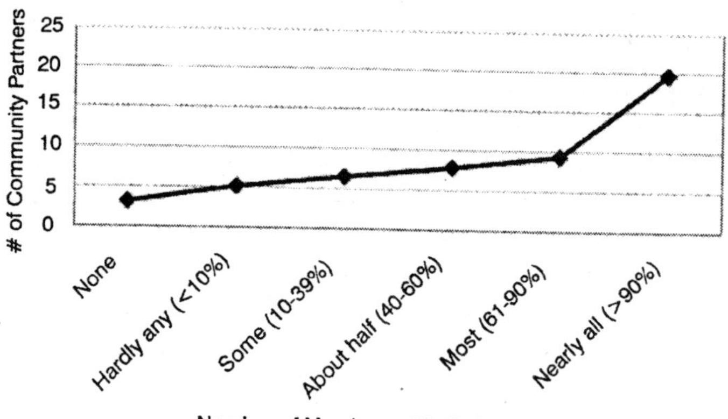

Fig. 1.11. Effect of Member Income on Community Involvement

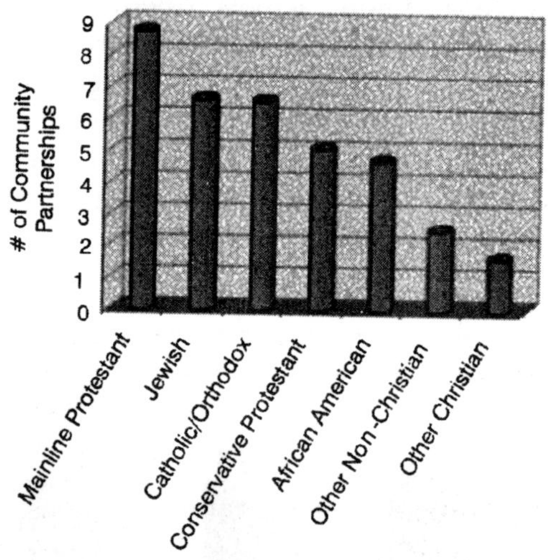

Fig. 1.12. Level of Involvement with Community Organizations
in Various Religious Traditions

Forming alliances with groups beyond one's own doors is an organizational strategy that exists in virtually all Christian and Jewish congregations, but it is a pattern that was historically set by the congregations in the Mainline Protestant tradition. All other things being equal, those congregations are still more heavily invested in community partnerships than are congregations in other religious traditions. In addition, their individual members are more likely to be personally involved in community organizations, politics, and giving monetary support to charitable work. Catholic and Jewish congregations are not far behind in their level of involvement. Those least involved with outside partnerships are the new immigrant (non-Christian) groups and the "other" Christian groups, such as Mormons and Jehovah's Witnesses. While denominational traditions make a significant difference in the degree to which congregations are involved in community partnerships, the particular "mission" orientation of the congregation makes a difference, as well. Even within a given denomination, some congregations have a more "activist" orientation, while others are "member oriented," and still others are "evangelistic." All other things being equal – that is, congregations in the same tradition, with similar budgets, in similar locations and with similar memberships – the particular theological orientation of the congregation makes a difference in how it relates to the community.

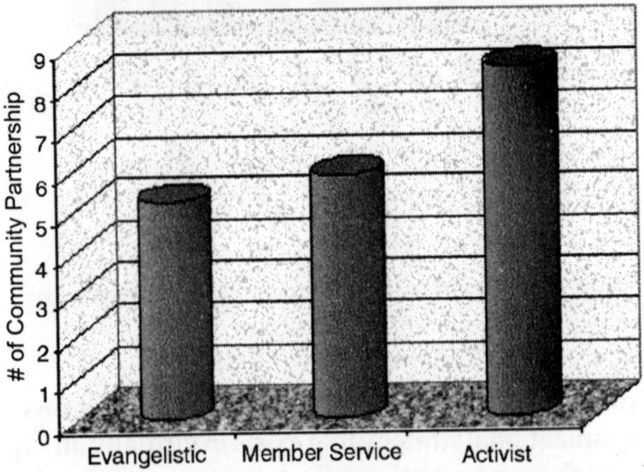

Fig. 1.13. Effects of Mission Orientation on Community Involvement

These mission orientations can characterize both

congregations and the individuals in them. Not every "activist" person is in an "activist" congregation, for instance. Congregations that define their mission in terms of social change are more involved in the community, but so are individuals who see their goals in life as seeking justice and serving the needy. The religious ideas and orientations that are nurtured in congregations shape both the activities of the congregation itself and the involvements of its individual members.

Denominational Connections

Some of what congregations do within a local area is channeled through their own particular denomination's agencies. A diocese, district, or other regional "judicatory" may maintain funds and programs that serve needy people, help to advocate for social reform, and contribute to community well-being in a variety of other ways. These efforts are not always very visible. Almost none of the regional judicatories we have examined makes policy advocacy a high and visible priority, although many channel resources to regional religious coalitions that more visibly lobby and work for change, often speaking in behalf of the whole religious community. One denominational leader described the role of ecumenical bodies as "sort of a lightening rod for some of the activists in the churches."

Because regional denominational bodies are often made up of quite diverse congregations, they may not advertise all the work they do, even when they are actively involved. We found that 20% of the congregations we surveyed mentioned at least one denominationally-sponsored local outreach effort they support. Those actively involved with other, non-denominational, local partnerships were neither more nor less likely to be involved with their denomination. People who fear that involvement with "parachurch" organizations will undermine denominational loyalty will find nothing to worry about in our findings. What congregations do through religious and secular non-profits, informal coalitions and government alliances, is in addition to, not instead of, what they do with their denominations. Both forms of connection help congregations to extend their care for the community, neither at the expense of the other.

Local denominational involvement is not a matter of demographics or resources or size. Rather, being involved in the community in a denominational mode seems to vary depending on the denomination in question. Catholics, for instance, are more likely to do work for their community through their local diocese than Protestants are to do work with their regional office (30% v 20%). Among Protestants, Episcopal churches, Southern Baptists, the Church of God in Christ, and Seventh-Day Adventists were more likely to report local outreach efforts undertaken through their denominations than are groups like Unitarians or Baptists (other than Southern Baptists).

An A.M.E. pastor in Chicago, describing his local A.M.E. ministers group, said, "We have a concern about our youth...We talked about doing a program jointly where [a nearby] college would have an opportunity to talk to first of all a lot of black ministers out there, and we would try to get a number of youth there too....Another initiative for us is health care. We're going to be setting the alliance up so that on a given day we can advertise that at any A.M.E. church you can get your blood pressure taken." An Albuquerque Catholic priest noted that "in the whole archdiocese, all the parishes participate. We have a mission weekend, to pray and financially help. We have about 7-8 collections a year for missions or mission programs." And a neighboring Episcopal parish in Albuquerque noted how connections in the diocese enabled them to enlarge a mission program they had started. "We opened it up a few years ago to anyone in the diocese that wanted to join us.

Last year for example, they took 3 different teams to Honduras for 2 weeks each." Even small and rural Southern

Baptist churches in Missouri and Alabama pointed with pride to their support for SBC-sponsored regional food pantries, children's homes, and retirement facilities. These denominational connections, then, add to the work congregations are doing through other organizations in the community, as well as facilitating connections that spread throughout the world. Here again, the pooled resources of many people make good work possible. There is a dense and complex web of connection in every community – a web that binds together the agencies that serve the community with the congregations in which people of faith gather. Those communities of faith are first and foremost places where people gather for spiritual strength and moral guidance, where they find a caring community in which to express themselves and find a home. Even when congregations have no overt ministries or other connections in the community, they serve us well by doing these basic religious tasks. But beyond what congregations do for their own members, they also participate in myriad ways in the supportive web that enhances community life. That web makes possible a wide array of services to needy people, as well as self-help groups and educational enrichment, evangelism and political activism.

As you think about your own participation in the nation's support network, we hope you will reflect on questions like these:

1. How might existing connections between congregations and service agencies be broadened? Which congregations need to be invited to become involved?
2. How can community needs be better communicated among a wider range of concerned groups?
3. What groups share common concerns and ought to be working more closely with each other?
4. How might congregations more intentionally explore the religious ideas and traditions that are the reason for this work? Do volunteers know why they do what

they do, and how does that sense of purpose give them strength? Do congregations know why they give, and does that sense of mission help them make well-considered decisions?

5. Social service agencies are often supported by a wide diversity of religious groups. How might agencies more intentionally provide opportunities for donors, volunteers, and clients to be more aware of each other, talking and working together so that their common concerns are discovered, experienced, and expressed?
6. What sorts of informal alliances can facilitate getting things done? When can we get along without a professional staff, and when are professionals essential?
7. How can congregations be creative partners with governmental organizations? What sorts of things can congregations do without risking "unnecessary entanglement"?
8. Which religious organizations, if any, are best positioned to take advantage of "charitable choice"? Which existing partnerships have lessons to teach as government urges new "faith-based" initiatives?
9. In the midst of all this, how can we protect the ability of congregations to do their religious work, valuing the diverse traditions they nurture and the spiritual perspectives they contribute to their members and to the community?

2

Contemporary Transnationalism

In recent years, Canada's relationship with its southern neighbour has been an overriding pre-occupation of politics, public policy and academic debate. There are good reasons for this. The United States received more than 80 percent of all Canadian exports in the 1990s, and supplied 67 percent of all imports. In the same decade, more than two-thirds of foreign direct investment stock in Canada was owned by U.S. interests, and over half of Canada's foreign direct investment was located there. Not unrelated to these economic linkages, Canadian foreign policy has become largely reactive to—if not always completely in accord with—the U.S. geopolitical agenda. At the same time, cultural flows across the border are extensive (and largely one-way).

If, however, a different set of measurements is taken, Canada's most significant global relation ships begin to look a little different. The 2001 census of Canada recorded 1.8 million residents who had arrived in the country over the previous decade. Of these, only 3 percent had come from the United States, while 58 percent had arrived from Asia—primarily China, India, the Philippines, Hong Kong, Sri Lanka, Pakistan and Taiwan (Statistics Canada 2003), The 2001 census even shows a visible 'minority'—and primarily Chinese and South Asian—population becoming a majority in a few suburban neighbourhoods. In Richmond, British Columbia, the visible minority population amounted to 59 percent of the total in 2001. In Markham, Ontario, the equivalent figure was 56 percent (Statistics Canada 2003).

Grassroots symbolic and material relations connecting societies across national borders expanded to historic levels during the last third of the 20th century. These transnational connections simultaneously affect more than one nation-state and are often generated from below by human migration, social movements, and nongovernmental organizations. The proliferation of grassroots transnational ties world- wide is a phenomenon of great significance but one that, so far, has received little attention in the sociological literature. Our goal in this chapter is to investigate one particular form of transnational engagement, namely the political activities conducted by contemporary immigrants across national borders, affecting communities, parties, and official institutions in the sending nations. From this analysis, we hope to draw general lessons modifying conventional expectations of what an immigrant is and what the process of adaptation to the host society is about. Our main concern is to probe the extent, implications, and social determinants of cross-border political relationships initiated and maintained by contemporary migrants to the United States.

Our analysis focuses specifically on the transnational political activities of three major Latin American immigrant groups residing in four major U.S. metropolitan areas. We seek to establish what types, scale, and intensity of political engagement prevail among these immigrants and to determine the individual and social factors that shape such participation. In the past few years, the term "transnational" has become commonly and conspicuously displayed in the titles of conferences and discussion panels at scholarly meetings in the United States and Europe. This surge in interest has been accompanied, however, by mounting theoretical ambiguity and analytical confusion in the use of the term. Thus, while some scholars have started to embrace and deploy the concept in their work, others have responded with intense skepticism. Seeking to clarify the meaning of the term, several scholars have provided explicit definitions of "transnational migration" and "transnational fields."

For Glick Schiller and Fouron, for example, "transnational migration is a pattern of migration in which persons, although they move across inter- national borders, settle, and establish relations in a new state, maintain ongoing social connections with the polity from which they originated. In transnational migration people literally live their lives across inter- national borders. Such persons are best identified as 'transmigrants.'" The problem with this definition is that it does not establish explicit criteria for differentiating those who participate in these activities from those who do not. If the simple act of sending remittances to families or travelling home occasionally qualifies a person as a "transmigrant," the entire field is subject to the charge of banality since it is well known that international migrants have always engaged in these activities. The main difficulty with the field of transnationalism, as developed so far, is that its empirical base relies almost exclusively on case studies.

While useful, these studies invariably sample on the dependent variables, focusing on those who take part in the activities of interest, to the exclusion of those who do not participate. The unintended result is to exaggerate the scope of the phenomenon by giving the impression that everyone in the studied communities is involved. While the occasional trip home or a sporadic financial contribution to a home country political party certainly helps to strengthen the transnational field, these intermittent activities do not justify by themselves the coining of a new term. It is the rise of a new class of immigrants, economic entrepreneurs or political activists who conduct cross-border activities on a regular basis, that lies at the core of the phenomenon that this field seeks to highlight and investigate. These are, to use Glick Schiller and Fouron's term, the true "transmigrants." In this chapter, we focus on the phenomenon of political transnationalism as it manifests itself among immigrant groups in the United States.

We have assembled data that allow us to answer or explore three fundamental questions:

1. Is there such a thing as a class of political transmigrants—immigrants who become involved in their home country polities on a regular basis?
2. If so, who are they and what are the main determinants of their participation in this form of activism?
3. If so, are there patterned differences across immigrant nationalities in the incidence and forms adopted by this phenomenon?

Political Transnationalism

The recent research literature on immigrant transnationalism has made several important claims that deserve attention as a prelude to our own analysis. Several scholars have argued that migrants' loyalty and commitment to their homelands from afar constitute an alternative political force that not only alters local traditional structures but also opens up new opportunities for their communities of origin. Migrants are depicted as agents of change, who support and promote local development initiatives through hometown associations, as well as active political participants and direct international investors. For many sending countries, such as Colombia, El Salvador, and the Dominican Republic, migrants' monetary remittances have already become a major source of hard currency and the cornerstone of their countries' macroeconomic and social stability.

Several immigrant communities also remain an important part of their country's electorate. Political parties from these countries have opened chapters in immigrant settlements, while political candidates regularly campaign among expatriates to gain their political favour and monetary support. In countries such as the Dominican Republic, migrants' financial contributions are estimated to be as much as 15% of major Dominican parties' annual fundraising revenues. Even people who have lived overseas for several decades are reported to maintain their involvement with their homelands either in support of or in opposition to the incumbent government. At the same time, an increasing number of states, including those of the countries included in our study, have introduced constitutional reforms to provide dual citizenship rights and formal political representation to their expatriates. Such a panoply of initiatives has transformed the way in which migrants incorporate themselves into the societies where they reside.

Incentives provided by sending countries are designed to maintain the loyalty of their expatriates and keep their remittances, investments, and political contributions flowing. At the same time, such incentives provide a new and stronger "voice" for organized immigrants in the politics of their country and home communities. The question is how and to what extent immigrants choose to avail themselves of these new opportunities for political action. This literature leaves little doubt about the existence of the phenomenon of political transnationalism and its transformative potential, but it says little about the actual numbers involved or their characteristics and motivations. The relative presence and causes of transnationalism represent the logical questions in need of answer at this time. To accomplish this task properly, we seek guidance from existing sociological theories bearing on the processes of immigrant settlement and incorporation.

Theoretical Perspectives and Hypotheses

Potential determinants of immigrant transnationalism can be drawn from three different theoretical literatures:

(a) classical theories of the role of individual factors in immigrant assimilation; (b) contemporary theories of contextual embedded ness as determinant of immigrants' incorporation to host societies; and (c) social network theory. Given the novelty of the phenomenon, the resulting hypotheses are tentative; we use them as an initial guide for exploring its onset and development. Individual Characteristics Affecting Assimilation Orthodox theoretical approaches to immigration, especially push-pull and assimilation theories, were based, for the most part, on the early-20th century European immigration experience to the United States and elsewhere. These theories continue to underlie the "canonical" view of how the process of assimilation plays itself out.

One of its guiding assumptions is of a world divided into well-defined sovereign national political units. Accordingly, migrants move from country A to country B and either settle for good (i.e., become "immigrants") or move back home after reaching their economic objectives (i.e., become "sojourners"). Immigrants who settle abroad are eventually expected to assimilate into the dominant society's socio-cultural and economic systems while simultaneously shedding their "old" cultural practices and political loyalties. The main hypothesis derived from this perspective is that the longer immigrants live and are socialized into the ways of the host society, the greater the likelihood of their becoming thoroughly absorbed in it. As far as transnationalism is concerned, the logical corollary here is that longer periods of U.S. residence should lead to progressive disengagement from old country loyalties and attachments.

The same theoretical perspective generally expects immigrants to have a single identity, national allegiance, and representation in one national polity. Accordingly, cultural identity and political membership are defined as well-bounded characteristics, such that acquiring new ones implies abandoning those held previously. The hypothesis derived from this reasoning is that immigrants who have naturalized as citizens would be much less likely to continue involving themselves in the politics of their home nation. Becoming a U.S. citizen should act as a "natural barrier" to the continuation of political transnationalism. Another important individual characteristic is education. However, the predictive role of this variable is ambiguous. For assimilation theory, education should lead to a decline in home country ties, insofar as it facilitates swifter integration and mobility in the host society.

Educated immigrants, therefore, would be significantly more inclined to shift allegiances and transfer their energies and interests toward their new country. This prediction is questioned by an extensive literature that shows that education increases political participation worldwide. Thus individuals who were already interested or active in the politics of their home countries continue these interests even after emigrating. In that case, higher education would lead to an increase in transnationalism. The way that these contradictory expectations play out in reality has not been elucidated.

Role of Gender

A recent literature on the relationship between gender and immigration finds that men and women have quite disparate views toward their receiving and sending countries. Commonly, males experience occupational downward mobility upon immigration. Women's experience tends to go the opposite way, as many of them become paid workers for the first time in the United States. Women's labour market incorporation brings about significant changes in how they perceive themselves and are perceived by men within and outside the household. More specifically, Jones-Correa has introduced a gendered view of migrants' political orientation and engagement.

Reinforcing earlier arguments, he asserts that Latin American immigrant men in the United States tend to have a stronger political perspective and are more likely than women to become involved in transnational political activities: "With the loss of status in the receiving country, men tend to form, participate in and lead ethnic organizations whose interests and focus is in the country of origin. In contrast, women [are] more likely to shift their orientation toward the United States".

In many sending countries, including those of Latin America, men have traditionally dominated politics. In this context, Jones-Correa's prediction should be understood as asserting that this traditional male hegemony continues after immigration but that it remains fixed in the countries and communities of origin to compensate partially for the status loss experienced by men in receiving ones. The data for our analysis allow us to examine both the role of gender and that of downward mobility as possible determinants of political transnationalism. Contexts of Migration Immigrant adaptation is affected not only by individual characteristics but also by their contexts of exit and reception.

An extensive literature dating back at least to the classic Midtown Manhattan Project supports the proposition that the greater the socio-cultural differences between newcomers and the host society, the more difficult their process of incorporation. Hence, it can be expected that people emigrating from remote rural places to metropolitan areas in the United States will be less likely to adapt easily and, by the same token, will remain more closely attached to their past. Referring to the experiences of European peasants migrating to U.S. metropolitan areas, Srole et al. concluded that "to compress the profound historical changes of a revolutionizing century into a few adult years can exact a high price." Expectations held by kin and friends about the proper duration of the journey abroad can also affect immigrants' economic and political behaviour. These "socially expected durations" (SEDs) were originally theorized by Merton as a decisive element in social life affecting a wide range of individual and collective activities. For the specific case of U.S. - bound migrants, Roberts applied Merton's concept to show that the propensity to engage in entrepreneurial ventures varies systematically with the SEDs of migration: those who are subject to strong normative expectations of return are less likely to launch businesses in the United States because they are strongly oriented toward saving for investments at home. Following Roberts' logic, we hypothesize that temporary SEDs— that is, normative expectations of return—will also increase transnationalism insofar as it helps preserve ties with the country and community of origin.

Contexts of reception in the United States also bear significantly on immigrants' economic and political adaptation. Governmental and societal reception of immigrant nationalities can range from a favourable or at least neutral stance to active hostility and discrimination. Differences in this respect among the three immigrant groups selected for study are described in the following section. For all immigrants, a more negative context of reception, marked by downward occupational mobility, should lead to the perpetuation of ties with the home countries. As several authors have noted, transnational activism can function, under these circumstances, as a compensatory mechanism for the immigrants' status loss.

Social Networks Sociologists have described migration as a network-building process that builds upon itself, facilitating the departure and settlement of newcomers and sustaining the movement when the original economic incentives have disappeared. The notion of cumulative causation has been invoked to describe the operation of networks of migration, whereby early departures pave the way for subsequent ones, lowering the costs and risks of the initial journey. We expect that the onset and continuation of transnational activities will follow the same logic. In the absence of large economic resources, the implementation of long-distance ventures must depend on the maintenance of a strong web of social contacts. The larger or more difficult the attempted transnational project is, the stronger the social networks required to sustain it. Thus we predict that, regardless of the motivations individuals have for engaging in political transnationalism, the latter will be conditioned by the size and spatial scope of their networks. The larger and more spatially diversified these are, the greater the chances for engaging in political initiatives across national borders.

Groups Studied

Salvadoran, Dominican, and Colombian immigrants form part of the newest wave of mass immigration in the United States. These groups make up approximately 15% of the Latin American immigrant population. Despite common cultural origins, these communities represent very different migratory experiences, shaped by the combined effects of global forces and national realities. We expect these national variations to affect, in predictable ways, the course of immigrant adaptation. For this reason, a brief introduction to the history of each group is in order. Immigrants from Colombia (which has a population of 43 million) first started to arrive in significant numbers in New York and Los Angeles in the wake of the Second World War. The first wave of Colombians was formed mostly by upper-middle-class and professional people.

After the 1965 immigration reform, the social composition of the inflow included mostly middle and working-class immigrants in search of economic improvement. Since the mid-1980s, a deepening political and economic crisis in Colombia and growth of the drug trade has resulted in a significant expansion of migration, primarily from urban areas. Recent research points to high levels of mutual distrust among Colombian immigrants stemming from insecurity at home and the shadow of the drug trade: Colombians seldom cluster in tightly knit communities and become dispersed instead in large metropolitan areas.

The major destination is New York City, where two-fifths of a U.S. Colombian population estimated at 750,000 resides. Even in New York, these immigrants remain relatively invisible, except in certain sections of Queens, such as Jackson Heights. Because of this spatial dispersion and their relatively high educational levels, Colombians have not been targets of extensive discrimination in the United States—notwithstanding the stigma of drug trafficking attached to Colombia. These circumstances, in addition to their alienation from traditional electoral politics and the convulsed socio-political situation of their country, lead us to predict limited involvement in political transnationalism. We suggest that this holds true despite the political rights, including voting rights from abroad and congressional representation, granted to them by the Colombian state. Relative to other groups, Colombians should tend to avoid continuous political engagement with their home nation. Emigration from the Dominican Republic was severely constrained during the 30-year Trujillo dictatorship, but it suddenly increased after the dictator's assassination in 1961.

At the time, a substantial number of opposition leaders were forcefully expatriated by a provisional government seeking to alleviate domestic pressures. The U.S. government expeditiously issued visas to these deportees and, later, "cooperated at the provisional government's request, by refusing to permit the deportees to leave the United States". This politically driven out-migration, concentrated in New York City, established the beachhead for subsequent waves of economic immigrants to the same area. By the end of the 1990s, approximately 10% of the Dominican population was residing in the United States. Areas with a high concentration of Dominicans in New York City, such as Washington Heights, and in some smaller northeast cities such as Providence, Rhode Island, have become sites for intense Dominican economic, cultural, and political activity.

Given the political roots of Dominican emigration and the active presence of national parties in this expatriate community, we expect political transnationalism to be relatively more common than among other migrants. The Dominican Republic is at peace and democracy has taken hold, so that active competition for office takes place regularly among the three largest national parties. Voting rights for Dominicans living abroad have been approved, and the consul general in New York has been selected in recent years from among leaders of that community. Such gestures contribute to reinforcing the web of transnational political ties between the sending nation and its emigrants. Salvadorans come from a small (6.4 million) and densely populated Central American country that has been highly dependent on U.S. economic and geopolitical interests. During the early 1960s, Salvadoran immigration to the United States increased and was dominated by professionals, technocrats, and investors. These well-to-do immigrants opened channels for labour migration by importing Salvadoran domestic workers.

The civil war between 1980 and 1992 set off a massive exodus to the United States, mostly from rural areas. By 1999, about half of the total Salvadoran immigrant population in the United States, estimated at over 800,000, resided in the Los Angeles metropolitan area. The Washington, D.C., metropolitan area hosts the second largest concentration of Salvadorans, with an estimated population of close to 250,000. Although the majority of Salvadorans left their country because of political violence, their claims to asylum were routinely denied by U.S. authorities, who classified them as illegal immigrants. Despite their precarious legal and economic status, Salvadoran migrants managed to maintain close ties with their communities and families of origin and to support them economically. Their remittances have consistently surpassed $1 billion per year during the last decade and constitute the country's single most important source of foreign exchange today. Most Salvadoran immigrants come from small towns and rural areas severely affected by the country's civil war. The strong bonds forged during that war were sustained and expanded after the country returned to peace. A still incipient democracy and frail political parties have failed to create many opportunities for migrant participation in Salvadoran electoral politics. Instead, expatriates and their organizations have concentrated their efforts at the local level, seeking to aid and improve their communities of origin. Salvadoran trans- nationalism can thus be expected to follow a distinct course, defined by the historical context under which the original migration took place: unlike Colombians, Salvadorans are expected to sustain strong ties with their country of origin; unlike Dominicans they do not channel such ties through national political parties but link directly with the towns and regions of origin.

As previously noted, all three sending nations have implemented policies designed to sustain the loyalty of their expatriates and to encourage a continuing flow of remittances and investments. Despite these common policies, we expect the three groups to differ systematically even after controlling for individual variables. These differences reflect their distinct histories of departure and resettlement, as just seen.

Data and Method

Data for this study come from the Comparative Immigrant Enterprise Project (CIEP), a collaborative effort focused on entrepreneurship and institutional development among the three groups described. The project included both qualitative and quantitative data gathered between fall 1996 and winter 1998. The first phase of the study consisted of in-depth interviews with 353 key informants in six areas of immigrant concentration in the United States (two for each nationality) and two cities, including the capital, of each country of origin. The second phase was a proba-bility survey of immigrant communities in four cities corres-ponding to the principal areas of concentration of the target nationalities. Dominicans were contacted and interviewed in the Washington Heights area of Manhattan and in Providence, Rhode Island; the Colombian survey took place in New York City, mainly in the borough of Queens; and the Salvadoran survey was conducted simultaneously in central and selected suburban areas of Los Angeles and Washington, D.C.

The CIEP survey was completed in 1998, gathering data on a total of 1,202 adult family heads. The survey can be considered representative of each immigrant nationality in its principal areas of concentration, especially because non-response rates were uniformly low. However, sampling fractions—the ratio of the sample to the eligible population in each area—varied significantly among surveyed communities. To adjust for this problem we developed a set of weights based on the estimated sampling fraction in each area. Sampling fractions were computed by dividing the final sample by 1990 Census figures of the adult population of the target nationality in each area. Weights are the reverse of these sampling fractions. The adjusted figures allow us to compare national samples and avoid unequal probability bias in the estimation of coefficients based on the full sample.

Conventionally, political participation is measured by electorally related indicators. However, immigrants also seek to be represented and participate in decision making through political means other than elections. Thus, under the concept of transnational political participation, we include both electoral and non-electoral activities aimed at influencing conditions in the home country. Each type of political participation is measured by a count of the number of activities in which respondents are involved on a regular basis. Transnational electoral participation includes membership in a political party in the country of origin, monetary contributions to these parties, and active involvement in political campaigns in the polity of origin. Transnational non-electoral politics includes membership in a hometown civic association, monetary contributions to civic projects in the community of origin, and regular membership in charity organizations sponsoring projects in the home country.

Non-electoral activities of this type are political because they influence local and regional governments by determining which public projects receive migrants' financial support. By so doing, they compel authorities to take immigrant wishes and priorities into account. As Levitt and Landolt have noted, helping finance local development projects or contributing to philanthropic works represent effective mechanisms to uphold high status and political influence in the localities of origin. 6 Questionnaire items measuring involvement in each of these six types of political activities provided three response categories: "never," "occasionally/once in a while," and "regularly." In keeping with the previous theoretical discussion concerning reasons for operationally restricting the meaning of transnationalism, our primary focus in the following analysis is on activities in which respondents were involved on a regular basis.

This definition identifies the class of migrants who have become most committed to transnational political action. As noted previously, however, the transnational field is also nurtured by the more occasional activities of other immigrants, and we also pay attention to these activities. Among independent variables, age, sex, marital status, and years of U.S. residence are self-measured by individual questionnaire items. National origin corresponds to the original survey screening question used to determine sampling eligibility. Education is measured as years completed, coded into three ordered achievement categories. U.S. citizenship acquisition is coded "1" if the respondent had naturalized American and "0" otherwise. Corresponding to the remaining hypotheses, urban/rural places of origin are coded into three mutually exclusive size categories (large city, small city, and rural); SEDs of migration is a dummy variable coded "1" if the respondent's family expected the journey abroad to be temporary and "0" otherwise; downward mobility is the ratio of the occupational status of the last regular job in the country of origin to the first in the United States.

Higher values of this variable, coded along a five-point status scale, indicate greater downward mobility. Network size is measured by the absolute number of persons in the respondent's social networks, and network spatial scope by the ratio of out-of-town contacts, including those living abroad, to those in the city of residence. Both measures are drawn from a name-generator module in the CIEP questionnaire, designed to elicit first names and characteristics of individuals on whom respondents could rely for both occupational and personal needs. The CIEP data set provides the first quantitative estimates of the phenomenon of transnationalism, allowing us to examine effects of both network size and spatial scope on each dependent variable.

Results

It shows that respondents are, on average, middle-aged and married; they arrived in the United States at a prime productive age, mainly from urban metropolitan areas, and have resided here for some 15 years. Close to one-third had become U.S. citizens by the time of the survey, but one-fourth still have children living in the country of origin and almost one-fifth travels there on a regular basis. Average group characteristics of the CIEP sample correspond in order of magnitude to figures from the 1990 census. Both indicate that Colombians are on average older, have higher levels of educational attainment and personal incomes, and the highest rate of naturalization (44%) of the three groups. Dominicans are mostly at the opposite end regarding educational attainment and income, while Salvadorans exhibit the lowest naturalization rate. The latter results show that the transnational field engages, in one form or another, up to a third of each immigrant group. Core transnational activists, on the other hand, are much less numerous, representing less than one-sixth of the sample. This figure contrasts markedly with past ethnographic descriptions of transnationalism as a form of political action adopted by entire immigrant communities.

Around these averages, however, there are statistically significant variations by nationality: Dominican immigrants are most likely to engage in electoral party politics and Salvadorans most likely to focus on hometown civic committees and community projects; close to one-fifth of the Salvadoran sample takes part in these kinds of activities on a regular basis. Differences by nationality correspond to our predictions based on the known contexts of exit and reception of each group. To separate these group effects from those of individual-level factors, we incorporate all predictors in models of political transnationalism, defined strictly and loosely.

Predictive Models

Our dependent variable, the number of transnational political activities in which immigrants become involved, is a count variable with a range of 0–6. Following the preceding definition, regular participation or involvement is coded "1" and occasional or no participation "0." The conditional mean of the negative binomial distribution is the same as the Poisson distribution, but the variance differs. The extent of over dispersion is estimated by the NBREG routine of Strata, which also provides a likelihood ratio test of significance. Predictor variables in our models follow the preceding theoretical discussion and include gender, education, size of community of origin, years in the United States, SEDs of migration, downward mobility, and national origin. As control variables, we add the linear and quadratic forms of age and marital status. The CIEP survey contains several different measures of respondents' social networks. Following the preceding discussion, we include network size (absolute number of respondent's social ties) and scope (the ratio of long-distance to local ties in the city of residence). The assumption is that larger and more geographically dispersed networks will be more conducive to transnational activism. NBR coefficients can be transformed into percentages indicating the net increase/decrease in the relative probabilities of the dependent variable associated with a unit increase in each predictor.

For clarity of presentation, we present these figures for all NBR coefficients that are statistically significant. The percentage change associated with significant coefficient has the advantage of not depending on the value of other predictors, unlike NBR coefficients that predict the actual count of trans- national activities contingent on other variables. We use robust variance estimators to correct for the two-stage cluster sample design in different cities. The corrected variances do not affect the actual coefficients, but they adjust for underestimation of errors that can lead to inflated Z-scores. Robust standard errors provide much more demanding criteria for statistical significance than ordinary ones so that regression coefficients that meet this criterion can be confidently tagged as reliable.

The first regresses political transnationalism, defined according to the strict criterion given above. These results provide the main source for our conclusions. The second column redefines the dependent variable based on a broader definition of transnationalism that codes as "1" both regular and occasional involvement in each of the activities counted as part of the index. These results allow us to examine to what extent determinants of political transnationalism vary according to the empirical definition of the concept. The first column of the table highlights the nonlinear effect of age, as indicated by a significant negative quadratic coefficient. This means that engagement in transnational politics increases substantially during adulthood but declines in old age. The gender and marital status coefficients show that transnational activists are overwhelmingly married males.

The column presenting the percentage change associated with each significant coefficient indicates that the gender effect is very strong, with males being over twice more likely to be involved in these activities. The tendency increases by an additional 13% for those married. Both high school and college graduations lead to significant increases in the probability of political transnationalism. The high school effect is the strongest, exceeding 10 times its standard error and increasing regular engagement in these activities by 173% relative to non-graduates. These results support predictions based on conventional theories of political participation rather than on those derived from assimilation theory. Other hypotheses derived from the same perspective are also unsupported by the data: U.S. citizenship acquisition has no effect on the dependent variables, and length of U.S. residence actually increases the probability of political transnationalism.

These findings suggest that it is not the least educated, more marginal, or more recent arrivals who are most prone to retain ties with their home country politics. While running contrary to conventional expectations concerning immigrant assimilation, a moment's reflection suffices to make sense of these results. Educated immigrants are more capable of following events in their home countries and seeking a role in them; the passage of time and acquisition of U.S. citizenship do not necessarily reduce this interest since their assimilative potential is balanced by the greater security and stability that they produce. A U.S. passport enables former migrants to travel back and forth without restrictions; greater time in the United States is usually associated with economic stability and more resources to invest in favored political causes. The hypothesis concerning significant effects of urban versus rural origins is not supported by the data, nor is that predicting greater trans national activism among the downwardly mobile.

We interpret these results as supportive of the previous findings, indicating that transnationalism is not a compensatory mechanism for migrants most affected by the traumas of adaptation to urban life or those suffering from status loss.

We further interacted downward mobility with gender to test Jones-Correa's (1998) notion that the proclivity of males to engage in home country politics is a consequence of status loss. Once again, it appears that trans nationalism is not a refuge for the marginal and downtrodden, but a practice associated with greater stability and greater resources brought from the home country. The hypothesis of socially expected duration is, however, strongly supported. Immigrants whose families expect them to return at some point (temporary SEDs) are significantly more likely to retain political ties with their countries than those never expected to return.

The increase in the count of regular transnational activities brought about by the temporary SEDs is 55%. Along the same lines, respondents with larger social net works are much more likely to participate. We find that it is the size of the networks rather than their physical location that makes the difference. Each additional tie, regardless of whether it is local or not, increases the count of transnational activities by 10%. Taken together, these findings indicate that political transnationalism is associated with well-connected migrants who remain normatively attached to their home communities by kin and friendship ties. With Dominicans as the reference category, results show that Colombian immigrants are the least likely to take part in home country politics, while Salvadorans and Dominicans are about equally likely to do so. The Colombian negative coefficient is very strong, exceeding 19 times its standard error.

This finding is important for two reasons: first, it confirms the influence of national origin and the associated contexts of exit and reception for each immigrant group; second, it fits well the history of each nationality and its particular resettlement experiences. Colombians want little to do with their country's politics, having escaped a situation of profound instability, official corruption, and widespread violence. The return to social peace in El Salvador and the relative political stability in the Dominican Republic facilitate regular cross-border ties by their expatriates, though, as we will see, their form and determinants also vary. For example, the gender effect is more than halved, while that of high school graduation drops 82 percentage points. Importantly, neither marital status nor length of U.S. residence has significant effects in this alternative definition of the dependent variable.

This suggests that the greater stability associated with marriage and permanent settlement in the United States increases the probability of regular, core transnational engagement but has no bearing on occasional participation. Broad political transnationalism emerges from this analysis as a diluted version of the strict version. It is affected by the same set of determinants, only less so. A probable reason is that occasional transnationalism is conjunctural and, hence, less dependent on the social and educational resources and political traditions that sustain regular involvement. Classic assimilation predictions are consistently rejected while those stemming from gender differences and contexts of exit and reception are supported. Political transnationalism is, in this analysis, strongly associated with national origin and a product of greater human capital, greater stability and experience in the receiving society, plus strong social connections and enduring moral ties with sending communities.

Interaction Effects

The resilient effects of national origin on both dependent variables suggest that different contexts of exit and reception may not only affect political transnationalism additively, but also interact with other predictors. We examine this possibility by running separate regressions for each immigrant nationality of political transnationalism on the same set of predictors considered previously. Because determinants of broad transnationalism continue to have parallel, albeit weaker effects than those bearing on a strict definition of the concept, we omit them from this analysis.

The overall trend is for Colombian transnationalism to be not only exceptional but also more weakly determined. This is shown by the corresponding R 2 and the few predictors that achieve statistical significance in this case. For Colombians, only place of origin and a college education affect the dependent variable. The original hypothesis concerning the positive effect of rural origins on the perpetuation of home country ties is supported in this instance. In addition, college graduation also increases participation in these activities. Hence, it appears that whatever transnational political activism exists among Colombian immigrants, it follows a bimodal pattern involving highly educated individuals and those coming from traditional rural areas.

As seen before, most Colombians show little inclination to engage in home country politics of any kind. Since migrants from that country come increasingly from urban areas and experience a dominant political culture of disengagement, our results suggest that this pattern of disinterest in transnational activities may become even stronger in the future. Dominicans and Salvadorans are much more vigorously involved in the politics of their home countries. The corresponding regressions introduce controls for city of residence, since both national samples were drawn from more than one city. No statistically significant differences between areas of residence were found in either case. In both cases, however, network size increases transnationalism significantly: each additional tie raises the net count of Dominican transnational activities by 16% and the count for Salvadorans by 9%.

The effect of education is also similar for both groups. Since so few Salvadoran or Dominican immigrants are college educated, the key human capital effect is that of high school graduation and it is quite strong in both cases. Differences between Salvadorans and Dominicans, on the one hand, and Colombians, on the other, in the effects of social networks are significant. Differences in the interaction effects between education and nationality approach, but fail to achieve, statistical significance. The same pattern is evident with gender effects. Unlike Colombians, among whom gender is an insignificant predictor, Dominican and Salvadoran males are much more likely to participate in transnational politics.

The effect is especially strong among Dominicans, where it exceeds six times its standard error. Temporary SEDs of migration have positive effects among Dominicans and Salvadorans, but only the latter effect is significant, increasing the count of transnational activities by 53%. By contrast, the effect of downward occupational mobility proves to be significant among Dominican immigrants only. In this instance, the direction of the effect runs contrary to the original hypothesis: instead of increasing the tendency to engage in transnational activity, downward mobility actually decreases it. The interaction between nationality and this variable is significant, as shown in the last column. Where Dominican and Salvadoran immigrants differ most is in the orientation of their respective political activities. With Dominicans as the reference category, the Salvadoran effect on party politics is significant and negative and that on civic community activism is significant and positive. As expected, Colombian effects are uniformly negative. These results support the conclusion that Dominican immigrants are more likely to concentrate on party politics, while Salvadorans bypass it to focus on the affairs of their local hometowns and regions. Thus, the meaning and scope of political transnationalism is not uniform. Although there are common forces bearing on all immigrants, the particular circumstances of each community also affect the extent and character of these activities. For some immigrants, transnational politics is a means to maintain an active presence in their country's centers of power; for others, it is a means to avoid such centers in order to provide direct assistance to their native regions; and for still others, it is a practice to be avoided in order to leave a violent and unsettling past behind.

An emerging transnational perspective has brought new vistas on inter- national migration. It has questioned conventional analyses that focus exclusively on assimilation to the host society, neglecting migrants' ties and ongoing relations with their countries of origin. Yet serious short comings and criticisms have been levelled at this perspective. Most early studies of political transnationalism were based on ethnographic evidence and often lacked clear operational definitions. A dearth of knowledge about the size, scope, and determinants of such practices has been a consistent weakness of this field. Comparing Colombian, Dominican, and Salvadoran immigrants in several areas of settlement, this study seeks to address these shortcomings. It provides empirical evidence of the scale and determinants of transnational activism among these populations.

Our first significant conclusion is that the transnational political field is not as extensive or evenly distributed among contemporary immigrants as proposed by previous accounts. In fact, the number of immigrants who are regularly involved in cross-border activism is relatively small. However, this proportion reaches up to one-third of the sample if we shift to a more inclusive definition of transnationalism. The fluctuation between a small core and a larger soft rim of transnational activists suggests its sensitivity to changing contextual conditions. Thus, while core transnationals stay involved in their home country politics via electoral or non- electoral means, others become active only at special junctures such as highly contested elections or natural disasters. A second set of findings is related to determinants of these practices in relation to predictions stemming from different theoretical schools. Our analysis shows that core transnational engagement is significantly different by gender and associated with migrants' age, human capital, and social capital. Results run counter to classical views of immigrant assimilation, still common in public understandings of the process.

Contrary to these views, results indicate that transnational political activities are not the refuge of marginalized or poorly educated immigrants. That conclusion holds, regardless of whether transnationalism is defined strictly or broadly. Along the same lines, length of residence in the United States does not reduce interest or involvement in home country politics but actually increases it. The uneven distribution of these practices by age and gender coincides with conventional power relations based on patriarchal structures that have historically dominated Latin American politics. The view that greater male participation is a result of downward mobility experiences in the United States is not supported since the corresponding main and interaction effects are insignificant. Support for the hypothesis of a strong gender effect must also be qualified by significant differences among national groups.

The male proclivity to participate is relatively strong among Dominicans (the group that gave rise to the hypothesis in the first place), but it is considerably weaker among other nationalities. In conclusion, our evidence demonstrates that a stable and significant transnational field of political action connecting immigrants with their countries of origin does exist. Within this field, we find a repertoire of cross-border electoral and non-electoral activities that warrant attention. The analysis shows that migrants' transnational political engagement is far from being socially unbounded and "de-territorialized," as some analysts have argued in the past. Transnational actions are socially bounded across national borders and occur in quite specific territorial jurisdictions. The transnational field is significant not only for home countries but also for the United States, since it affects the way immigrants incorporate themselves and alters conventional expectations about their assimilation.

The presence and dynamics of this phenomenon certainly contradicts a normative view of the assimilation process that places a premium on the rapid shedding of old loyalties and identities. This does not mean, however, that acculturation to the host society is not occurring or that transnational activism necessarily precludes successful integration. The old-line exclusivist views of how assimilation is supposed to occur are contradicted by the fact that the immigrants most involved in transnational activities are better educated, longer residents of the host society, and more likely to become involved in local politics there.

Similarly, transnational activism often seeks to reproduce in home country national and local politics the discourses and institutional practices of probity and respect for civil rights learned in the United States. By and large, transnational activism is a constructive phenomenon through which people respond to long-distance social obligations and belonging and seek to transform political practices in their sending countries. By the same token, it endows immigrants with a renewed sense of efficacy and self-worth that facilitates their integration into the political institutions of their new country. Recent ethnographic studies have documented the existence of significant transnational ties connecting contemporary migrants and their places of origin, but have failed to provide both consistent theoretical formulation and quantitative estimates of the actual scale of transnational social action. This chapter addresses some of these shortcomings and presents evidence of the scale, relative intensity, and social determinants of immigrants' transnational political engagement.

It demonstrates that a stable and significant transnational field of political action connecting immigrants with their polities of origin does indeed exist. Our results help temper celebratory images of the extent and effects of transnational engagement provided by some scholars. We show that migrants' habitual transnational political engagement is far from being as extensive, socially unbounded, "deterritorialized," and liberatory as previously argued.

Transnational political action, we argue, is regularly undertaken by a small minority, is socially bounded across national borders, occurs in quite specific territorial jurisdictions, and appears to reproduce pre-existing power asymmetries. The potential of transnationalism for transforming such asymmetries within and across countries has Jet to be determined. Grassroots symbolic and material relations connecting societies across national borders expanded to historic levels during the last third of the twentieth century. These transnational connections simultaneously affect more than one nation state and are often generated from below by human migration, social movements, and non-government organizations. The proliferation of grassroots transnational ties worldwide is a phenomenon of great significance but one which, so far, has received little attention in the sociological literature. Our goal in this chapter is to investigate one particular form of transnational engagement, namely the political activities conducted by contemporary immigrants across national borders, affecting communities, parties, and official institutions in the sending nations.

From this analysis, we hope to draw general lessons modifying conventional expectations of what an immigrant is and what the process of adaptation to the host society is about. Our main concern is to probe the extent, implications, and social determinants of cross-border political relationships initiated and maintained by contemporary migrants to the United States. Our analysis focuses specifically on the transnational political activities of three major Latin American immigrant groups residing in tour major U.S. metropolitan areas. We seek to establish what types, scale and intensity of political engagement prevail among these immigrants and determine the individual and social factors that shape such participation.

In the past few years, the term "transnational" has become commonly and conspicuously - displayed in the titles of conferences and discussion panels at scholarly meetings in the U.S. and Europe. This surge in interest has been accompanied, however, by mounting theoretical ambiguity and analytical confusion in the use of the term. Thus, while some scholars have started to embrace and deploy the concept in their work, others have responded with intense skepticism. Seeking to clarify the meaning of the term, several scholars have provided explicit definitions of "transnational migration" and "transnational fields". For Glick-Schiller and Fouron for example:

Transnational migration is a pattern of migration in which persons, although they move across international borders, settle, and establish relations in a new state, maintain ongoing social connections with the polity from which they originated. In transnational migration people literally live their lives across transnational borders. Such persons are best identified as "transmigrants".

The problem with this definition is that it do is not establish explicit criteria for differentiating who participates in these activities and who does no to If the simple act of sending remittances to families or travelling home occasionally qualities a person as a "transmigrant", the entire field is subject to the charge of banality since it is well-known that international migrants have always engaged in these activities. The main difficulty with the field of transnationalism, as developed so far, is that its empirical base relies almost exclusively on case studies? While useful, these studies invariably sample on the dependent variables, focusing on those who take part in the activities of interest, to the exclusion of those who do not participate. The result is to exaggerate the scope of the phenomenon by giving the impression that everyone in the studied communities is involved.

While the occasional trip home or a sporadic financial contribution to a home country political party certainly help strengthen the transnational field, they do not justify by themselves the coining of a new term. It is the rise of a new class of persons, economic entrepreneurs or political activists, who conduct cross-border activities on a regular basis that lies at the core of the phenomenon that this field seeks to highlight and investigate. These are, to use Glick Schiller and Fouron's term, the true "transmigrants". In this chapter, we focus on the phenomenon of political transnationalism as it manifests itself among immigrant groups in the United States.

We have assembled data that allow us to answer or explore three fundamental questions:

1. Is there such a thing as a class of political transmigrants -immigrants who become involved in their home country polities on a regular basis?
2. If so, who are they and what are the main determinants of their participation in this form of activism?

3. If so, are there patterned differences across immigrant nationalities in the incidence and forms adopted by this phenomenon?

Political Transnationalism

The recent research literature on immigrant transnationalism has made several important claims that deserve attention as a prelude to OUT own analysis. Several scholars have argued that migrants' loyalty and commitment to their homelands from afaı constitute an alternative political force that not only alters local traditional structures, but also opens up new opportunities for their. communities of origin Migrants are depicted as agents of change, who support and promote local development initiatives through hometown associations, as well as active political participants, and-direct international investors. For many sending countries, like El Salvador and the Dominican Republic, migrants' monetary remittances have already become a major source of hard currency and the cornerstone of their, countries' macroeconomic and social stability. Several immigrant communities also remain an important part oft heir country's electorate.

Political parties from these countries have opened chapters in immigrant settlements, while political candidates regularly campaign among expatriates to gain their political favor and monetary support. In countries like the Dominican Republic, migrants' financial contributions are estimated to be as much as 15 percent of major Dominican parties' annual fundraising revenues. Even people who have lived overseas for several decades are reported to maintain their involvement with their homelands either in support of or in opposition to the incumbent government. At the same time, an increasing number of states, including those of the countries included in our study, have introduced constitutional reforms to provide dual citizenship rights and formal political representation to their expatriates. Such a panoply of initiatives has trans-formed the way in which migrants in corporate themselves into the societies where they reside.

Incentives provided by sending country states are designed to maintain the loyalty of their expatriates and keep their remittances, investments, and political contributions flowing. At the same time, such incentives provide a -new and stronger "voice" for organized immigrants in the politics of their country and home communities. The question is how and to what extent immigrants choose to avail themselves of these new opportunities for political action. This literature leaves little about the existence of the phenomenon of political transnationalism and its transformative potential, but says little I about the actual numbers involved or their characte-ristics and motivations. The relative presence and causes of transnationalism represent the logical questions in need of answer at this time. To accomplish this task properly, we seek guidance from existing sociological theories bearing on the processes of immigrant settlement and incorporation.

Theoretical Perspectives and Hypotheses

Potential determinants of immigrant transnationalism can be drawn from three different theoretical literatures: a) classical theories of the role of individual factors in immigrant assimilation; b) contemporary theories of contextual embedded ness as determinant of immigrants' incorporation to host societies; and c) social network theory. Given the novelty of the phenomenon, the resulting hypotheses are tentative; we use them as an initial guide for exploring its onset and development.

a. Individual Characteristics

Affecting Assimilation Orthodox theoretical approaches to immigration, especially push-pull and assimilation theories were based, for the most part, on the early twentieth century European immigration experience to the United

States and elsewhere. These theories continue to underlie the "canonical" view of how the process of assimilation plays itself out. One of its guiding assumptions is of a world divided into well-defined sovereign national political units. Accordingly, migrants move from country A to country B and either settle for good (i.e., become "immigrants") or move back home after reaching their economic objectives (i.e., become "sojoumers"). Immigrants who settle abroad are eventually expected to assimilate into the dominant society's socio-cultural and economic systems, while simultaneously shedding their "old" cultural practices and political loyalties.

The main hypothesis derived from this perspective is that the longer immigrants live and are socialized into the ways of the host society, the greater the likelihood of becoming thoroughly absorbed in it. As far as transnationalism is concerned, the logical corollary is that longer periods of U.S. residence should lead to progressive disengagement from old country loyalties and attachments. The same theoretical perspective generally expects immigrants to have a single identity, national allegiance, and representation in one national polity. Accordingly, cultural identity and political membership are defined as well-bounded characteristics, such that acquiring new ones implies abandoning those held previously.

The hypothesis derived from this reasoning is that immigrants who have natural-ized as citizens would be much less likely to continue involving themselves in the politics of their home nation. Becoming a U.S. citizen should act as a "natural barrier" to the continuation of political transnationalism. A third important individual characteristic is education. However, the predictive role of this variable is ambiguous. For assimilation theory, education should lead to a decline in home country ties, in so far as it facilitates swifter integration and mobility in the host society. Educated immigrants, therefore, would be significantly more inclined to shift allegiances and transfer their energies and interests toward their new country. This prediction is questioned by an extensive literature that shows that education increases political participation worldwide. Thus individuals who were already interested or active in the politics of their home countries continue these interests even after emigrating. In that case, higher education would lead to an increase in transnationalism. The way that these contradictory expectations play out in reality has not been elucidated.

b. The Role of Gender

A recent literature on the relationship between gender and immigration finds that men and women have quite disparate views toward their receiving and sending countries. Commonly, males experience occupational downward mobility upon immigration. Women's experience tends to go the opposite way as many of them be come paid workers for the first time in the United States. Women's labor market incorporation brings about significant changes in how they perceive themselves and are perceived by men within and outside the household. More specifically, Jones-Correa (1998) has introduced a gendered view of migrants political orientation and engagement. Reinforcing earlier arguments, he asserts that Latin American immigrant men in the United States tend to have a stronger political perspective and are more likely than women to become involved in transnational political activities: With the loss of status in the receiving country, men tend to form, participate in and lead ethnic organizations whose interests and focus is in the country of origin. In contrast, women [are] more likely to shift their orientation toward the United States. In many sending countries, including those of Latin America, men have traditionally dominated politics. In this context, Jones Correa's prediction should be understood as asserting that this traditional male hegemony continues after immigration, but that it remains fixed in the countries and communities of origin to partially compensate for the status loss experienced by men in receiving ones. The data for our analysis allows us to examine both the role of gender and that of downward mobility as possible determinants of political transnationalism.

c. Contexts of Migration

Immigrant adaptation is not only affected by individual characteristics, but also by their contexts of exit and reception. An extensive literature dating back at least to the classic Midtown Manhattan Project supports the proposition that the greater the socio-cultural differences between newcomers and the host society, the more difficult their process of incorporation. Hence, it can be expected that people emigrating from remote rural places to metropolitan areas in the United States will be less likely to adapt easily and, by the same token, would remain more closely attached to their past. Referring to the experiences of European peasants migrating to U.S. metropolitan areas, Srole et. al. concluded that "to compress the profound historical changes of revolutionizing century into a few adult years can exact a high price."

Expectations held by kin and friends about the proper duration of the journey abroad can also affect immigrants' economic and political behaviour. These "socially expected durations" (SEDs) were originally theorized by Merton (1984) as a decisive element in social life affecting a wide range of individual and collective activities.

For the specific case of U.S.-bound migrants, Roberts (1995) applied Merton's concept to show that the propensity to engage in entrepreneurial ventures varies systematically with the SEDs of migration: those who are subject to strong normative expectations of return are less likely to launch businesses in the United States because they are strongly oriented toward saving for investments at home. Following

Roberts' logic, we hypothesize that temporary SEDs, that is normative expectations of return will al so increase transnationalism insofar as it helps preserve ties with the country and community of origin. Contexts of reception in the United States also bear significantly on immigrants' economic and political adaptation.

Governmental and societal reception of immigrant nationalities can range from a favorable or at least neutral stance to active hostility and discrimination. Differences in this respect among the three immigrant groups selected for study are described in the following section. For all immigrants, a more negative context of reception, marked by downward occupational mobility, should lead to the perpetuation of ties with the home countries. As several authors have noted, transnational activism can function, under these circumstances, as a compensatory mechanism for the immigrants' status loss.

d. Social Networks

Sociologists have described migration as a network-building process that builds upon itself, facilitating the departure and settlement of newcomers and sustaining the movement when the original economic incentives have disappeared. The notion of cumulative causation has be en invoked to describe the operation of networks of migration, as early departures pave the way for subsequent ones, lowering the costs and risks of the initial journey. We expect that the onset and continuation of transnational activities will follow the same logic.

In the absence of large economic resources, the implementation of long-distance ventures must depend on the maintenance of a strong web of social contacts. The larger or more difficult the attempted transnational project is, the stronger the social networks required to sustain it. Thus we predict that, regardless of the motivations individuals have for engaging in political transnationalism, the latter will be conditioned by the size and spatial scope of their networks. The larger and more spatially diversified these are, the greater the chances for engaging in political initiatives across national borders.

Groups Studied

Salvadoran, Dominican, and Colombian immigrants form part of the newest wave of mass immigration in the United States. These groups comprise approximately 15 percent of the Latin American immigrant population. Despite common cultural origins, these communities represent very different migratory experiences shaped by the combined effects of global forces and national realities. We expect these national variations to affect, in predictable ways, the course of immigrant adaptation. For this reason, a brief introduction to the history of each group is in order. Immigrants from Colombia (population 41 million) first started to arrive in significant numbers in New York and Los Angeles in the wake of the Second World War. The first wave of Colombians was formed mostly by upper-middle class and professional people.

After the 1965 immigration reform, the social composition of the inflow included mostly middle- and working- class immigrants in search of economic improvement. Since the mid-1980s, a deepening political and economic crisis in Colombia and growth of the drug trade has resulted in a significant expansion of migration, primarily from urban areas. Recent research points to high levels of mutual distrust among Colombian immigrants stemming from insecurity at home and the shadow of the drug trade: Colombians seldom cluster in tightly-knit communities and become dispersed instead in large metropolitan areas.

The major destination is New York City, where two-fifths of a Colombian population estimated at three quarters of a million resides. Even in New York, these immigrants remain relatively invisible, except in certain sections of Queens such as Jackson Heights. Because of this spatial dispersion and relatively high educational levels, Colombians have not been targets of extensive discrimination in the United States. These circumstances, in addition to their alienation from traditional electoral politics and the convulsed sociopolitical situation of their country lead us to predict limited involvement in political transnationalism. Relative to other groups, Colombians should tend to avoid continuous engagement with their home nation.

Emigration from the Dominican Republic was severely constrained during the 30-year Trujillo dictatorship, but suddenly increased after the dictator's assassination in 1961. At the time, a substantial number of opposition leaders were forcefully expatriated by a provisional government seeking to alleviate domestic pressures. The U.S. government expeditiously issued visas to these deportees and, later, "cooperated at the provisional government's request, by refusing to permit the deportees to leave the United States". This politically-driven out migration, concentrated in New York City, established the beachhead for subsequent waves of economic immigrants to the same area. By the end of the 1990s, approximately 10 percent of the 7 million Dominican population was residing in the United States. Areas with high concentration of Dominicans in New York City, such as Washington Heights, and some smaller northeast cities such as Providence, have become sites for intense Dominican economic, cultural, and political activity.

Given the political roots of Dominican emigration and the active presence of national parties in this expatriate community, we expect political transnationalism to be relatively more common than among other migrants. The Dominican Republic is at peace and democracy has taken hold so that active competition for office takes place regularly among the three national parties. There is an elected representative of the New York immigrant community in the Dominican congress and the consul general in New York has be en selected in recent years from among leaders of that community. Such gestures contribute to reinforce the web of transnational political ties between the sending nation and its emigrants.

Salvadorans come from a small (5.2 million) and densely populated Central American country that has been highly dependent on U.S. economic and geopolitical interests. During the early 1960s, Salvadoran immigration to the United States increased and was dominated by professionals, technocrats, and investors. These well-to-do immigrants opened channels for labour migration by importing Salvadoran domestic workers. The civil war between 1980 and 1992 set off a massive exodus to the United States, mostly from rural areas. By 1999, about half of the total Salvadúran immigrant population in the United States, estimated at over 800,000, resided in the Los Angeles metropolitan area. The Washington D.C. metropolitan area hosts the second largest concentration of Salvadorans, with an estimated population of close to a quarter of a million.

Although the majority of Salvadorans left their country because of political violence, I their claims to asylum were routinely denied by U.S. authorities who classified them as illegal immigrants. Despite their precarious legal and economic status, Salvadoran migrants managed to maintain close ties with their communities and families of origin and to support them economically. Their remittances have consistently surpassed one billion dollars per year during the last decade and constitute the country' s single most important source of foreign exchange today. Most Salvadoran immigrants come from small towns and rural areas severely affected by the country's civil war. The strong bonds forged during that war were sustained and expanded after the country returned to peace. A still.incipient democracy and frail political parties have failed to create many opportunities for migrant participation in Salvadoran electoral politics.

Instead, expatriates and their organizations have concentrated their efforts at the local level, seeking to aid and improve their communities of origin. Salvadoran transnationalism can thus be expected to follow a distinct course, defined by the historical context under which the original migration took place: unlike Colombians, Salvadorans are expected to sustain strong ties with their country of origin; unlike Dominicans such ties are not channeled through national political parties, but link them directly with the towns and regions of origin. As previously noted, all three sending nations have implemented policies designed to sustain the loyalty of their expatriates and encourage a continuing flow of remittances and investments. Despite these common policies, we expect the three groups to differ systematically even after controlling for individual variables. These differences reflect their distinct histories of departure and resettlement, as just seen.

Data and Method

Data for this study come from the Comparative Immigrant Enterprise Project (CIEP), a collaborative effort between universities on the East and West Coasts focused on entrepreneurship and institutional development among the three groups described. The project included both qualitative and quantitative data gathered between the fall of 1996 and winter of 1998. The first phase of the study consisted of in-depth interviews with 353 key informants in six areas of immigrant concentration in the United States (two for each nationality) and two cities, including the capital, of each country of origin. The second phase was a probability survey of immigrant communities in four cities corresponding to the principal areas of concentration of the target nationalities. Dominicans were contacted and interviewed in the Washington Heights area of Manhattan and in Providence, Rhode Island; the Colombian survey took place in New York City, mainly in the borough of Queens; and the Salvadoran survey was conducted simultaneously in central and selected suburban areas of Los Angeles and Washington, D.C. The CIEP survey was completed in 1998, gathering data on a total of 1,202 adult family heads.

The survey can be considered representative of each immigrant nationality in its principal areas of concentration, especially because non-response rates were uniformly low. However, sampling fractions -the ratio of the sample to the eligible population in each area- varied significantly among surveyed communities. To adjust for this problem we developed a set of weights based on the estimated sampling fraction in each area. Sampling fractions were computed by dividing the final sample by 1990 Census figures of the adult population of the target nationality in each area. Weights are the reverse of these sampling fractions. The adjusted figures allow us to compare national samples and avoid unequal probability bias in the estimation of coefficients based on the full sample.

Conventionally, political participation is measured by electorally-related indicators. However, immigrants also seek to be represented and participate in decision-making through different political means, not just elections. Thus, under the concept of transnational political participation, we include both electoral and non electoral activities aimed at influencing conditions in the home country. Each type of political participation is measured by a count of the number of activities in which respondents are involved on a regular basis. Transnational electoral participation includes membership in a political party in the country of origin, monetary contributions to these parties, and active involvement in political campaigns in the polity of origin. Transnational non electoral politics includes membership in a hometown civic association, monetary contributions to civic projects in the community of origin, and regular membership in charity organizations sponsoring projects in the home country.

Non-electoral activities are political because they influence local and regional governments by determining which public projects receive migrants' financial support. By so doing, they compel authorities to take immigrant wishes and priorities into account. As Levitt and Landolt have noted, helping finance local development projects or contributing to philanthropic works represent effective mechanisms to uphold high status and political influence in the localities of origin. Questionnaire items measuring involvement in each of these six types of political activities provided three response categories: "never" occasionally/ once in a while; and 'regularly'. In keeping with the previous theoretical discussion concerning reasons for operationally restricting the meaning of transnationalism, we focus the following analysis on activities in which respondents were involved on a regular basis.

This definition identifies the "; class of migrants who have become most committed to transnational political action. As noted previously, however, the transnational field is also nurtured by the more occasional activities of other immigrants which, for this reason, also merit attention. We consider both types of activism, in the following analysis, but pay primary attention to the core of migrants committed to transnational action on a regular basis. Among independent variables, age, sex, marital status, and years of U.S. residence are self-measured by individual questionnaire items.

National origin corresponds to the original survey screening question used to determine sampling eligibility. Education is measured as years completed, coded into three ordered achievement categories. U.S. citizenship acquisition is coded 1 if the respondent had naturalized American and Q otherwise. Corresponding to the remaining hypotheses, urban/rural places of origin are coded into three mutually exclusive size categories (large city, small city, and rural); SEDs of migration is a dummy variable coded 1 if the respondent's family expected the journey abroad to be temporary and 0 otherwise; downward mobility is the ratio of the occupational status of the last regular job in the country of origin to the first in the United States.

Higher values of this variable, coded along a 5-point status scale, indicate greater downward mobility. Network size is measured by the absolute number of persons in the respondent's social networks and network spatial scope by the ratio of out-of-town contacts, including those living abroad, to those in the city of residence. Both measures are drawn from a name-generator module in the CIEP questionnaire, designed to elicit first names and characteristics of individuals on whom respondents could rely for both occupational and personal needs. The CIEP data set provides the first quantitative estimates of the phenomenon of transnationalism, allowing us to examine effects of both network size and spatial scope on each dependent variables.

Results

General Characteristics of the Sample

It shows that respondents are, on average, middle-aged and married; they arrived in the U.S. at a prime productive age, mainly from urban metropolitan areas and have resided here for so me 15 years. Close to one-third had become U.S. citizens by the time of the survey, but one-fourth still have children living in the country of origin and almost one fifth travels there on a regular basis. Average group characteristics of the CIEP sample correspond in order of magnitude to figures from the 1990 Census. Both indicate that Colombians are on average older, have higher levels of educational attainment and personal incomes, and the highest rate of naturalization (44%) of the three groups. Salvadorans are mostly at the opposite end. The latter results show that the transnational field engages, in one form or another, up to a third of each immigrant group. Core transnational activists, on the other hand, are much less numerous, representing less than one-sixth of the sample. This figure contrasts markedly with past ethnographic descriptions of transnationalism as a form of political action adopted by entire immigrant communities. Around these averages, however, there are statistically significant variations by nationality: Dominican immigrants are most likely to engage in electoral party politics and Salvadorans most likely to focus on hometown civic committees and community projects; close to one-fifth of the Salvadoran sample takes part in these kinds of activities on a regular basis. Differences by nationality correspond to our predictions based on the known contexts of exit and reception of each group. To separate these group effects from those of individual-level factors, we incorporate all predictors in models of political transnationalism, defined strictly and loosely.

Predictive Models

Our dependent variable, the number of transnational political activities in which immigrants become involved is a count variable with a range of 0 to 6. Following the preceding definition, regular participation or involvement is coded 1 and occasional or no participation 0. The use of linear regression for this dependent variable can result in inconsistent, inefficient, or biased estimates. The distribution of such variables is commonly modeled as a Poisson process. Deviations of the univariate distribution from Poisson are usually accounted by heterogeneity in the average rate, and are modeled accordingly. Poisson regression models rarely fit the data, however, because of the assumption of equidispersion in the conditional distribution, $x = y = \exp(yw)$, In practice, the variance frequently exceeds the mean. Preliminary analysis shows that this condition, known as over dispersion, is present in our data. Negative binomial regression models (NBRM) obviate this constraint by replacing the conditional mean x by a random variable x where: x = exp (yw + e) where e is random error uncorrelated with y. The conditional mean of the NB distribution is the same as the Poisson distribution, but the variance differs. The extent of over dispersion is estimated by the NBREG routine of Strata, which also provides a likelihood ratio test of significance.

Predictor variables in our models follow the preceding theoretical discussion and include gender, education, size of community of origin, years in the United States, SEDs of migration, downward mobility, and national original. As control variables, we add the linear and quadratic forms of age and marital status. The CIEP survey contains several different measures of respondents' social networks. Following the preceding discussion, we include network size -absolute number of respondent's social ties -and scope- the ratio of long-distance to local ties in the city of residence. The assumption is that larger and more geographically dispersed networks will be more conducive to transnational activism.

NBR coefficients can be transformed into percentages indicating the net increase/decrease in the relative probabilities of the dependent variable associated with a unit increase in each predictor. For clarity of presentation, we present these figures for all NBR coefficients that are statistically significant. The percentage change associated with significant coefficients has the advantage of not depending on the value of other predictors, unlike NBR coefficients which predict the actual count of transnational activities contingent on other variables. We use robust variance estimators to correct for the two-stage cluster sample design in different cities. The corrected variances do not affect the actual coefficients, but they adjust for underestimation of errors that can lead to inflated Z-scores. Robust standard errors provide a much more demanding criteria for statistical significance than ordinary ones so that regression coefficients that meet this criterion can be confidently tagged as reliable. The first regresses political transnationalism, defined according to the strict criterion given above. These results provide the main source for our conclusions. The second panel redefines the dependent variable based on a broader definition of transnationalism that codes as 1 both regular and occasional involvement in each of the activities counted as part of the index. These results allow us to examine to what extent determinants of political transnationalism vary according to the empirical definition of the concept. The first panel of the table highlights the non-linear effect of age, as indicated by a significant negative quadratic coefficient. This means that engagement in transnational politics increases substantially during adulthood, but declines in old age. The gender and marital status coefficients show that transnational activists are overwhelmingly married males.

The column presenting the percent change associated with each significant coefficient indicates that the gender effect is very strong, with males being aver twice more likely to be involved in these activities. The tendency increases by an additional 13 percent for those married. Both high school and college graduation lead to significant increases in the probability of political transnationalism. The high school effect is the strongest, exceeding ten times its standard error and increasing regular engagement in these activities by 173 percent relative to non-graduates. These results support predictions based on conventional theories of political participation rather than those derived from assimilation theory. Other hypotheses derived from the same perspective are also unsupported by the data: U.S. citizenship acquisition has no effect on the dependent variable and length of U.S. residence actually increases the probability of political transnationalism.

These findings suggest that it is not the least educated, more marginal, or more recent arrivals whom are most prone to retain ties with their home country politics. While running contrary to conventional expectations concerning immigrant assimilation, a moment's reflection suffices to make sense of these results. Educated immigrants are more capable of following events in their home countries and seeking a role in them; the passage of time and acquisition of U.S. citizenship do not necessarily reduce this interest since their assimilative potential is balanced by the greater security and stability that they produce. A U.S. passport enables former migrants to travel back and forth without restrictions; greater time in the United States is usually associated with economic stability and more resources to invest in favored political causes.

The hypothesis concerning significant effects of urban vs. rural origins is not supported by the data, nor is that predicting greater transnational activism among the downwardly mobile. We interpret these results as supportive of the previous findings, indicating that transnationalism is not a compensatory mechanism for migrants most affected by the traumas of adaptation to urban life or those suffering from status loss. We further interacted downward mobility with gender to test Jones Correa's notion that the proclivity of males to engage in home country politics is a consequence of status loss. Once again, it appears that transnationalism is not a refuge for the marginal and downtrodden, but a practice associated with greater stability and greater resources brought from the home country.

The hypothesis of socially expected duration is, however, strongly supported: Immigrants whose families expect them to return at some point (temporary SEDs) are significantly more likely to retain political ties with their countries than those never expected to return. The increase in the count of regular transnational activities brought about by temporary SEDs is 55 percent. Along the same lines, respondents with larger social networks are much more likely to participate. We find that it is the size of the networks rather than their physical location that makes the difference. Each additional tie, regardless of whether it is local or not, increases the count of transnational activities by 10 percent. Taken together, these findings indicate that political transnationalism is associated with well-connected migrants who remain normatively attached to their home communities by kin and friendship ties.

With Dominicans as the reference category, results show that Colombian immigrants are the least likely to take part in home country politics, while Salvadorans and Dominicans are about equally likely to do so. The Colombian negative coefficient is very strong, exceeding 19 times its standard error. This finding is important for two reasons: first, it confirms the influence of national origin and the associated contexts of exit and reception for each immigrant group; second, it fits well the history of each nationality and its particular resettlement experiences. Colombians want little to do with their country's politics, having escaped a situation of profound instability, official corruption, and widespread violence. The return to social peace in El Salvador and the relative political stability in the Dominican Republic facilitate regular cross-border ties by their expatriates though, as we will see, their form and determinants also vary.

For example, the gender effect is almost halved, as is that of high school graduation. Importantly, neither marital status nor length of U.S. residence have significant effects in this alternative definition of the dependent variable. This suggests that the greater stability associated with marriage and permanent settlement in the United States increases the probability of regular, core transnational engagement, but have no bearing on occasional participation. Broad transnationalism emerges from this analysis as a diluted version of the strict version. It is affected by the same set of determinants, only less so. A probably reason is that occasional transnationalism is conjunctural and, hence, less dependent on the social and educational resources and gendered political traditions that sustain regular involvement. Classic assimilation predictions are consistently rejected while those stemming from gender differences and contexts of exit and reception are supported. Political transnationalism is, in this analysis, a product of greater human capital, greater stability and experience in the receiving society, plus strong social connections and enduring moral ties with sending communities.

Interaction Effects

The resilient effects of national origin on both dependent variables suggests that different contexts of exit and reception may not only affect political transnationalism additively, but also interact with other predictors. We examine this possibility by running separate regressions for each immigrant nationality of political transnationalism on the same set of predictors considered previously. Because determinants of broad transnationalism continue to have parallel, albeit weaker effects than those bearing on a strict definition of the concept, we omit them from this analysis. The overall trend is for Colombian transnationalism to be not only exceptional, but also more weakly determined. This is shown by the corresponding R2 and the few predictors that achieve statistical significance in this case. For Colombians, only place of origin and a college education affect the dependent variable. The original hypothesis concerning the positive effect of rural origins on the perpetuation of home country ties is supported in this instance. In addition, college graduation Also increases participation in these activities. Hence, it appears that whatever transnational political activism exists among Colombian immigrants, it follows a bi-modal pattern involving either highly educated individual s or those coming from traditional rural areas. As seen before, most Colombians show little inclination to engage in home country politics of any kind. Since migration from that country comes increasingly from urban areas, our results suggest that this pattern of disinterest in transnational activities may be come even stronger in the future.

Dominicans and Salvadorans are much more vigorously involved in the politics of their home countries. The corresponding regressions introduce controls for city of residence since both national samples were drawn from more than one city. No statistically significant differences between areas of residence were found in either case. In both instances, however, network size increases transnationalism significantly: each additional tie raises the net count of Dominican transnational activities by 16 percent and the count for Salvadorans by 9 percent. The effect of education is also similar for both groups. Since so few Salvadoran or Dominican immigrants are college educated, the key human capital effect is that of high school graduation and it is quite strong in both cases. Differences between Salvadorans and Dominicans, on the one hand, and Colombians, on the other, in the effects of social networks are significant. Differences in the interaction effects between education and nationality approach, fail to achieve, statistical significance.

The same pattern is evident with gender effects. Unlike Colombians, among whom: gender is an insignificant predictor, Dominican and Salvadoran males are much more likely to participate in transnational politics. The effect is especially strong among Dominicans where it exceeds six times its standard error. Temporary SEDs of migration have positive effects among Dominicans and Salvadorans, but only the latter effect is significant, increasing the count of transnational activities by 53 percent. By contrast, the effect of downward occupational mobility proves to be significant among Dominican immigrants only. In this instance, the direction of the effect runs contrary to the original hypothesis: instead of increasing the tendency to engage in transnational activity, downward mobility actually decreases it. The interaction between nationality and this variable is significant, as shown in the last column. Where

Dominican and Salvadoran imm-igrants differ most is in the orientation of their respective political activities. With Dominicans as the reference category, the Salvadoran effect on party politics is significant and negative and that on civic community activism is significant and positive. As expected, Colombian effects are uniformly negative. These results support the conclusion that Dominican immigrants are more likely to concentrate on party politics, while Salvadorans bypass it to focus on the affairs of their local hometowns and regions. Thus, the meaning and scope of political transnationalism is not uniform. Although there are common forces bearing on all immigrants, the particular circumstances of each community also affect the extent and character of these activities. For some immigrants, transnational politics is a means to maintain an active presence in their country' s centers of power; for others, it is a means to avoid such centers in order to provide direct assistance to their native regions; and still for others, it is a practice to be avoided in order to leave a violent and unsettling past behind.

An emerging transnational perspective has brought new vistas on international migration. It has questioned conventional analyses that focus exclusively on assimilation to host society, neglecting migrants' ties and ongoing relations with their countries of origin. Yet serious shortcomings and criticisms have been leveled at this perspective. Most early studies of political transnationalism were based on ethnographic evidence and often lacked clear operational definitions. A dearth of knowledge about the size, scope, and determinants of such practices has been a consistent weakness of this field. Comparing Colombian, Dominican, and Salvadoran immigrants in several are as of settlement, this study seeks to address these shortcomings. It. provides empirical evidence of the scale and determinants of transnational activism among these populations. Our first significant conclusion is that the transnational political field is not as extensive or evenly distributed among contemporary immigrants proposed by previous accounts. In fact, the number of immigrants who are regularly involved in cross-border activism is relatively small. However, this proportion reaches up to one-third of the sample if we shift to a more inclusive definition of transnationalism. The fluctuation between a small core and a larger soft rim of transnational activists suggests its sensitivity to changing contextual conditions. Thus, while core transnationals stay involved in their home country politics via electoral or non electoral means, others be come active only at special junctures such as highly contested elections or natural disasters. A second set of findings is related to determinants of these practices in relation to predictions stemming from different theoretical schools.

Out analysis shows that core transnational engagement is significantly different by gender and associated with migrants' age, human capital, and social capital. Results run counter to classical views of immigrant assimilation, still common in public understandings of the process. Contrary to these views, results indicate that transnational political activities are not the refuge of marginalized or poorly educated immigrants. That conclusion holds, regardless of whether transnationalism is defined strictly or broadly. Along the same lines, length of residence in the United States does not reduce interest or involvement in some country politics, but actually increases it. The uneven distribution of these practices by age and sex coincides with conventional power relations based on patriarchal structures that have historically dominated Latin American politics. The view that greater mal e participation is a result of downward mobility experiences in the United States is not supported since the corresponding main and interaction effects are insignificant. Support for the hypothesis of a strong gender effect must also be qualified by significant differences among national groups. The male proclivity to participate is stronger among Dominicans (the group that gave rise to the hypothesis in the first place), but considerably weaker among other nationalities. Our evidence demonstrates that a stable and significant transnational field of political action connecting immigrants with their countries of origin does exist. Within this, field, we find a repertoire of cross border electoral and non-electoral activities that warrant attention. The analysis shows that migrant~' transnational political engagement is far from being socially unbounded and "deterritorialized", as so me analysts have argued in the past. Transnational actions are socially bounded across national borders and occur in quite specific territorial jurisdictions.

The transnational field is significant not only for home countries, but also for the United States, as it affects the way immigrants incorporate themselves and alters conventional expectations about their assimilation. The presence and dynamics of this phenomenon certainly contradicts a normative view of the assimilation process that places a premium on the rapid shedding of old loyalties and identities. This does not mean, however, that acculturation to the host society is not occurring or that transnational activism necessarily precludes successful integration. The old-line exclusivist views of how assimilation is supposed to occur are contradicted by the fact that the immigrants most involved in transnational activities are better educated, longer residents of the host society, and more likely to become involved in local politics there. Similarly, transnational activism often seeks to reproduce in home country national and local politics the discourses and institutional practices of probity and respect for civil rights learned in the United States. By and large, transnational activism is a constructive phenomenon through which people respond to long-distance social obligations and belonging, and seek to transform political practices in their sending countries. By the same token, it endows immigrants with a renewed sense of efficacy and self-worth that facilitates their integration into the political institutions of their new country.

3

Religion and the Process of Migration

The rapid and drastic process of secularization in western Europe over the last decades has not diminished the continuing unease with which Europe considers the Islamic religion and Muslims in its midst. In this benchmark essay from 2004, José Casanova argues that the "Islam problem" is an indicator of the disparity between liberal and illiberal strands of European secularism. Since the signing of the Treaty of Rome in 1957 that established the EEC and initiated the ongoing process of European integration, western European societies have undergone a rapid, drastic, and seemingly irreversible process of secularization. In this respect, one can talk of the emergence of a post-Christian Europe. At the same time, the process of European integration, the eastward expansion of the European Union, and the drafting of a European constitution have triggered fundamental questions concerning European identity and the role of Christianity in that identity. What constitutes "Europe"? How and where should one draw the external territorial and the internal cultural boundaries of Europe?

The most controversial and anxiety-producing issues, which are rarely confronted openly, are the potential integration of Turkey and the potential integration of non-

European immigrants, who in most European countries happen to be overwhelmingly Muslim. It is the interrelation between these phenomena that I would like to explore in this chapter. The progressive, though highly uneven, secularization of Europe is an undeniable social fact. An increasing majority of the European population has ceased to participate in traditional religious practices, at least on a regular basis, while still maintaining relatively high levels of private individual religious beliefs. In this respect, one should perhaps talk of the unchurching of the European population and of religious individualization, rather than of secularization.

Grace Davie has characterized this general European situation as "believing without belonging". At the same time, however, large numbers of Europeans even in the most secular countries still identify themselves as "Christian," pointing to an implicit, diffused, and submerged Christian cultural identity. In this sense, Danièle Hervieu-Léger is also correct when she offers the reverse characterization of the European situation as "belonging without believing." "Secular" and "Christian" cultural identities are intertwined in complex and rarely verbalized modes among most Europeans. The most interesting issue sociologically is not the fact of progressive religious decline among the European population, but the fact that this decline is interpreted through the lenses of the secularization paradigm and is therefore accompanied by a "secularist" self-understanding that interprets the decline as "normal" and "progressive", that is, as a quasi-normative consequence of being a "modern" and "enlightened" European.

It is this "secular" identity shared by European elites and ordinary people alike, that paradoxically turns "religion" and the barely submerged Christian European identity into a thorny and perplexing issue when it comes to delimiting the external geographic boundaries and to defining the internal cultural identity of a European Union in the process of being constituted. I would like to explore some of the ways in which religion has become a perplexing issue in the constitution of "Europe" through a review of four ongoing controversial debates: the role of Catholic Poland, the incorporation of Turkey, the integration of non-European immigrants, and the place of God or of the Christian heritage in the text of the new European constitution.

Catholic Poland in post-Christian Europe

The fact that Catholic Poland is "re-joining Europe" at a time when western Europe is forsaking its Christian civilizational identity has produced a perplexing situation for Catholic Poles and secular Europeans alike. In a previous issue of Transit, I examined the convoluted, long historical patterns of convergence and divergence in Polish and western European religious developments. It suffices to state here that throughout the Communist era, Polish Catholicism went through an extraordinary revival at the very same time when western European societies were undergoing a drastic process of secularization. The reintegration of Catholic Poland into secular Europe can be viewed therefore as "a difficult challenge" and/or as "a great apostolic assignment".

Anticipating the threat of secularization, the integralist sectors of Polish Catholicism have adopted a negative attitude towards European integration. Exhorted by the Polish Pope, the leadership of the Polish church, by contrast, has embraced European integration as a great apostolic assignment. The anxieties of the "Europhobes" would seem to be fully justified since the basic premise of the secularization paradigm, that the more a society modernizes, the more secular it becomes, seems to be a widespread assumption, also in Poland. Since modernization, in the sense of catching up with European levels of political, economic, social, and cultural development, is one of the goals of European integration, most observers tend to anticipate that such a modernization will lead to secularization also in Poland, putting an end to Polish religious "exceptionalism".

Poland becoming at last a "normal" and "unexceptional" European country is after all one of the aims of the "Euroenthusiasts". The Polish Episcopate, nevertheless, has accepted enthusiastically the papal apostolic assignment and has repeatedly stressed that one of its goals once Poland rejoins Europe is "to restore Europe for Christianity". While it may sound preposterous to western European ears, such a message has found resonance in the tradition of Polish messianism. Barring a radical change in the European secular zeitgeist, however, such an evangelistic effort has little chance of success. Given the loss of demand for religion in western Europe, the supply of surplus Polish pastoral resources for a Europe-wide evangelizing effort is unlikely to prove effective.

The at best lukewarm, if not outright hostile European response to John Paul II's renewed calls for a European Christian revival points to the difficulty of the assignment. I've suggested that a less ambitious, though no less arduous, apostolic assignment could perhaps have equally remarkable effects. Let Poland prove the secularization thesis wrong. Let Polonia Simper Fidelis keep faith in its Catholic identity and tradition while succeeding in its integration into Europe, thus becoming a "normal" European country. Such an outcome, if feasible, could suggest that the decline of religion in Europe might be not a teleological process necessarily linked with modernization but a historical choice that Europeans have made.

A modern religious Poland could perhaps force secular Europeans to rethink their secularist assumptions and realize that it is not so much Poland which is out of sync with modern trends, but rather secular Europe which is out of sync with the rest of the world. Granted, such a provocative scenario is only meant to break the spell which secularism holds over the European mind and over the social sciences. Could a democratic Muslim Turkey ever join the European Christian club. Or, which is the torn country? While the threat of a Polish Christian crusade awakens little fear among secular Europeans confident of their ability to assimilate Catholic Poland on their own terms, the prospect of Turkey joining the European Union generates much greater anxieties among Europeans, Christian and post-Christian alike, but of the kind which cannot be easily verbalized, at least not publicly. Turkey has been patiently knocking on the door of the European club since 1959, only to be told politely to keep waiting, while watching latecomer after latecomer being invited first in successive waves of accession. The formation of the European Coal and Steel Community (ECSC) in 1951 by the six founding members and its expansion into the European Economic Community (EEC) or "common market" in 1957 was predicated upon two historic reconciliations: the reconciliation between France and Germany, two countries which had been at war or preparing for war from 1870 to 1945; and the reconciliation between Protestants and Catholics within Christian Democracy. Indeed ruling or prominent Christian Democrats in all six countries played the leading role in the initial process of European integration.

The Cold War, the Marshall Plan, NATO, and the newly established Washington-Rome Axis formed the geopolitical context for both reconciliations. Greece in June 1959 and Turkey in July 1959, hostile enemies yet members of NATO, were the first two countries to apply for association to the EEC. That same July, the other western European countries formed EFTA as an alternative economic association. Only Franco's Spain was left out of all initial western European associations and alliances. The EEC always made clear that candidates for admission would have to meet stringent economic and political conditions. Ireland, The United Kingdom, and Denmark formally applied for admission in 1961 but only joined in 1973.

Spain and Portugal were unambiguously rebuffed as long as they had authoritarian regimes, but were given clear conditions and definite timetables once their democracies seemed on the road to consolidation. Both joined in 1986. Greece, meanwhile, had already gained admission in 1981 and with it de facto veto power over Turkey's admission. But even after Greece and Turkey entered a quasi-détente and Greece expressed its readiness to sponsor Turkey's admission in exchange for the admission of the entire island of Cyprus, Turkey still did not receive an unambiguous answer, being told once again to go back to the end of the queue. The fall of the Berlin Wall once again rearranged the priorities and the direction of European integration eastward. In 2004, ten new members, eight ex-Communist countries plus Malta and Cyprus are set to join the European Union.

Practically all the territories of Medieval Christendom, that is, of Catholic and Protestant Europe, will now be reunited in the new Europe. Only Catholic Croatia and "neutral" Switzerland will be left out, while "Orthodox" Greece as well as Greek and Turkish Cyprus will be the only religious "other". "Orthodox" Romania and Bulgaria are supposed to be next in line, but without a clear timetable. Even less clear is if and when the negotiations for Turkey's admission will begin in earnest. The first open, if not yet formal, discussions of Turkey's candidacy during the 2002 Copenhagen summit touched a raw nerve among all kinds of European "publics". The widespread debate revealed how much "Islam" with all its distorted representations as "the other" of Western civilization was the real issue rather than the extent to which Turkey was ready to meet the same stringent economic and political conditions as all other new members.

About Turkey's eagerness to join and willingness to meet the conditions, there could be no doubt now that the new, officially no longer "Islamic" government had reiterated unambiguously the position of all the previous Turkish "secularist" administrations. Turkey's "publics", secularist and Muslim alike, had spoken in unison. The new government was certainly the most representative democratic government of all of Turkey's modern history. A wide consensus had seemingly been reached among the Turkish population, showing that Turkey, on the issue of joining Europe and thus "the West", was no longer a "torn country". Two of the three requirements stated by Samuel Huntington for a torn country to redefine successfully its civilizational identity had clearly been met: "First, the political and economic elite of the country has to be generally supportive of and enthusiastic about this move. Second, the public has to be at least willing to acquiesce in the redefinition of identity." It was the third requirement that apparently was missing: "The dominant elements in the host civilization, in most cases the West, have to be willing to embrace the convert."

The dream of Kemal, "Father of the Turks", of begetting a modern Western secular republican Turkish nation-state modeled after French republican laicize has proven not easily attainable, at least not on Kemalist secularist terms. But the possibility of a Turkish democratic state, truly representative of its ordinary Muslim population, joining the European Union, is today for the first time real. The "six arrows" of Kemalism (republicanism, nationalism, secularism, statism, populism, and reformism) could not lead towards a workable representative democracy. Ultimately, the project of constructing such a nation-state from above was bound to fail because it was too secular for the Islamists, too Sunni for the Alevis, and too Turkish for the Kurds.

A Turkish state in which the collective identities and interests of those groups that constitute the overwhelming majority of the population cannot find public representation cannot possibly be a truly representative democracy, even if it is founded on modern secular republican principles. But Muslim Democracy is as possible and viable today in Turkey as Christian Democracy was half a century ago in western Europe. The still Muslim, but officially no longer Islamist party in power has been repeatedly accused of being "fundamentalist" and of undermining the sacred secularist principles of the Kemalist constitution which bans "religious" as well as "ethnic" parties, religion and ethnicity being forms of identity which are not allowed public representation in secular Turkey. One wonders whether democracy does not become an impossible "game" when potential majorities are not allowed to win elections, and when secular civilian politicians ask the military to come to the rescue of democracy by banning these potential majorities, which threaten their secular identity and their power.

Practically every continental European country has had religious parties at one time or another. Many of them, particularly the Catholic ones, had dubious democratic credentials until the negative learning experience of Fascism turned them into Christian Democratic parties. Unless people are allowed to play the game fairly, it may be difficult for them to appreciate the rules and to acquire a democratic habitus. One wonders who the real "fundamentalists" are here. "Muslims" who want to gain public recognition of their identity and demand the right to mobilize in order to advance their ideal and material interests, while respecting the democratic rules of the game, or "secularists" who view the Muslim veil worn by a duly elected parliamentary representative as a threat to Turkish democracy and as a blasphemous affront against the sacred secularist principles of the Kemalist state? Could the European Union accept the public representation of Islam within its boundaries? Can "secular" Europe admit "Muslim" democratic Turkey?

Officially, Europe's refusal to accept Turkey so far is mainly based on Turkey's deficient human rights record. But there are not-too-subtle indications that an outwardly secular Europe is still too Christian when it comes to the possibility of imagining a Muslim country as part of the European community. One wonders whether Turkey represents a threat to Western civilization or rather an unwelcome reminder of the barely submerged yet inexpressible and anxiety-ridden "white" European Christian identity. The widespread public debate in Europe over Turkey's admission showed that Europe was actually the torn country, deeply divided over its cultural identity, unable to answer the question whether European unity, and therefore its external and internal boundaries, should be defined by the common heritage of Christianity and Western civilization or by its modern secular values of liberalism, universal human rights, political democracy, and tolerant and inclusive multiculturalism. Publicly, of course, European liberal secular elites could not share the Pope's definition of European civilization as essentially Christian.

But they also could not verbalize the unspoken "cultural" requirements that make the integration of Turkey into Europe such a difficult issue. The spectre of millions of Turkish citizens already in Europe but not of Europe, many of them second-generation immigrants, caught between an old country they have left behind and their European host societies unable or unwilling to fully assimilate them, only makes the problem the more visible. "Guest workers" can be successfully incorporated economically. They may even gain voting rights, at least on the local level, and prove to be model or at least ordinary citizens. But can they pass the unwritten rules of cultural European membership or are they to remain "strangers"? Can the European Union open new conditions for the kind of multiculturalism that its constituent national societies find so difficult to accept?

Comparative Perspectives from the American Experience of Immigration

Throughout the modern era, western European societies have been immigrant-sending countries, indeed the primary immigrant-sending region in the world. During the colonial phase, European colonists and colonizers, missionaries, entrepreneurs, and colonial administrators settled all corners of the globe. During the age of industrialization, from the 1800s to the 1920s, it is estimated that ca. 85 million Europeans emigrated to the Americas, to Southern Africa, to Australia and Oceania, 60 per cent of them to the United States alone. In the last decades, however, the migration flows have reversed and many western European societies have instead become centres of global immigration.

A comparison with the United States, the paradigmatic immigrant society (despite the fact that from the late 1920s to the late 1960s it also became a society relatively closed to immigration), reveals some characteristic differences in the contemporary western European experience of immigration. Although the proportion of foreign immigrants in many European countries (United Kingdom, France, Holland, West Germany before reunification), at approximately 10 percent is similar to the proportion of foreign born in the United States, most of these countries still have difficulty viewing themselves as permanent immigrant societies or viewing the native second generation as nationals, irrespective of their legal status. But it is in the different ways in which they try to accommodate and regulate immigrant religions, particularly Islam, that European societies distinguish themselves not only from the United States but also from one another.

European societies have markedly different institutional and legal structures regarding religious associations, very diverse policies of state recognition, of state regulation, and of state aid to religious groups, as well as diverse norms concerning when and where one may publicly express religious beliefs and practices. In their dealing with immigrant religions, European countries, like the United States, tend to replicate their particular model of separation of church and state and the patterns of regulation of their own religious minorities. France's etatist secularist model and the political culture of laicité require the strict privatization of religion, eliminating religion from any public forum, while at the same time pressuring religious groups to organize themselves into a single centralized church-like institutional structure that can be regulated by and serve as interlocutor to the state, following the traditional model of the concordat with the Catholic Church. Great Britain, by contrast, while maintaining the established Church of England, allows greater freedom of religious associations which deal directly with local authorities and school boards to press for changes in religious education, diet, etc, with little direct appeal to the central government.

Germany, following the multi-establishment model, has tried to organize a quasi-official Islamic institution, at times in conjunction with parallel strivings on the part of the Turkish state to regulate its Diaspora. But the internal divisions among immigrants from Turkey and the public expression and mobilization of competing identities (secular and Muslim, Alevi, and Kurd) in the German democratic context have undermined any project of institutionalization from above. Holland, following its traditional pattern of pillarization, seemed, until very recently at least, bent on establishing a state-regulated but self-organized separate Muslim pillar. Lately, however, even liberal tolerant Holland is expressing second thoughts and seems ready to pass more restrictive legislation setting clear limits to the kinds of un-European, un-modern norms and habits it is ready to tolerate.

If one looks at the European Union as a whole, however, there are two fundamental differences with the situation in the United States. In the first place, in Europe immigration and Islam are almost synonymous. The overwhelming majority of immigrants in most European countries, the UK being the main exception, are Muslims and the overwhelming majority of western European Muslims are immigrants. This identification appears even more pronounced in those cases when the majority of Muslim immigrants tend to come predominantly from a single region of origin, e.g., Turkey in the case of Germany, the Ma'ghreb in the case of France. This entails a superimposition of different dimensions of "otherness" that exacerbates issues of boundaries, accommodation and incorporation. The immigrant, the religious, the racial, and the socio-economic disprivileged "other" all tend to coincide.

In the United States, by contrast, Muslims constitute at most 10 percent of all new immigrants, a figure that is actually likely to decrease given the strict restrictions to Arab and Muslim immigration imposed after September 11 by the increasingly repressive American security state. Since the US Census Bureau, the Immigration and Naturalization Service, and other government agencies are not allowed to gather information on religion, there are no reliable estimates on the number of Muslims in the United States. Available estimates range widely between 2,8 million and 8 million. Moreover, it is estimated that from 30 to 42 percent of all Muslims in the United States are African-American converts to Islam, making more difficult the characterization of Islam as a foreign, un-American religion. Furthermore, the Muslim immigrant communities in the United Sates are extremely diverse in terms of geographic region of origin from all over the Muslim world, in terms of discursive Islamic traditions, and in terms of socio-economic characteristics.

As a result, the dynamics of interaction with other Muslim immigrants, with African-American Muslims, with non-Muslim immigrants from the same regions of origin, and with their immediate American hosts, depending upon socio-economic characteristics and residential patterns, are much more complex and diverse than anything one finds in Europe. The second main difference has to do with the role of religion and religious group identities in public life and in the organization of civil society. Internal differences notwithstanding, western European societies are deeply secular societies, shaped by the hegemonic knowledge regime of secularism. As liberal democratic societies they tolerate and respect individual religious freedom. But due to the pressure towards the privatization of religion, which among European societies has become a taken-for-granted characteristic of the self-definition of a modern secular society, those societies have a much greater difficulty in recognizing some legitimate role for religion in public life and in the organization and mobilization of collective group identities.

Muslim organized collective identities and their public representations become a source of anxiety not only because of their religious otherness as a non-Christian and non-European religion, but more importantly because of their religiousness itself as the other of European secularity. In this context, the temptation to identify Islam and fundamentalism becomes the more pronounced. Islam, by definition, becomes the other of Western secular modernity. Therefore, the problems posed by the incorporation of Muslim immigrants become consciously or unconsciously associated with seemingly related and vexatious issues concerning the role of religion in the public sphere, which European societies assumed they had already solved according to the liberal secular norm of privatization of religion.

By contrast, Americans are demonstrably more religious than the Europeans and therefore there is a certain pressure for immigrants to conform to American religious norms. It is generally the case that immigrants in America tend to be more religious than they were in their home countries. But even more significantly, today as in the past religion and public religious denominational identities play an important role in the process of incorporation of the new immigrants. The thesis of Will Herberg concerning the old European immigrant, that "not only was he expected to retain his old religion, as he was not expected to retain his old language or nationality, but such was the shape of America that it was largely in and through religion that he, or rather his children and grandchildren, found an identifiable place in American life," is still operative with the new immigrants.

The thesis implies that collective religious identities have been one of the primary ways of structuring internal societal pluralism in American history. One should add as a corrective to the thesis that not religion alone, as Herberg's study would seem to imply, and not race alone, as contemporary immigration studies tend to imply, but religion and race and their complex entanglements have served to structure the American experience of immigrant incorporation, indeed are the keys to "American exceptionalism". Today, once again, we are witnessing various types of collision and collusion between religious identity formation and racial identity formation, processes that are likely to have significant repercussions for the present and future organization of American multiculturalism. Religion and race are becoming, once again, the two critical markers identifying the new immigrants either as assimilable or as suspiciously "alien".

Due to the corrosive logic of racialization, so pervasive in American society, the dynamics of religious identity formation assume a double positive form in the process of immigrant incorporation. Given the institutionalized acceptance of religious pluralism, the affirmation of religious identities is enhanced among the new immigrants. This positive affirmation is reinforced moreover by what appears to be a common defensive reaction by most immigrant groups against ascribed racialization, particularly against the stigma of racial darkness. In this respect, religious and racial self-identifications and ascriptions represent alternative ways of organizing American multiculturalism. One of the obvious advantages of religious pluralism over racial pluralism is that, under proper constitutional institutionalization, it is more reconcilable with principled equality and non-hierarchic diversity, and therefore with genuine multiculturalism. American society is entering a new phase.

The traditional model of assimilation, turning European nationals into American "ethnics", can no longer serve as a model of assimilation now that immigration is literally world-wide. America is bound to become "the first new global society" made up of all world religions and civilizations, at a time when religious civilizational identities are regaining prominence on the global stage.

At the very same moment that political scientists like Samuel Huntington are announcing the impending clash of civilizations in global politics, a new experiment in intercivilizational encounters and accommodation between all the world religions is taking place at home. American religious pluralism is expanding and incorporating all the world religions in the same way as it previously incorporated the religions of the old immigrants.

A complex process of mutual accommodation is taking place. Like Catholicism and Judaism before, other world religions, Islam, Hinduism, Buddhism are being "Americanized" and in the process they are transforming American religion, while the religious Diasporas in America are simultaneously serving as catalysts for the transformation of the old religions in their civilizational homes, in the same way as American Catholicism had an impact upon the transformation of world Catholicism and American Judaism has transformed world Judaism.

This process of institutionalization of expanding religious pluralism is facilitated by the dual clause of the First Amendment which guarantees the "no establishment" of religion at the state level, and therefore the strict separation of church and state and the genuine neutrality of the secular state, as well as the "free exercise" of religion in civil society, that includes strict restrictions on state intervention and on the administrative regulation of the religious field.

It is this combination of a rigidly secular state and the constitutionally protected free exercise of religion in society that distinguishes the American institutional context from the European one. In Europe one finds on the one extreme the case of France, where a secularist state not only restricts and regulates the exercise of religion in society but actually imposes upon society its republican ideology of laïcité, and on the other the case of England, where an established state church is compatible with a wide toleration of religious minorities and a relatively unregulated free exercise of religion in society.

As liberal democratic systems, all European societies respect the private exercise of religion, including Islam, as an individual human right. It is the public and collective free exercise of Islam as an immigrant religion that most European societies find difficult to tolerate precisely on the grounds that Islam is perceived as an "un-European" religion. The stated rationales for considering Islam "un-European" vary significantly across Europe and among social and political groups.

For the anti-immigrant, xenophobic, nationalist Right, represented by Le Pen's discourse in France and by Jörg Haider in Austria, the message is straightforward. Islam is unwelcome and un-assimilable simply because it is a "foreign" immigrant religion. Such a nativist and usually racist attitude can be differentiated clearly from the conservative "Catholic" position, paradigmatically expressed by the Cardinal of Bologna when he declared that Italy should welcome immigrants of all races and regions of the world, but should particularly select Catholic immigrants in order to preserve the Catholic identity of the country. Liberal secular Europeans tend to look askance at such blatant expressions of racist bigotry and religious intolerance. But when it comes to Islam, secular Europeans tend to reveal the limits and prejudices of modern secularist toleration. One is not likely to hear among liberal politicians and secular intellectuals explicitly xenophobic or anti-religious statements. The politically correct formulation tends to run along such lines as "we welcome each and all immigrants irrespective of race or religion as long as they are willing to respect and accept our modern liberal secular European norms". The explicit articulation of those norms may vary from country to country. The controversies over the Muslim veil in so many European societies and the overwhelming support among the French citizenry, including apparently a majority of French Muslims, for the recently passed restrictive legislation prohibiting the wearing of Muslim veils and other ostensibly religious symbols in public schools, as "a threat to national cohesion", may be an extreme example of illiberal secularism. But in fact one sees similar trends of restrictive legislation directed at immigrant Muslims in liberal Holland, precisely in the name of protecting its liberal tolerant traditions from the threat of illiberal, fundamentalist, patriarchal customs reproduced and transmitted to the younger generation by Muslim immigrants.

Revealingly enough, Prime Minister Jean-Pierre Raffarin, in his address to the French legislature defending the banning of ostensibly religious symbols in public schools made reference in the same breath to France as "the old land of Christianity" and to the inviolable principle of laïcité, exhorting Islam to adapt itself to the principle of secularism as all other religions of France have done before. "For the most recently arrived, I'm speaking here of Islam, secularism is a chance, the chance to be a religion of France." The Islamic veil and other religious signs are justifiably banned from public schools, he added, because "they are taking on a political meaning", while according to the secularist principle of privatization of religion, "religion cannot be a political project".

Time will tell whether the restrictive legislation will have the intended effect of stopping the spread of "radical Islam" or whether it is likely to bring forth the opposite result of radicalizing further an already alienated and maladjusted immigrant community. The positive rationale one hears among liberals in support of such illiberal restriction of the free exercise of religion is usually put in terms of the desirable enforced emancipation of young girls, if necessary against their expressed will, from gender discrimination and from patriarchal control. This was the discourse on which the assassinated liberal politician Pim Fortuyn built his electorally successful anti-immigrant platform in liberal Holland, a campaign which is now bearing fruit in new restrictive legislation.

While conservative religious people are expected to tolerate behaviour they may consider morally abhorrent such as homosexuality, liberal secular Europeans are openly stating that European societies ought not to tolerate religious behaviour or cultural customs that are morally abhorrent in so far as they are contrary to modern liberal secular European norms. What makes the intolerant tyranny of the secular liberal majority justifiable in principle is not just the democratic principle of majority rule, but rather the secularist teleological assumption built into theories of modernization that one set of norms is reactionary, fundamentalist, and anti-modern, while the other set is progressive, liberal, and modern. Does one need references to God or to its Christian heritage in the new European constitution or does Europe need a new secular "civil religion" based on Enlightenment principles?

Strictly speaking, modern constitutions do not need transcendent references nor is there much empirical evidence for the functionalist argument that the normative integration of modern differentiated societies requires some kind of "civil religion". In principle, there are three possible ways of addressing the quarrels provoked by the wording of the Preamble to the new European Constitution. The first option would be to avoid any controversy by relinquishing altogether the very project of drafting a self-defining preamble explaining to the world the political rationale and identity of the European Union. But such an option would be self-defeating in so far as the main rationale and purpose of drafting a new European constitution appears to be an extra-legal one, namely to contribute to European social integration, to enhance a common European identity, and to remedy the deficit in democratic legitimacy.

A second alternative would be the mere enumeration of the basic common values that constitute the European "overlapping consensus", either as self-evident truths or as a social fact, without entering into the more controversial attempt to establish the normative foundation or to trace the genealogy of those European values. This was the option chosen by the signatories of the Declaration of American Independence when they proclaimed "We Hold These Truths To Be Self-Evident". But the strong rhetorical effect of this memorable phrase was predicated on the taken-for-granted belief in a Creator God who had endowed humans with inalienable rights, a belief shared by republican deists, Establishmentarian Protestants, and radical-pietist sectarians alike. In our post-Christian and post-modern context, it is not that simple to conjure such self-evident "truths" that require no discursive grounding.

The 2000 Solemn Proclamation of the Charter of Fundamental Rights of the European Union attempts to produce a similar effect with its opening paragraph: "Conscious of its spiritual and moral heritage, the Union is founded on the indivisible, universal values of human dignity, freedom, equality, and solidarity." But the proclamation of those values as a basic social fact, as the common normative framework shared by most Europeans, could hardly have the desired effect of grounding a common European political identity. It simply reiterates the already existing declarations of most national European constitutions, of the 1950 European Convention on Human Rights, and most importantly of the 1948 Universal Declaration of Human Rights of the United Nations. Without addressing explicitly the thorny question of Europe's "spiritual and moral heritage" and its disputed role in the genesis of those supposedly "universal values", it is unlikely that such a proclamation can have the desired effect of inscribing those values as uniquely, particularly, or simply poignantly "European".

The final and more responsible option would be to face the difficult and polemical task of defining through open and public debate the political identity of the new European Union: Who are we? Where do we come from? What constitutes our spiritual and moral heritage and the boundaries of our collective identities? How flexible internally and how open externally should those boundaries be? This would be under any circumstance an enormously complex task that would entail addressing and coming to terms with the many problematic and contradictory aspects of the European heritage in its intra-national, inter-European, and global-colonial dimensions. But such a complex task is made the more difficult by secularist prejudices that preclude not only a critical yet honest and reflexive assessment of the Judeo-Christian heritage, but even any public official reference to such a heritage, on the grounds that any reference to religion could be divisive and counterproductive, or simply violates secular postulates.

The purpose of my argument is not to imply that the new European constitution ought to make some reference to either some transcendent reality or to the Christian heritage, but simply to point out that the quarrels provoked by the possible incorporation of some religious referent in the constitutional text would seem to indicate that secularist assumptions turn religion into a problem, and thus preclude the possibility of dealing with religious issues in a pragmatic sensible manner. Firstly, I fully agree with Bronislaw

Geremek that any genealogical reconstruction of the idea or social imaginary of Europe that makes reference to Greco-Roman antiquity and the Enlightenment while erasing any memory of the role of Medieval Christendom in the very constitution of Europe as a civilization evinces either historical ignorance or repressive amnesia.

Secondly, the inability to openly recognize Christianity as one of the constitutive components of European cultural and political identity means that a great historical opportunity may be missed to add yet a third important historical reconciliation to the already achieved reconciliation between Protestant and Catholics and between warring European nation-states, by putting an end to the old battles over Enlightenment, religion, and secularism. The perceived threat to secular identities and the biased overreaction to exclude any public reference to Christianity belies the self-serving secularist claims that only secular neutrality can guarantee individual freedoms and cultural pluralism. What the imposed silence signifies is not only the attempt to erase Christianity or any other religion from the public collective memory, but also the exclusion from the public sphere of a central component of the personal identity of many Europeans.

To guarantee equal access to the European public sphere and undistorted communication, the European Union would need to become not only post-Christian but also post-secular. Finally, the privileging of European secular identities and secularist self-understandings in the genealogical affirmation of the common European values of human dignity, equality, freedom, and solidarity may not only impede the possibility of gaining a full understanding of the genesis of those values and their complex process of societal institutionalization and individual internalization, but also preclude a critical and reflexive self-understanding of those secular identities. David Martin and Danièle Hervieu-Léger have poignantly shown that the religious and the secular are inextricably linked throughout modern European history, that the different versions of the European Enlightenment are inextricably linked with different versions of Christianity, and that cultural matrixes rooted in particular religious traditions and related institutional arrangements still serve to shape and encode, mostly unconsciously, diverse European secular practices.

The conscious and reflexive recognition of such a Christian encoding does not mean that one needs to accept the claims of the Pope or of any other ecclesiastical authority to be the sole guardians or legitimate administrators of the European Christian heritage. It only means to accept the right of every European, native and immigrant, to participate in the ongoing task of definition, renovation, and transmission of that heritage. Ironically, as the case of French laic etatism shows, the more secularist self-understandings attempt to repress this religious heritage from the collective conscience, the more it reproduces itself subconsciously and compulsively in public secular codes. The four issues analyzed in this chapter, the integration of Catholic Poland in post-Christian Europe, the integration of Turkey into the European Union, the incorporation of non-European immigrants as full members of their European host societies and of the European Union, and the task of writing a new European constitution that both reflects the values of the European people and at the same time allows them to become a self-constituent European demos, all are problematic issues in themselves. But the paper has tried to show that unreflexive secular identities and secularist self-understandings turn those problematic issues into even more perplexing and seemingly intractable "religious" problems.

Role of Religion in the Migration Process

This theme can be looked at from many different angles. The Churches Commission for Migrants in Europe (CCME) is representing European Protestant and Orthodox Churches who are active in advocacy and integration work with migrants and refugees. The issue of religion finds in CCME a collocation in the programme "Uniting in Diversity".

Where is religion playing a role in the life of migrants? Religion has a role at different levels of community life:

- It can be simply a very personal issue of the spiritual life of an individual.
- It may be an aspect of community building, or even the basic reason for community life.
- At states level religion can be an instrument for political and social cohesion or on the opposite a state chooses to leave religious issues completely in the private sphere.

It can also become a major cause of conflicts within a state. All three aspects may play a role for migration processes. There are individual implications, but also community life and the internal cohesion within a country may be influenced by this factor.

Religion and the Individual

a Religion and personal identity: for many persons religion is a component of their personal identity. A specific creed is part of the life of persons. The teachings, the traditions and the habits of a specific religion will influence these people in their behaviour, their way to approach situations and how they relate to each other. The personal value system will be based on the religion the person belongs to. Religion can be an important part of an individual, and even if such a person will migrate to another country he or she will carry with her these elements of faith.

Even if loosing all material possessions this religious capital will stay with this migrant. It is known that religion can become an important part of the identity of a migrant, even if he had rather little interest in religious matters until leaving his home country. In the new situation, having left behind family and social links and feeling the need to defend his identity, religion becomes an important factor. It depends on what the person will find in the host country if this part of identity will become a positive or negative element for the personal integration process. Will religion become an isolating force or a possibility to find a sense of belonging. Faith and religion may become an instrument and opportunity to experience a transnational identity. The migrant may find a way to define for him a new identity made out of components from both societies. This would not be just a summary of two cultures but something new, which could be important for both societies. Precondition for this is an open and tolerant receiving society, where also the local faith communities practice these values.

b Religion may play a role in many parts of daily life: religious convictions and rules influence the life of a believer nearly in all parts of daily life: health and health care are affected. For instance migrant women may find it difficult to access health services because of their religious education. The education of children depends widely on religious values, so as the whole issue of family life. The well-known conflict between first and second generation in migrant communities is also a consequence of this. Religious laws influence the working conditions, the rhythm of the workday and free time; clothing and food rules may not allow people to work in certain places. The question of equal rights for men and women may create critical situations.

Religion and Community Life

Often religion is not only a personal conviction; the believer may be requested to participate actively in community life, as non-renounceable part of his faith. If these believers migrate abroad they will put much energy into finding or rebuilding in the host country some kind of faith community where to live their faith. Religious migrant communities can have a positive or a negative role within the integration process. They may give to the migrant in the first phase of integration, a feeling of home and belonging which will give him or her a sense of security and mutual support, but if these communities are closed and/or marginalised by the host society creating a ghetto like situation this could be contra-productive for the integration process.

Parallel societies may rise and communication between the host society and that of the migrants could become difficult. On the other hand if such a community is an open or even a mixed community with migrant and autochthonous members, where a common faith is the binding link this may become a bridge, and allow a smoother integration process. Finally the religious community has an important role in directing migration movements. It is known that migrants often choose the country or even the town they aim to because of having religious links in that place. They may know that in a certain city lives a community which professes the same creed and where it will be easier to feel at home and to receive support. In this way religion may even become a pull factor for migration.

Religion and State

As long as society was considered homogenous Governments did not consider the question of religion a priority although no society has ever been totally homogeneous. Migration has always existed. Today migration is a structural factor of all states and all must cope with heterogeneous societies, and latest with the events of 11th September in New York the religious question has become an issue in migration politics. The role of religion within the legal system and the functioning of a state is very different in the various parts of the World. There can be total division between religion and state, or there are other states where religion is a dominant factor for legislation and functioning of all parts of the state. In between these two solutions there is a large spectrum of diverse approaches to the question. Problems may arise if migrants who come from one system must cope with the opposite situation in the host country.

An example could be a person or a whole community which comes from a state with Sharia law and will now have to live in a secularised state of the industrialised World. The religious needs, the strong convictions and values the person is carrying with her may create conflicts with the legislation and the way of life in the host country. Social cohesion may be at risk. This becomes even more important if religious institutions of the country of origin continue to influence the life of migrant communities in a country of immigration. As we saw before religion can be important for all parts of daily life and legislation and public administration will have to keep this in mind. The public health system may be affected.

Labour legislation needs to consider the issue. In schools and all educational institutions the problem may arise. I only mention the whole issue of religious schools, which are for various faith communities of basic importance. Commerce and industry may be influenced by consumer behaviour based on religious rules; the same may be said for cultural and scientific work.

Reassuming these reflections it can be said:

1. Migrants need to express and to live their religious creed. This can be a tool for stabilisation, avoiding marginalisation, meanwhile the loss of religious identity will lead to the loss of ethical values and these migrants will be even more disoriented and uprooted in the host society.
2. Similar religious communities of the host society and of the migrant communities should promote exchange and sharing, becoming like this a bridging tool for integration, avoiding marginalisation and frustration of migrant faith communities which may lead to radicalisation. CCME is

working in this direction with its programme "Uniting in Diversity- To be Church Together"

3. The religious communities of the host society may be enriched by the contributions of migrant religious communities. Intercultural experiences can be experienced and eventually transferred into other sectors of social life. The so-called social capital, of basic importance for social cohesion, will be incremented if the religious factor of migration movements is governed correctly. All components of the society and governments will have to work together to pursue this aim.

What could be the role of Christian churches in this context? Why should churches feel the need or the wish to become active in this field? Churches are faith communities and as such have a religious mandate, which makes them act. The basis of the Christian mandate is a book, the Bible and from this text in a theological process Christians elaborated their code of conduct. As far as migrants are concerned there are precise rules which Churches should respect.

The role of churches can be looked at from two points of view. On the basis of their creed churches may be involved in the field of migration in different ways:

1. In order to protect human dignity, rights and freedom churches will become active parts of the society, similar to other social actors.
2. Churches will also act as faith communities, which have their creed in common with certain migrant communities.

Churches as active players in the society defending migrants' and refugees' rights: Churches are faith communities and as such feel like responsible parts of the organised civil society. They cannot live in a spiritual ghetto. This responsibility within the state makes them active players as far as social cohesion is concerned. They intend to be involved in advocacy for the respect of Human Rights and the dignity of all human beings. They should do this in the same conditions as other parts of the society and should not claim for a privileged status - this is at least the position of many Protestant Churches. Working for issues of social and economic justice they will not distinguish between migrants of their own faith and those belonging to other creeds.

They will work in two directions:

a. Advocacy work on migration and asylum policy and legislation.
b. Solidarity programmes to support individuals.

As far as migration policy is concerned they will monitor and lobby decision making processes in order to promote a correct migration policy which respects values so as human rights, solidarity, burden sharing, non-discrimination. In many parts of the World churches do not have the possibility and freedom to act like this.

Recently we worked together with other Christian organisations on fair conditions for forced return measures, in order to insist on the respect of basic rights of migrants and asylum seekers. CCME prepared a document with 12 basic criteria for a correct migration and asylum policy. It opposed the EU Directive on family reunification, which is not respecting the rights of children and the right to live in a family. Anti-discrimination measures have been an important issue of our commitment, so as the fight against trafficking. Speaking on religious issues churches will also have to lobby and to monitor on religious freedom, not only freedom for their own communities but also for the freedom of other creeds and faith communities.

Churches must insist on correct legislation on religious freedom. There must be full respect for religious minorities, also if these are not Christian. In this context the whole debate on common values and on how far faith communities can push their right to promote certain religious rules which may seem not compatible with values which are perceived basic in the host community. A balance must be found between religious freedom of a certain religious community and the basic values and the freedom of all other citizens and communities which the state must protect. Solidarity and support to individuals: In Europe churches promote their own programmes of mutual support for migrants in order to allow their integration and full access to equal rights in all parts of civil life. They run programmes on housing, education, access to the labour market, counselling for migrants and refugees, legal assistance and empowerment by leadership training and support to migrant associations. They promote language schools and courses for vocational training, support refugees who wish to study at university. They run homes for refugees and for unaccompanied minors, for mothers with small children and other vulnerable groups. They protect women who became victims of trafficking and violence.

Churches of the host societies in collaboration with Christian migrant churches "Uniting in Diversity – To be Church Together": A particular question arises when migrants and refugees confess the same creed as a church of the hosting state. Many migrants are Christians. In this case we do not speak of assisting migrants for social needs or giving them legal assistance in order to defend their rights. The link is here totally different; it is a spiritual link with important theological implications. Migrants who are Christians and belong to our churches are not guests but equal partners in our churches. This is important to state, although our churches are not always aware of this fact. It is a big opportunity that in church we can meet on equal footing. There economic, social or cultural levels should not be of any importance.

We are partners with equal rights and duties. This may sound nice and is the basic understanding of churches. Nevertheless the realty is not always like this. Speaking from a European point of view I know very well that our churches in the host countries do not always behave according to this affirmation. We very often handle the issue still as a question of patronising assistance and do not face the deeper questions, so as partnership and empowerment. Migrant churches are questioning our being church. The missionary process starts to be inverted. It is no longer primarily going from North to South, but Christians from the Southern hemisphere often have a strong missionary attitude towards the secularised industrialised World.

It is not always easy to accept this. A migrant Christian who accepts to be a guest in my community is heartily welcomed but if he or she wishes to be a full member, participating also in decision making processes problems arise. If these migrant Christians wish to change our liturgy or to introduce new theological thinking many European churches get into difficulties and may try to stop the process. Within the Christian churches in Europe a similar process is taking place as in the European society as a whole. How can we live together in a multi- or intercultural context? Churches have probably an even bigger responsibility in finding ways, as this is part of their creed. "...no longer guest but citizens..." is said in a letter of S. Pauls.

Churches must find ways to make this a reality. Lets have a quick look at what is happening in European Churches. At the end of 2003, following the dossier of Caritas Italia, there were ca. 24 million migrants in the European Union. About 48,5% of these belong to Christian churches, about 30,9% are Moslems, about 20,5% belong to other religions. The European churches are approaching the situation in very different ways:

- In some countries the local churches choose the way of separate development: Migrant churches grew and are in some countries now the majority churches.
- In others the phenomena was only seen as a question of assistance. Migrant churches started to develop and the local churches supported them often financially

without trying to build up a real mutual understanding and exchange.

- We find a particular approach in local minority churches so as the Protestant churches in Southern European countries: for instance in Italy where Protestants are a very small minority.

Migrants are today at least half of the Protestants, present in Italy. Migrants are worshipping in all Italian Protestant churches. In many communities migrants are the majority, often more than 60%. The Italian Protestant churches found themselves in a totally new situation and must live up to this. These churches must face the question how migrant believers can become fully equal members of the local churches. How can cultural and theological differences become a resource and not a reason for conflict in a multi- or intercultural community?

Also in the Italian Protestant churches various models of cohabitation, sharing and learning from each other are experienced. It may be still to early to judge which one is really reaching the aim of an intercultural community where all parts find there correct placement and will have equal rights, where empowerment of all parts will become a reality. Many migrant Christians prefer to build their own churches where they may live their faith as they did at home. They may use their mother tongue and reproduce their religious traditions. This is a model specially, first generation Christians often choose. It certainly gives a sense of belonging and offers a feeling of home, but if the links with the rest of the society are weak it may not be very helpful for the integration process. The model of the mixed congregation where local people and migrants worship could be another approach, which can lead to very different results: the local church is promoting a process of assimilation and insisting that migrants accept to live their faith exactly in the same way as local people do. This will produce a loss of identity and values of one part of the congregation. The other possibility would be that all parts of the congregation try to grow together learning from each other, developing something new. This would correspond to the Christian believe in the Universal Church where all are equal and have equal rights and duties. It would be a model of empowerment of all members, of real partnership. This is the model Italian Protestant churches are actually aiming for. It is a very challenging aim and we have still a long way to go.

Nevertheless Christians have a big responsibility. To be successful in reaching this objective of a faith community where each member has equal rights and possibilities is of double importance: on one side it means to fulfill the requirements of the Christian faith which is important looking at the question from the inside, but looking at the situation from a secular point of view this approach is important for the integration process of migrants into our societies. If positive religious integration takes place this could become a tool for the whole integration process of migrants. Churches or other faith communities of the receiving countries could become important bridge-makers where a positive value exchange could take place.

Values of the secular society, so as democracy, human rights and active participation could be transferred by this channel, so as important inputs from the migrants could find their way into the receiving society, so as community sense, mutual support and solidarity, cultural contributions and other expertise. Summarising it can be said that churches and all faith communities of the receiving countries have a role to play in the migration process. They can become a bridging tool between different cultures and communities, but if they are not living up to this responsibility, if they are exclusive or dominant, if they are not sharing values, power and goods they may contribute to a negative process of alienation, frustration and marginalisation of migrants. In order to allow faith communities to play this important role positively the states will have to guaranty a correct legislation first of all on migration and asylum issues and second on religious freedom where a balance can be found between the needs of all faith communities, the respect of the freedom of all citizens and the values, considered fundamental for the dignity of human beings and the functioning of the civil society.

A combination of the doctrines of traditional and "modern" religions; ethnicity; marginalization and external forces played complementary roles in the rise and sustenance of the terrorist forms of rebel movements in Uganda. In comparing the insurgent groups of the Holy Spirit Movement (HSM) and that of the Lord's Resistance Army (LRA) in Uganda with similar movements in other parts of the World, the article clearly portrays the uniqueness of the two movements. They used traditional and religious methods combined with violence as a method of mobilizing and indoctrinating recruits, more so from their own people. Several factors led to the popularity and rapid expansion (from about 150 fighters to almost 10,000 fighters) of the short lived HSM of Alice Auma Lakwena (popularly known as Lakwena). Ethnic solidarity that emerged out of the marginalization of northern Uganda, a legacy left by the Colonial government, played a big role in mobilizing fighters (mostly former soldiers of former President Tito Okello, an Acholi) against the government of President Museveni (an Ankole from Western Uganda).

The local people already believed in Lakwena as a healer and this made it easy for her to mobilize followers towards her "vision of removing Museveni's government and proclaiming the word of the Holy Spirit". Lakwena instilled a strong sense of discipline in her combatants and this made her fighters more popular than the government soldiers who were involved in torturing and looting property of the local people. Therefore, the creation of a rebel movement with a strong mix of spirits and some Biblical lineage raised the moral of the Acholi fighters against the government forces. No wonder the HSM forces encountered many problems as their forces expanded to other ethnic tribes in Eastern Uganda. The defeat of the HSM by the government was not felt because Kony swiftly took over as the leader of a more aggressive rebel movement: The LRA. Apart from using spirits and religion, this time a combination of Christianity and Islam, Kony introduced violence on the civilians as a strategy to mobilize his fighting force and sustaining them. Looting, abducting, torturing, rapping and killing became so normal in northern Uganda and Acholi land in particular. The brutality of the government soldiers on the same civilians just added injury to an already bad situation. Most of the "rebel combatants" the government claims to be killing are from among the over 10,000 children abducted by the LRA, some of whom have been killed by leaders of the LRA when ever they attempted to escape.

A blessing in disguise for the LRA is the claim of Uganda government support to the Sudanese People's Liberation Army (SPLA), which resulted to an open support to the LRA by the Sudan government. Thus, making them a powerful force to sustain pressure from the Uganda People's Defense Force (UPDF) and although the Sudan government is said to have stopped giving support to the LRA and allowed the UPDF to fight the LRA inside their territory, the war has not ended. Despite the costly war, in terms of resources, suffering, and "human blood," talking peace to end it is not an alternative being considered by both the government and the LRA. There is simply no trust between the two forces, yet they are also uncomfortable with peace initiatives from outside. The Acholi Religious Leaders' Peace Initiative is trying but there is no sign of breaking through.

Migrants' use of Religion in the Migration Process

Religion plays throughout the migration process and the religious component to migration has been overlooked by most research and literature in sociology and immigration studies. They explain how religion plays a very important role in the migration process, by providing spiritual resources, informing the decision to migrate, influencing attitudes of migrants, and creating social networks. The authors study a Maya community from the western highlands of Guatemala, and their ties to Houston, Texas. Through field study in both the highlands of Guatemala and Houston, the authors have found migrants and their families to increasingly turn to the Pentecostal church as a result of the increasing dangers of migration.

The town the researchers focused on in Guatemala has strong ties to Houston, as a great number of townspeople have migrated there. The cost of undocumented travel to the U.S. both in terms of expense and danger has increased a great deal in the past few years, causing residents to turn increasingly towards the Pentecostal church for counsel, prophesizing and religious services. The authors paid special attention to services called *ayunos,* which are informal prayer services, where pastors who lead them are believed to have the power to hear the will of God and to predict the future. Many people attend *ayunos,* in order to hear the pastor's final decision on if their migration should take place and if so when their migration should take place.

The authors found that as undocumented travel becomes more difficult, the number of *ayunos,* and the people attending them increases dramatically. The authors support the idea that for many Pentecostal Maya: "The decision to migrate, though driven by economic considerations, can ultimately be based on the advice or premonitions of Pentecostal pastors... (and) helps the migrants and their families feel more comfortable with whatever decision is made." The authors divide the migration process into six stages: deciding whether or not to migrate, preparing for the journey, the journey, the arrival, the role of the ethnic church in immigrant settlement, and the development of transnational religious linkages. Through out the migration process, the migrants keep in touch with their home community, family, and pastors through phone calls, mail and in the later stages by visiting family in Guatemala.

The concluding hypothesis the authors make is that migrants come to rely more heavily on religion when they feel little or no control over their situation, and when they must confront many risks during their journey. This being the case, the authors believe that religion will be an important component/resource for other groups of undocumented migrants around the world. They see evidence of their hypothesis in other groups such as undocumented catholic Mexicans. They briefly mention that particular religious beliefs and practices of Pentecostalism may account for the use of religion in undocumented travel, but more research across religious groups must be undertaken to test this hypothesis.

4

The Evolution of Remittances from Family to Faith

The suburb of expensive homes with neatly-trimmed lawns and SUVs seems like any other well-to-do American community. But the mailboxes reveal a twist: almost all are labeled "Patel" or "Bhagat." Over the past twenty years, these Indian immigrants have moved from the villages and small towns of Gujarat State on the west coast of India, initially to rental apartment complexes in northeastern Massachusetts and then to their own homes in subdivisions outside Boston. Watching these suburban dwellers work, attend school, and build religious congregations here, casual observers might conclude that yet another wave of immigrants has successfully joined in the pursuit of the American dream.

A closer look, however, reveals they are pursuing Gujarati dreams as well. They send money back to India to open businesses or improve family homes and farms. They work closely with religious leaders to establish Hindu communities in the United States and also to strengthen religious life in their homeland. Indian politicians at the state and national level now court these emigrants' contributions to Indian political and economic life. The

Gujarati experience illustrates a growing trend among immigrants to the United States and Europe. In the 21st century, many people will belong to two societies at the same time. Researchers call those who maintain strong, regular ties to their homelands and who organize aspects of their lives across national borders transnational migrants. They assimilate into the countries that receive them while sustaining strong ties to their homelands. Assimilation and transnational relations are not mutually exclusive; they happen simultaneously and influence each other. More and more, people earn their livings, raise their families, participate in religious communities, and express their political views across national borders. The host-country experiences of some migrants remain strongly influenced by their continuing ties to their country of origin and the fate of sending communities is inextricably linked to its immigrant members.

Transnational Perspectives on Migration

What do we gain by using a transnational lens to understand the immigrant experience? For one thing, it reveals the many layers and sites that make up the social spaces that they occupy. The relationship between Salvadoran villagers and their migrant family members in urban Los Angeles is not just a product of these narrow, local connections. It is also strongly influenced by ties between the Salvadoran and the U.S. states and between the U.S. and Salvadoran national Catholic Churches. Ties to Salvadorans living in Europe and Mexico also affect these dynamics. Similarly, a complete account of the religious lives of Brazilian immigrants in Massachusetts must go beyond the connections between specific congregations in Boston and Brazil and locate these ties within the thick, multi-layered web of links between national denominations in the United States and Brazil.

Transnational social fields, then, encompass the many sites of migrant and non-migrant connection. They also include the many levels of cross border ties that emerge in response. Furthermore, seeing migrants and non-migrants as occupying the same social space also drives home that becoming incorporated into the United States and sustaining strong ties to one's homeland are not at odds with each other. Rather, the migrant experience is more like a gauge that, although anchored, pivots back and forth between sending, receiving-country, or other orientations, at different stages of life. Migrants do not trade one membership for another. Instead, they change how they direct their energy and resources in response to election campaigns, wars, economic downturns, life-cycle events, and natural disasters. By doing so, they contradict the expectation that newcomers will either fully incorporate or remain entirely transnational and suggest that most people will craft some combination of the two.

Finally, a transnational perspective drives home the point that sometimes migration is as much about the people who stay behind as it is about those who move. In some cases, the ties between migrants and non-migrants are so strong and widespread that migration radically transforms the lives of individuals who remain at home. Actual movement is not required to participate across borders. People, money, and social remittances — or the ideas, practices, identities and social capital that migrants remit home, permeate the daily lives of those who remain behind, altering their behavior, and transforming notions about gender relations, democracy, and what states should and should not do. Non-migrants hear enough stories, look at enough photographs, and watch enough videos of birthday parties and weddings to begin imagining their own lives elsewhere. They covet clothes and accessories that have become part of the dress code.

They want to play by the rules they think are at work in the United States which they learn about each time they talk on the phone, receive e-mail, or someone comes to visit. In such cases, migrants and non-migrants, though separated by physical distance, still occupy the same social space. Although laws and political borders limit movement and formal citizenship within it, their lives are strongly connected by a range of economic, political, and religious activities that cross borders. What happens to those in the U.S. cannot be separated from what happens to those who remain in the homeland because their fates are inextricably linked. In the last decade, migrant economic remittances have been hailed as a development panacea. These debates largely overlook the social remittances that are exchanged between migrants and non-migrants and their potential role in the development equation. The remainder of this chapter discusses what social remittances are, how they are transmitted and what determines their impact, and how they change the lives of women.

Defining and Specifying Social Remittances

There are at least three types of social remittances — normative structures, systems of practice, and social capital. Normative structures, are ideas, values, and beliefs. They include norms for behavior, notions about family responsibility, principles of neighborliness and community participation, and aspirations for social mobility. They encompass ideas about gender, race, and class identity. They also include values about how organizations should work, incorporating ideas about good government and good churches and about how politicians and clergy should behave. Systems of practice are the actions shaped by normative structures.

These include how individuals delegate household tasks, the kinds of religious rituals they engage in, and how much they participate in political and civic groups. They also include organizational practices such as recruiting and socializing new members, goal setting and strategizing, establishing leadership roles, and forming interagency ties. Both the values and norms on which social capital is based, and social capital itself, also constitute social remittances. Social and political leaders can sometimes harness the status they acquire in the host country to advance their cause in the homeland. The non-migrant family members of the hometown association leader in California, for example, can access the social capital he or she has accrued back in Mexico.

Decreases in migrant social capital also register. If someone was a respected community leader in Los Angeles, but has fallen out of favor, the family also feels this back in Mexico. Social remittance exchanges occur when migrants return to live in or visit their communities of origin; when non-migrants visit those in the receiving country; or through exchanges of letters, videos, cassettes, e-mails, and telephone calls. The mechanisms of social remittance transmission differ from other types of global cultural dissemination in several ways. First, while it is often difficult to distinguish how global culture is disseminated, it is possible to specify how social remittances flow. They travel through identifiable pathways; their source and destination are clear. Migrants and non-migrants can state how they learned of a particular idea or practice and why they decided to adopt it.

A second feature differentiating social remittances from global cultural flows is that they are transmitted systematically and intentionally. A social remittance occurs when migrants speak directly to a family member about a different kind of politics and encourage them to pursue reforms. In cases such as these, ideas are communicated intentionally to a specific recipient or group. People know when and why they changed their mind about something or began to act in a different way. A third distinguishing feature is that remittances are usually transferred between individuals who know one another or who are connected by mutual social ties. A familiar person who comes "with references" delivers them. The personalized character of this kind of communication stands in contrast to the faceless, mass-produced nature of global cultural diffusion. A fourth difference between social remittances and global culture is the timing with which they are communicated. In many cases, a staged process occurs whereby macro-level global flows precede and pave the way for social remittance transmission. Since many non-migrants are eager to emulate the consumption patterns they observe in the media, they are more receptive to the new political and religious styles migrants bring back. Social remittances do not arise out of the blue. They are part and parcel of an ongoing process of cultural diffusion. Gradual transmission sets the stage for future remittance transfers that, as a result, make more sense.

A variety of factors determine the nature and magnitude of social remittance impact:

- The nature of the remittance itself - Social remittance impact is, in part, a function of how easy it is to transmit a particular remittance. Some remittances are difficult to package. They do not translate easily into neat data packets because they are slippery, unstable, and unwieldy to send. They are sometimes so complex that they are difficult to communicate or theorize. They have to be broken down into smaller pieces to be exchanged.
- The features of transnational organizations and the social networks through which remittances are communicated also influence their impact. Remittances flow more efficiently through tightly connected, dense systems because they consist of similar parts and use similar technologies. Transfers within more open, informal systems are sloppier, less efficient, and more prone to interference by other cultural exchanges. As in the child's game of "telephone," each time a message is re-communicated; it becomes increasingly distorted in the translation. Remittance impact also changes at different stages of organizational development. New

organizations or organization in flux are more malleable or amenable to change and, thus, more open to remittance acceptance.

- The character of the messenger also influences remittance impact. Individuals occupying higher status positions get listened to more. These tend to be men, people with money, older community members, or established community leaders. In some cases, these individuals get listened to because others depend on them for economic support. In others, people adopt remittances because they want to emulate their peers. Since everyone belonging to a certain class is doing it, they want to keep up with the Jones'.
- Remittance impact also depends on the gender, class, and life-cycle stage of the receiver. Individuals with more resources and power, who have more control over their lives, have more freedom to accept or reject remittances.
- Social remittance impact is influenced by relative differences between sending and receiving countries. If the value structures and cognitive models migrants import are similar to host- country norms, then social remittances are likely to be assimilated more quickly. If the new patterns of social relations have elements in common with those already in places, then social remittances are also more likely to be adopted. If the remittance is a completely new idea or behavior, then it will face greater barriers to acceptance. In this sense, remittance adoption, as well as evolution, is path dependent, in that existing normative, cognitive, and structural constraints condition future choices.
- Some remittances have a stronger effect because they travel with other remittances. When those introduced first are accepted, receptivity to those that follow is heightened. Remittances traveling through multiple pathways, or those reinforced by global cultural flows, also have a more significant effect.

Finally, the force of transmission affects remittance impact. If many remittances are transmitted consistently during a short time, their impact is greater than when they are transferred periodically. If there are many, simultaneous calls for a particular change, and numerous examples of people who have adopted it, than non-migrants are more likely to change than if they were exposed to only infrequent, isolated examples of a particular behavior.

Changing Gender Dynamics

There are numerous examples of how social remittances change the status of migrant and non-migrant women. Let me mention three brief examples: • Many of the young women in the Dominican village of Miraflores from which, during the 1990s, more than 65 percent of the households sent migrants to Boston, completely changed their ideas about the kind of men they wanted to marry. They learned that since both men and women have to go out to work in Boston, the man helps out much more with the children and the housework when they return home at night. They observed that when married couples came back to visit, they seemed to make decisions together and that the husband seemed to treat his wife with more respect. In response to these social remittances, they demanded a different kind of partnership. They did not want to marry a man who had never migrated and who continued to treat women in the "old" way. They wanted to be with someone who would treat them as equals.

Most of the people who belong to the Islamic Center of New England are Pakistanis. On the whole, they are well-educated professionals who belonged to the upper middle-class before they migrated and have maintained their status in the U.S. Because Pakistan is an Islamic country, they never had to think much about what it meant to be Muslim. But in the United States, they are forced to figure out what their faith means to them and how to pass it along to their children. This transforms the mosque from a center of prayer, with no formal leadership structure, to a social and cultural center with tax-deductible status and a board of directors. Enter women. In Pakistan, most women do not go to the mosque to pray. In Boston, they not only pray alongside men, they run the mosque alongside them as well. News of these changes travels back to Karachi where some women say, "This is all well and good but we still want to pray at home." Others, however, are galvanized by these changes and try to create new spaces where women can collectively pray and study together.

Many of the Brazilian migrants who have settled in Boston come from the city of Governador Valadares. As more and more women start their own housecleaning and office cleaning companies, they have also assumed a prominent role in organizational life of this community. Women started one of the branches of the Brazilian Business Network as well as many of the community's social and cultural organizations. Some of the women in Valadares who have learned about this followed suit and became leaders of their churches or neighborhood groups. Others simply revisited their assumptions about political participation, acknowledging that women can play a much more central role than they ever thought possible and that it is important for them to participate, albeit only with their vote.

Social Remittances and Development

Not all migrants are transnational migrants nor do all those who participate in transnational activities do so all the time. But when a small group is regularly involved in their sending country, and others participate periodically, their combined efforts add up. Taken together and over time, these activities constitute a social force with tremendous transformative significance that can modify the economy, values, and everyday lives of entire regions. Social remittances play a key role in bringing about such changes.

Not all social remittances are positive, however. What some consider a force for greater democratization and accountability, others hold responsible for rising materialism and individualism. Furthermore, culture does not flow only one way. Migrants introduce new ideas and practices to the countries that receive them which transform the host culture, in both positive and negative ways as well. Social remittances are under-utilized development resources that have the potential to be purposefully harnessed to improve socioeconomic outcomes in both sending and receiving countries.

This can happen in several ways:

1. To improve socioeconomic indicators - To the extent that migrants and non-migrants are embedded in transnational social fields, the forces shaping their health, education, and class status are also transnational. By systematically encouraging flows of information about health and education back to the source country and by stimulating a parallel flow of information to the host country, practitioners and policymakers will better understand the factors determining socioeconomic outcomes in a transnational field. By paying attention to social remittances, teachers and health care providers will understand the assumptions and expectations underlying health and educational behavior better. They will also have more powerful, effective tools with which to improve them.
2. Defining social categories like race, class, and gender- Those who live in transnational social fields are managing two sets of, often conflicting, ideas about race, gender, and class. How people thing about race in Latin America is, in many ways, the exact opposite of how it is conceived in the United States. One drop of black blood meant being black in the United States while the slightest link to whiteness made it possible to ascend the racial hierarchy in Latin America.

Migrants and non-migrants use social remittances to square these conflicting social expectations. Dominicans who migrated to Boston, for example, thought of themselves as white before they moved to the United States. Soon after their arrival, they realized they were being slotted into a different racial category in the U.S. and they told those who remained behind about this.

This exposure made non-migrants reconsider their relations with their Haitian neighbors. Some became more tolerant while others more firmly asserted their whiteness in the face of this new threat. In this example, racial identities were transnationally determined, largely in response to social remittance flows. These dynamics do not confine themselves to class. Those who live across borders earn their living and measure their success in two different socioeconomic contexts. How should class be defined when migrants receive government assistance toward their housing costs in the United States at the same time that they are building homes in their sending communities? What about those who have trouble paying their rent because they continue to support family members in their homelands? In cases such as these, both remaining poor and getting ahead, and where one locates oneself in the class hierarchy, are influenced by home and host-country factors. Therefore, shouldn't programs aimed at alleviating poverty take both contexts into account?

3. Culture as an asset - Culture is an under-explored, under-utilized development asset. Poverty alleviation and development require not only getting the structures right. They also require getting the heart and soul right. Culture is a valuable asset in creating communities, helping communities identify problems, and in coming up with solutions to them. It is a safe way for factions within communities, divided by gender or generation, to clarify their positions and achieve consensus. The more culture is harnessed to build strong, viable

communities that know what they want and how to achieve it, the more such groups will be able to protect their interests and make claims *vis a vis* the policymakers, development professionals, and state officials they work with.

Until recently, the importance of the money migrants send home to developing countries has been little studied, with foreign direct investment and official development assistance receiving most of the attention. When migration experts and economists have taken an interest in migrants' remittances, they have done so in the form of country case studies or limited surveys. But as remittances have swelled in recent years, they have drawn more attention—as a raw financial flow, as an opportunity to expand financial services in the developing world, as a well of funds for money launderers, and as a source of capital with significant development potential. For example, the 2003 edition of the World Bank's Global Development Finance (GDF) brought migrant workers' remittances to the attention of a broad audience of professionals and experts in development finance.

And, for the past few years, the Multilateral Investment Fund of the Interamerican Development Bank has raised awareness and catalyzed initiatives related to remittances in Latin America and the Caribbean. In October 2003 the first international conference on migrant workers' remittances will highlight the range of developmental, policy, and regulatory issues surrounding remittances and their relation to migration and financial systems and services. The conference builds on initiatives of the World Bank and the U.K. Department for International Development with strong and shared interest from other funding and investment agencies. This study is a contribution to the conference. Africa, and particularly Sub-Saharan Africa, has received little attention in studies or discussions of remittances. This may be explained in part by the relatively low share of remittances going to the African continent (15 percent of total flows to developing countries) and the even lower share going to Sub-Saharan Africa (5 percent), and by the relatively small number of international migrants from Africa, as well as their greater dispersion, compared to migrants from other developing regions.

Remittances to Africa are nevertheless an important financial flow—with significant developmental effects. Moreover, their level is probably much higher than official data indicates. Many transactions go unrecorded or unreported, in large part because financial systems and services are weak in much of Africa. That weakness creates obstacles for the efficient transfer of remittances through formal money transfer services and limits the potential of remittances to contribute to development (for example, through investment). Regulatory and policy impediments block private-sector solutions to the problem. In analyzing remittance flows, it is helpful to distinguish between cross-border (or international) and domestic (in-country) flows as well as between officially recorded and unrecorded flows. Most published figures on migrant remittances are based on officially recorded flows, meaning flows passing through banks or other formal financial institutions and captured as part of the balance of payments data reported by each country to the International Monetary Fund (IMF) and published annually in IMF's Balance of Payments Statistics Yearbook.

Fewer than two-thirds of all African countries, and just one-third of Sub-Saharan countries, report official figures. Those figures include only cross-border flows captured by central banks as part of international transactions. As for domestic remittance transfers, nowhere in Africa are these captured as a separate category of domestic transactions; they can be traced only through household surveys. An unknown but substantial portion of overall remittance flows goes unrecorded either because imperfect systems fail to capture the transactions involved or because the remittances pass through informal channels that do not report data. The range of informal transfer systems includes personal carriage of cash or goods by migrants, their relatives, their friends, or trusted agents. Other informal services operate as a side business to an import-export operation, retail shop, or currency dealership. Most keep little paper or electronic documentation. Transactions are communicated by phone, fax, or e-mail to a counterpart who will make the payment. Details vary.

The best known of the informal services are *hawala* and *hundi,* which operate in a similar fashion. The terms can be used interchangeably, but *hawala* is typically used in the context of the Middle East and Arab countries and their migrant populations, whereas *hundi* is usually connected with South Asia (especially Bangladesh). Drawing on relevant literature and experts in the field, this study surveys remittances in the African context, emphasizing their relation to financial systems and services. After analyzing available documentation to shed light on the motives behind migration, sending money home, the uses of remittances, and the choice of transfer channels and services, the study explores the actual and potential contributions of remittances to development. A subsequent analysis of remittance services and related regulatory and policy issues identifies obstacles to effective and efficient transfers. The study concludes with a brief summary of key findings and provides research and policy recommendations. Sub-Saharan Africa is the principal locus of the study. We concentrate on the region's distinct migration and remittance patterns, which differ from those of North Africa.

Remittance Flows

Remittances from migrant workers to their families in developing countries more than doubled over the past decade, from $33.1 billion in 1991 to $80 billion in 2002. The 10 percent increase from 2001 to 2002 illustrates how growth in remittances has accelerated. Remittances now constitute the second largest flow of external finance, well behind foreign direct investment but far ahead of official development assistance. Remittances also have proved more stable than other sources of finance, and most experts now believe that remittances create a steady net positive transfer. Informal transfers and formal but unrecorded transfers add another order of magnitude to remittance flows, bringing the estimated total to as much as $200 billion, more than foreign direct investment. Also unrecorded but not included in most estimates are domestic remittance flows resulting from rural-to-urban and rural-to-rural migration. These can be substantial sources of income for many more households, more so than overseas remittances. Domestic remittance transactions are typically much lower in value than international ones, but their cumulative value is believed substantial, although this belief has been substantiated only in isolated case studies.

Officially reported remittance flows to Africa are relatively low compared to flows to other developing regions. Official figures provide a skewed and incomplete picture, however, because data collection in the region is exceptionally poor and spotty. For Sub-Saharan Africa, for example, only about one-third of countries report data, much of which is of low quality. Thus, although remittance flows to Africa are heavily underreported, even the officially recorded flows indicate the significant financial inflow they constitute. Africa received some $12 billion in officially recorded workers' remittances in 2002, about 15 percent of global remittance flows to developing countries in 2002. Split regionally, Sub-Saharan Africa received $4 billion, or 5 percent of the global total, whereas the Middle East and North Africa together received $14 billion (18 percent). North Africa alone accounted for about $8 billion (10 percent). Whereas remittances to developing countries have more than doubled over the last decade, remittances to Africa have grown little and, as a result, have declined in relative share. Total remittance receipts to Africa over the past decade peaked in 1992 (at $10.7 billion) and were at their lowest in 2000 ($7.8 billion). For Sub-Saharan Africa, the share of global workers' remittances to developing countries dropped from some 8 percent in 1980 to 5 percent in 2002, reflecting the growth of flows to other regions rather than any absolute reduction in flows. The strong and consistent flow of remittances to North Africa reflects patterns of migration to Europe and the Middle East. Most remittances to Africa over the past decade were received in North Africa (72 percent), followed by East Africa (13 percent), and Southern and West Africa (7 and 5 percent). Central Africa records less than one percentage point in remittances. The most pronounced change in Sub-Saharan Africa over this period is that remittances to West Africa have decreased relative to total flows to the continent, whereas remittances to East Africa have increased.

This change could be due partly to liberalization of the financial sector, as in Uganda, to increased refugee flows into East Africa, and to the expansion of money transfer operators in the East African market since the mid-1990s. Only a thorough analysis of changes in both regions—one that included unrecorded flows, changes in data-collection definitions, and changes in available services—could offer a persuasive interpretation. No estimate of unrecorded flows (formal or informal) is available specifically for Africa. If one were to extrapolate from global estimates, total flows would be 2.5 times the official data. In Africa, however, unrecorded flows appear to be exceptionally high, especially in certain countries. In Sudan, for example, informal remittances are estimated to account for 85 percent of total remittance receipts. Overall, the weakness or absence of financial systems on the continent and the high proportion of intraregional migration suggest that informal remittances are likely to be a substantial share of total remittances. What is certain is that the official figures grossly underreport remittance levels.

Top Receiving Countries

A few countries dominate the remittance picture in Africa. It will be seen that migration patterns explain that dominance. Until 2001, Egypt was the largest receiver on the continent for a decade (in annualized nominal terms). In 2001, Morocco's remittance receipts overtook those of Egypt. In Sub-Saharan Africa the single largest receiver was Nigeria, which receives between 30 and 60 percent of remittances to the Sub-Saharan region, followed by Lesotho, Sudan, Senegal and Mauritius. Tunisia, Sudan, and Mozambique were also important recipients. Among the small African states, the top receivers were Mauritius, Lesotho, Cape Verde, and Botswana, although they also are the only four small countries with continuous data records. The other nine small African nations had no data for most of the years 1990 to 2001. Remittances for the small states have been declining compared to flows for the whole continent. While the data set is too small and weak to permit any solid conclusions, the apparent downward trend may reflect developments such as decreasing opportunities in South Africa for Basotho mineworkers, resulting in reduced remittances to Lesotho. Looking at individual countries, however, the flows can be quite erratic, an effect that may be traceable to inconsistent data reporting.

Key Source Countries

The continent's top five remittance sending countries for the period 1990 to 2001 were South Africa, Ivory Coast, Angola, Egypt, and Botswana. Egypt and Côte d'Ivoire are thus key receivers as well as senders, a reflection also of migration patterns. Both have gone through various phases of immigration. Due to economic downturn and war many migrants have left in recent years and remittance outflows have dropped. The world's top sources of workers' remittances to developing countries in 2001 were the United States, Saudi Arabia, Germany, Belgium, Switzerland, and France. The U.S. total of $28.4 billion may be grossly over reported, as the United States is the main hub of correspondent bank transactions. Although disaggregated data are not readily available for overseas remittance transfers to Africa specifically, it is very likely that the top sending countries are the same as the top destinations for migrants—France, Italy, Saudi Arabia, and the United States.

Remittances and Migration in Africa

Remittances are inherently linked to migration. Whether for economic or other reasons, migrants from developing countries leave their homes to improve their own livelihood and opportunities as well as to support the family back home. Worldwide, one of every 35 people, an estimated 175 million, live outside their country of origin, up from 75 million in 1965. The prime motivator for migration has been and remains economic, but colonial history and the increasing ease of travel have profoundly shaped its patterns. Migration is projected to grow at an annual rate of 2 to 3 percent. Remittances to developing countries have far outpaced migration over the past decade. While not statistically correlated, migration patterns and remittance flows are clearly congruent. Migration is the undercurrent that drives remittances. Motives for migration, choice of destination, and the purposes and means for sending home money are thus important contextual aspects of remittances that should inform policymakers and providers of money transfer services.

Migratory Patterns and Trends

Like people in other developing regions, Africans migrate to reduce economic or political insecurity and to earn a better livelihood both for themselves and the family they leave behind. Migrant workers send money home from their host countries overseas or, as is often the case for African migrants, from neighboring urban centers or nearby countries. The prime motivator for most African migrants is still economic, although war and political insecurity are increasingly compelling reasons. Refugees are a key group of African migrants. Most are displaced to neighboring countries, but some move overseas. North African and Sub-Saharan African migrant flows differ substantially. As African migration has been heavily defined by former colonial links and by cultural and linguistic affinities, North Africans have tended to move to Europe, the Middle East, and (to a lesser extent) North America. In contrast, Sub-Saharan migrants have tended to stay on the continent, moving within the region or their country.

The same patterns hold true for short-term and seasonal migration. Except for North Africans, distance and the cost of migration from the African continent are relatively high. For selected countries, migration can be substantial. For instance, in Nigeria two-thirds of all households are estimated to have had emigrants, and about one-tenth of Nigerians now live outside their country of birth. Migration can also be strongly segmented by cultural group. Different tribes or ethnic groups may be more prone to migration. In one area of dry-land Mali, for example, migration is frequent within the Bambara group and less so among the Fulani or the Maure. As the following sections discuss in more detail, seasonal or internal migrants often have low incomes and seek employment in urban centers or short-term income during peak agricultural seasons.

Internal and Seasonal Migration

Many African countries have a high rate of internal migration. De Haan estimated that during the 1980s one-third of Kenyan rural heads of household migrated. Similarly, in South Africa approximately 1 million people, mostly unskilled laborers, moved from other parts of the country to Gauteng (with Johannesburg as the major city) or the Western Cape (Cape Town). Seasonal migration is often internal but also intraregional; occasionally it leads overseas. It tends to increase with poor growing conditions or other hardships at home. A survey in the early 1990s in Eritrea showed that villages relied heavily on income from seasonal migration, to nearby towns or as far away as Saudi Arabia. In Mali migration is used to improve food security, as it relieves pressure on food stocks during the lean season. For migrants, the boundaries of internal and intraregional migration are often of little consequence. Tribal, ethnic, or cultural boundaries often transcend those of nation states, and most migrants are more concerned with income opportunities than political boundaries.

Intraregional Migration

Intraregional migration is very common in Africa, a fact reflected in the continent's migrant stock. Africa is home to about 9 percent of migrants globally, compared to 6 percent for Southeast Asia and Latin America and the Caribbean, 23 percent for North America, and 11 percent for Western Europe. Within Africa, West and East Africa have the largest share of the continents' migrant stock—42 and 28 percent, respectively. Each African region contains one or two centers of attraction for immigration. The establishment of regional economic bodies has also tended to generate labor mobility. Within ECOWAS, for instance, Côte d'Ivoire and Nigeria attract immigration from Sub-Saharan Africa; within SADC Botswana and South Africa play the same roles. West Africa and Southern Africa have gone through several phases of internal and intraregional migration. *West Africa* has a long but irregular tradition of labor migration facilitated by shared socio-cultural bonds that transcend language divisions. Côte d'Ivoire's liberal immigration policies over three decades made it a major hub for migrants and one of the top remittance- Migrant Stock by African Region sending countries on the continent until war and economic difficulties caused them to leave. Until recently it was home to some three million migrants—about one-quarter of the population in the country. Many worked as manual laborers on cotton, cocoa, and coffee plantations.

Overall, one in three West Africans was estimated to be living outside his village or district of birth. In *Southern Africa* migration has for decades been characterized by contract labor, predominantly within the mining industry. South Africa thus has long been a magnet for unskilled labor from the region. It is home to an estimated 3 to 8 million migrants, many from Zimbabwe, Lesotho, and Mozambique. Most are employed in the mining industry. Although the flows of contractual labor increased markedly in the post-apartheid era, the demand for foreign labor in the mines has since declined as a result of economic weakness. *East Africa* is best known for its movements of refugees, especially around the Horn of Africa and the Great Lakes region, and less known for labor migration (IOM 2000). Tanzania, Guinea, and Sudan have the largest numbers of refugees in nominal terms, whereas Guinea, Congo, and Zambia have the highest proportion of refugees to total population.

Overseas Migration

Overseas emigration from Africa, especially Sub-Saharan Africa, is less pronounced than for other developing regions. Nonetheless, it is still significant. Europe and the Middle East have been the prime destinations. Historical, cultural, and linguistic bonds have produced a strong flow of skilled and unskilled migrants between African nations and their former colonies. Many Sub-Saharan Africans have stayed on after training at institutions of higher education in Belgium, France, Portugal, Spain, and the United Kingdom. *Western Europe* had a population of some 3.4 million African nationals in 2000, of whom about 2.3 million originated from North Africa. Malians, though predominantly drawn to Ivory Coast, also have substantial migrant communities in France. Schoorl and others estimated that 10 to 20 percent of Ghanaians lived overseas during the 1980s and early 1990s. Overall, however, Africans people made up only about 5 percent of the total foreign and foreign-born population of the OECD countries in 2002.

The *United States* is home to far fewer African migrants than is Europe. Some 400,000 Sub-Saharan Africans and 110,000 North Africans migrated to the United States between 1978 and 1998 (IOM 2002). Overseas migrants, especially to developed countries, have tended to be highly educated. For instance, African-born migrants in the United States had the highest levels of education of any immigrant group. Professional and economic rewards are often their key motivations. Skilled and professional migrants tend to spend more time abroad than others. In Côte d'Ivoire, for example, the median number of years spent abroad was four for the less skilled and six for elite returnees. In a survey of Ghanaians, more than half of the elite returnees had spent over ten years abroad, whereas most of the less skilled had returned after six years.

Migration Trends

Recent changes in African migration, ascribable mainly to developments in the socio- political and economic environments, represent a fundamental shift in what has always been a complex pattern—a phenomenon markedly different from the relatively consistent patterns and trends observed for Asia or Latin America. Although the probable outcomes of those changes have yet to emerge—and although data are generally lacking and unreliable—pressures for emigration are seen to be growing. Net migration estimates for 1990–2000 show a trend of increased emigration from Sub-Saharan Africa to developed countries. Together with new outflows of North African workers to Kuwait and Saudi Arabia, the increase in Sub-Saharan emigration contributed to a rise in net migration from Africa during the 1990s. Increased emigration can be attributed partly to economic stagnation and downturn in Southern Africa, West Africa, and elsewhere. Low-skilled laborers, who have traditionally migrated within the region, are found to have expanded their horizons to Europe, the Middle East, and Asia. Conversely, however, more highly skilled professionals have moved to take up professional opportunities on the continent—in Botswana and South Africa—rather than in Europe. War and civil strife are growing drivers of African migration. This trend has ancillary effects, as refugees tend to set off or shape migration patterns on departure as well as on return. In their host destination, they can contribute to or cause conflict, leading to displacement of other groups. On return to their home countries, they can generate internal migration; for example, toward urban centers. When war affects a country of immigrants, such as Côte d'Ivoire, economic migrants can become refugees. The motives for and patterns of migration are often gendered. In Ghana, for instance, the main reason for male migration has been economic, whereas for women it has been family related.

Gender differences may also occur between regions in a country. In Benin, for example, male migrants predominate in the north, female migrants in the center and south. Overall, African migration has is becoming "feminized," as more women are migrating alone. Although the feminization of migration has been a global trend for some time, it is a fairly new phenomenon in Sub-Saharan Africa, one that contrasts starkly with the traditional pattern of migrating males who leave their immediate family at home. Female migration tends to be linked to socioeconomic issues different from those of male migration, including vulnerability to exploitation (such as trafficking and domestic labour).

The Effect of Migration on Remittances

As African migration is generally on the rise, remittances are bound to remain a substantial and important flow. In fact, one would expect remittances to have grown with migration, although such growth has not been observed in official remittance data. It may be that growth occurred in informal or unrecorded formal remittances. Typically, migration and remittance patterns do not mirror each other readily, nor do their respective flows correlate statistically, as discussed below. Rankings among the top remittance- receiving and sending countries in Africa are only partially explained by migration patterns—distortions in the allocation of flows account for the rest. Distortions may arise because the value of the remittances of international migrants far exceeds those of intraregional and domestic migrants, even though international migrants are fewer in number. Another source of potential distortion is that refugees quite often remit to, or receive in, neighboring countries rather than their home countries.

Moreover, levels of remittances differ by migrant group and migrational intent as well as duration, among other factors, as further discussed in the next section. A very simple comparison of some hubs of African migration and remittances illustrates the relatively high level of congruency between the two phenomena—and also some differences. Remittances are one of the developmental effects of migration. As shown in the next section, such effects are felt most distinctly at the individual or household level, but also at the community and national levels.

Developmental Effects of Remittances

Remittances make substantial developmental contributions to recipients and to their national economies. For Africa, as for other regions, remittances constitute a major source of foreign exchange and influence, often quite significantly, the national balance of payments. They also make up a fair share of gross domestic product in many countries and may outstrip other financial flows, all ancillary effects of a private flow of funds intended primarily as family support and directed at individuals and households. Remittances to Eritrea were 194 percent of exports and 19 percent of GDP in 1999.

For Cape Verde the same values were 51 percent and 12 percent; for Comoros, 24 percent and 6 percent; for Egypt, 26 percent and 4 percent; and for Morocco, 18 percent and 5 percent. For remittance receivers, these funds are often an important or vital source of income and have an important income-smoothing effect. Although remittances are generally spent for consumption and other individual or household needs, a small portion is invested, usually in property or a business. Similarly, communal or collective remittances, while making up a tiny fraction of total remittances, are typically invested in community improvements. These applications are discussed in more detail below.

Macro Effects

The volume and share of remittances relative to other financial flows is smaller in Africa than in other developing regions. Africa, and especially Sub-Saharan Africa, is the most aid- dependent of all developing regions—with official development assistance accounting for about one-half of all financial inflows, compared to a global average for developing countries of about one-tenth. The economic effect of remittances to Sub-Saharan Africa is nonetheless pronounced and significant. Counting only officially recorded receipts, remittances in 2002 represented 1.3 percent of GDP for Sub-Saharan Africa and 2.2 percent of GDP for the Middle East and North Africa. This compares to 1.3 percent of GDP for all developing countries and to 2.5 percent of South Asia's GDP. (South Asia has the highest proportion of remittances to GDP.) Remembering that data for Africa are exceptionally spotty and unreliable, only four African countries were among the top 20 remittance-receiving developing countries in 2001. Remittances contribute substantially to the balance of payments in several countries. During the 1980s international remittances covered 80 percent of the current account deficit in Botswana; they were equal to almost three-quarters of total commodity export earnings in Sudan; and constituted more than half of

Lesotho's foreign exchange earnings. In Lesotho in the 1990s, Basotho mine workers' remittances from South Africa accounted for as much as 67 percent of GDP. In Ghana in 1998, remittances constituted the fourth biggest source of foreign exchange after cocoa, gold, and tourism. Somaliland receives an estimated $500 million annually, four times the value of livestock, the main export.

Micro Effects

Aggregate remittance figures tell us little about the benefits to individual recipients or about how recipients use the funds. Anthropological and migration research, as well as household surveys, however, indicate strongly the importance of this flow as part of an income stream for remittance receiving households. Remittances contribute to:

- Improved standards of living?
- Better health and education?
- Human and financial asset formation.?

Average Remittance Values

Most international migrants send between $100 and $1,000 per transaction. Intraregional and domestic remittances are generally significantly lower. Ratha cites $200 as a global average transaction value, an estimate based on extensive research on remittances between the United States and Latin America. Remittances to African countries are less well researched. Data are sketchy on the percentage of their incomes migrants actually send home. Anecdotal evidence suggests that remitting up to one-third is not uncommon, and some surveys have recorded remittances of between 30 and 60 percent (McDonald). Variations are subject to myriad factors—among them the migrant's profile, salary level, cost of living in the host country, volatility of the home currency, and differentials in interest on savings between the host and the home country. The migration period also affects sending patterns. A fairly common pattern is for temporary migrants to send larger shares of their income home, often up to half, whereas longer- term migrants and follow-on generations tend to send less. Anecdotal evidence suggests that the amount Ethiopian migrants send home falls the longer they stay abroad. The remittances of Mexican migrants are curvilinear—recent migrants and those who stay more than 10 years send less.

Turkish migrants, even of the second generation, are found to continue to send money home. The following examples of remittance patterns are drawn from various studies:

- Senegalese migrants in France sent home between FF 6,500 and 8,500 annually in the ?mid-1990s; Malian migrants sent between FF 800 and 3,900 annually during the same period.
- Ghanaians sent home between $1,000 and $14,000 annually in 1999 and 2000; males sent more than female migrants; and "family-influenced" migrants sent more than those who were not influenced.
- Migrants from Côte d'Ivoire sent home $6,000 to $9,300 annually in 2000; women sent as much or more as men; family-influenced migrants sent more than those who were not influenced.
- Migrants in South Africa sent home an average of R 2,300 in 2000.
- Egyptians in the United States sent home an average of about $300.

Uses of Remittances

Remittances are an important contribution to recipients' total income. Although no data are readily available to show how many households receive remittances and in what amount, the earlier GDP analysis indicates that officially recorded international remittances alone provide a significant contribution. When recorded remittances are combined with informal and other unrecorded remittances, their contributions to household and national are clearly substantial even if not readily quantifiable. In many parts of Africa, unrecorded remittances include urban-to-rural payments that are not captured in official statistics. Estimates suggest these domestic remittances could contribute as much as three-quarters of non-farm earnings in areas close to major cities and one fifth of non-farm earnings in more remote areas.

Typically remittances constitute a net positive transfer from relatively richer to relatively poorer individuals or households. They form a family welfare system that smoothes consumption, alleviates liquidity constraints, and provides a form of mutual insurance. The vast majority of remittances go to family members who are either spouses or parents. Women head many recipient households. The bulk of remittances are used for consumption or investment in human capital (education, health, better nutrition), as data from a number of surveys and much anecdotal evidence indicates. Investment in land, livestock, and in building or improving a home is also relatively common but secondary to daily needs and human capital expenses. Still less is used for investments, such as in savings or business, or to repay debt, such as a loan for the expenses of going abroad. Insecurity tends to be the main motivator for investment; the type of insecurity affects the type of investment. The high proportion of remittances devoted to consumption reflects that migration and remittances are part of the strategies of individual migrants and their families to escape poverty and raise their standard of living. In Zimbabwe, for example, households with migrants were found to have less cultivated land than households without migrants, but slightly higher education levels. A household survey in Burkina Faso in the mid-1990s found that about 15 percent of households received international and domestic remittances; these tended to benefit the poorest households and rural, female-headed households. It was estimated that international remittances reduced the headcount poverty of rural households by about 7 percent and of urban households by about 3 percent. Consumption, land, and other purchases, as well as investments financed by remittances, also constitute contributions to the local economy. In Western Kenya, for example, an area with a poor climate for agriculture, remittances were found to fuel a sustained demand for local non- farm goods and services such as construction and education. Remittances spent by rural households may thus have a larger multiplier effect than those spent by urban ones, as the former tend to consume more domestically produced goods and services.

Communal use of Remittances

Most remittances are transfers between individuals or families, but some migrants participate in community or church groups that make collective remittances to their home communities. Often they are collected through fundraisers and applied to a range of investments, including building or renovating schools or churches. Because they are communal or collective, however, such remittances are very different from household or individual remittances, both in their intended use and in their low volume. Although no comprehensive survey of communal or collective remittances to Africa has been done, there are references in the literature to communal or collective sending and use of remittances, such as by Malians and Senegalese in France. The best documented and profiled cases in English describe the "hometown associations" of Latin Americans in the United States. Unlike the hometown associations, associations of African migrants in France, such as the Malians, often link up with municipalities and nongovernmental organizations, both in the host and home communities. African migrants' groups take the form of associations, cultural or church groups, refugee groups, ethnic professional groups (such as the Society of Black Lawyers), and virtual organizations that use the Internet (Somali Forum).

AFFORD also highlights the example of the Somali Diaspora that built the University of Hargeisa. The Kayes region of Mali, home to the great majority of migrants to France, has benefited from support by some 40 immigrant associations in France, most of which have counterparts in Kayes.

In the span of a decade, these associations supported 146 projects with a total budget of about three million euros, of which some 94 percent came from immigrant savings and the rest from donor-funded NGOs. AFFORD (2001), quoting Libercier and Schneider, estimates that over 60 percent of the infrastructure in the villages of Kayes can be attributed to the Diaspora in France.

The success of the individual projects has depended largely on the level of involvement of local villagers. Where expatriates covered the full cost, villagers took least interest and were difficult to engage. The sustainability of projects has been imperiled whenever returning migrants start projects that do not meet the needs of villagers. Many Ghanaian expatriates participate in ethnic- and town-based associations abroad. In the 1980s and early 1990s, some health institutions in Ghana were kept afloat with donations from these foreign-based Ghanaian associations. Nigerian migrants reportedly make individual or pooled remittances through "home improvement unions"

Opportunity Costs of and Obstacles

The developmental effects of remittances depend on their continued flow, which in turn depends on the ease with which money can be transferred. Weak financial infrastructure and limited availability of efficient and low-cost money transfer services constitute opportunity costs, or hurdles, that reduce the potential developmental effect of remittances. The cost of transfer services, in particular, has been discussed in the media, in migrant circles, and by donor agencies. If it were economical to send smaller amounts, or if other hurdles were reduced, the volume of remittances might swell.

Ratha estimates that if transaction costs were lowered by even 5 percent overall remittances to developing countries would increase by $3.5 billion. Certainly a larger share would pass through formal channels. Because remittances constitute many small transactions between geographically dispersed senders and the receivers, prevailing fees have remained high. Fees also reflect service characteristics such as accessibility, speed, and reliability.

Before jumping to conclusions on the need for lower cost transactions, therefore, it is important to understand the underlying cost factors affecting senders, receivers, and service providers, as well as differences in markets and in the cost structures of existing services, such as banks and money transfer operators. To date, these areas have received little documented attention, in the absence of which any directive intervention could well have a negative effect, such as reducing the availability of services. Although transaction costs are important, other aspects of the remittance process can be even more discouraging, both at the sending and receiving end.

For example, migrants have few opportunities to manage their finances, including remittances, in their home countries. The existence of services that send goods or vouchers for goods reflect, in part, the desire of migrants to support recipients *in a particular way*, rather than to send cash. Currently it is not possible to send money home with instructions that some of the money be credited to a savings account and the rest paid out to a specific individual. Saving in any form (let alone in foreign denominations to reduce foreign exchange losses) and products to build up financial assets in migrants' home countries are extremely rare and very limited.

Other investments, such as land purchases and construction, must be made in person or through a family member and cannot exceed the savings available. Mortgage products are few and far between in most African countries; where available, they are not easily accessible to a migrant. The following sections explore financial-service infrastructure related to remittances and the policy and regulatory environments surrounding financial services, foreign exchange, and investments.

5

Remittance Channels and Financial Infrastructure

Most remittances are made in the form of money. To a much lesser extent they take the form of goods (such as staple foods or electronic items) or services (religious ceremonies or airline tickets). The focus here is on the financial infrastructure for money transfers. Other modes of remittance are touched on to remind readers of the demand for non-financial remittance services. Remittance channels to and within Africa are similar to those in other parts of the developing world. They are classified in two categories: formal and informal. 36 Both include financial and nonfinancial service providers. Each of the principal remittance channels has advantages and disadvantages, differing from others in accessibility, service, and cost.

Formal Channels

Formal channels include money transfer services by banks and non-bank financial institutions, such as foreign exchange bureaus and dedicated money transfer operators (MTOs), the best known of which are Western Union and MoneyGram. The vast majority of MTO transactions in developing countries are receipts of funds. Other MTOs tend to have much smaller networks serving geographic niches or specific populations. Some are Internet based; a few include the option to have goods delivered or to purchase vouchers to be redeemed in shops in the home country. On a very small scale, some Diaspora associations facilitate remittance transfers of money and goods, formally or informally. In some areas domestic and intraregional remittances are made by bus, coach, and courier companies that transport money or goods as part of their regular and official service.

Informal Channels

Informal systems of remittance transfers in Africa are similar to those found in other regions, such as Asia or the Middle East. The similarities are probably due in part to the longstanding trade and migration links between those regions and Africa. It is still very common to send money with friends, relatives, and drivers of taxis or buses—or to carry it oneself. Other informal systems are modeled on *hawala* or *hundi* services or are single-destination services provided by individual business people. Indian Diaspora and Somali refugee communities in East Africa, for example, have long had such systems. In Eastleigh, a neighborhood of Nairobi known as "Mogadishu," informal agents with radio or satellite phones to Somalia handle money transfers home.

Similarly, certain homes or businesses of Ghanaians, Ugandans, and other nationalities living overseas are known among migrants to provide transfer services from a back office. Informal channels are common in many African countries. Because the formal financial infrastructure is weak in much of Africa, access to financial services, especially for rural and low- income populations, is very limited. Internal and intraregional migrants, of which Africa has a disproportionate share, are even more likely than overseas migrants to use informal channels for transfers. The prevalence of informal channels can vary by ethnic groups and nationalities as well. Whereas some groups are said to have very strong codes of trust, such as the Somalis, others fear what one Nigerian called "the Nigerian factor"—a lack of trust. Several studies of microfinance, savings, and money transfer in East Africa have revealed a noticeable decline in trust in informal systems and a heightened sense of vulnerability to theft and robberies.

User Preferences

Informal channels are used with particular frequency wherever the financial sector is weak, mistrusted (for example, due to bankruptcies), or missing altogether (as in Somalia and other countries in conflict or emerging from conflict). Severe controls on foreign exchange also tend to stimulate use of informal channels. Conversely, the use of formal channels increases in liberalized economies with a strong financial sector. The inefficiencies and market failures of weak or mistrusted banks in Africa have left a gap that has been filled by informal services and prepared the ground for formal MTOs. MTO services are already popular in many countries—some migrant groups prefer them to informal services. In addition to their other drawbacks, banks have limited outreach. Post offices, which offer access to an extended network, are spurned by clients in receiving countries who have experienced their inefficiency and poor service. Stories of insufficient cash on hand and other delays in receiving funds are common in East Africa and elsewhere.

At the same time, where post offices do operate effectively, as in many parts of South Africa, postal money orders are a preferred option, especially for domestic remitters. Even in South Africa, however, not all post offices in the country can handle money orders because of the cost and risks involved. Overall, a broad range of factors influences a migrant's choice of remittance channels. External factors, such as foreign exchange fluctuations and controls in their home countries, and subjective factors, such as preference for a service whose staff speak their language or share their cultural values, shape choices. Other factors include *accessibility* to the service at the sending and receiving ends, a concept that involves awareness, familiarity, and trust as well as physical proximity—all of which can be as important as the cost of the service. Formal services, particularly those offered by banks, are often less accessible than informal ones. Generally, though not always, their fees are higher than those of informal services, especially for low-value transactions like remittances.

Transfer Costs and Other Service Characteristics

Globally, the average cost of a remittance is about 13 percent of its value. Although research is scarce on the costs of transfers to African countries, some general parameters are known. Costs vary by the amount remitted, service used, destination, and origin; they range from a low of 0.2 percent to about 20 percent. Costs tend to be highest for small transactions, as most of the transfer services charge a minimum fee. While some studies find that certain migrant groups are highly sensitive to cost, others find that familiarity or convenience can often lead to the use of a more expensive service. On average, transfers through MTOs costs more than transfers between accounts, such as wire transfers through the SWIFT system. At the same time, MTOs have a more demand-oriented network of points of sale, much shorter average transaction times, and do not require that customers maintain an account. Speed and reliability is part of their service—and their marketing strategy.

In recent years, competition among service providers has begun to lower costs. This trend has been observed in parts of the Latin American market—notably from the United States to Mexico—but also for some African destinations. Remittances from and to high-volume markets are often cheaper than those to other destinations, especially if there is competition in the markets—either among MTOs or between MTOs and informal services. Western Union, for example, maintains a single set of standard rates for transactions from some of its markets, but in London it offers lower rates for money transfers to selected high-volume destinations, such as Ghana and Nigeria. For global MTOs such as Western Union and Money Gram fees start at about $15, with actual fees depending on the sending and receiving country. Fees are often structured by brackets of transfer values. Smaller MTOs typically charge a commission, commonly 5 percent, though it can be higher. Banks usually combine a minimum fee with a percentage fee.

Minimum fees at banks range from $5 to $50 depending on the sending and receiving country as well as the product. Percentage fees are sometimes flat, sometimes bracketed on a declining percentage for larger amounts. Most informal services charge 3–5 percent, although substantially higher rates are not uncommon. The fees of informal services are often lower than those of MTOs in their market; such services adopt foreign exchange rates falling between the highs and lows of commercial rates of banks and foreign exchange bureaus. Some informal services charge no fees, realizing revenue solely from gain on foreign exchange. Informal services and MTOs offer attractive services that banks and other formal agents have neglected or deliberately shunned in choosing to focus on corporate clients and high-income individuals. These include access, proximity, outreach, speed, ease, familiarity, awareness, and innovations such as those described in the following paragraphs.

Access – Access to the transfer service at both the sending and the receiving end is a critical factor. While capitals and other urban centers offer fairly good access to financial services, rural regions tend to be much less well served. Many remitters, however, need to send money to locations with poor financial infrastructure in which banks in their host country have little or no contact. A study of Sahelian migrants sending remittances home from France, for instance, found that fully one-third sent their remittances by hand, another third by post office, and only 6 percent through banks. Similarly, Sudanese emigrants send remittances informally or to neighboring countries such as Uganda and Kenya for lack of transfer services in Sudan. The interface of formal international remittance services with service points in the sending and receiving country is also an important aspect. Many formal remittance channels weaken or break down beyond an initial arrival point in the migrant's home country.

For instance, only banks that are part of the SWIFT network or similar systems, or that have correspondent banks, can receive international transfers. In some countries, this fact excludes postal banks. In Kenya, for example, postal banks can receive international transfers only as agents of Western Union. Where they have sprung up and are expanding, ATM systems are often not yet integrated—remaining limited to a specific bank and for use only with their cards, or to one or another network, such as VISA *or* Mastercard (as in Uganda). Such constraints are costly to the sender and to the receiver. A study in South Africa estimated that as much as 40 percent of the total value of a remittance of R200 to a rural recipient could go toward banking charges and transport costs. *Proximity and Outreach* – Many MTOs and informal services are successful because they work with migrants in "micro-markets"—often limited to certain cities or even neighborhoods within those cities. The Kenya Post Office Savings Bank, the main Western Union agent in Kenya, reported that the loss of a point of sale in a key migrant area in the United States had noticeably reduced transactions. Having a service point in the right neighborhood and with the right "feel" (such as service in the migrant's native tongue) can make all the difference in attracting business. Teba Bank in South Africa is a good example of a dedicated financial institution in a high-volume market: it is closely linked with its core clientele of miners, for whom it provides money transfer services. Most banks, unlike MTOs, choose not to pursue the "low-end" remittance clientele; in many more cases they lack the retail network to serve that clientele effectively.

Speed and Ease – MTOs and informal systems such as *hawala* and *hundi* are fast. Some services are almost instantaneous; others take one to three days. Most bank transfers, by contrast, are quoted as taking three to five business days. MTOs and informal systems are also the most straightforward and least complicated person-to-person transfer services; unlike bank transfers, neither the sender nor the receiver need have an account, although some MTOs require identification.

Familiarity – The choice of a transfer service may turn on comfort or familiarity. Many remitters are unfamiliar with banks and fear, often rightly, that they will not be welcomed as clients. Banks can be intimidating to people not used to dealing with them, and many banks frankly prefer to deal with wealthy individuals and corporate clients. Those preferences are reflected in access barriers such as account fees and minimum balances on accounts.

Awareness – Another common factor is lack of awareness of services. Many banks, post offices, and other providers fail to market their services or to purse segmented strategies, such as advertising in different languages or recruiting multilingual staff. Recognizing this failure, some recipient-country governments, such as Mali's, compensate by informing their migrant communities of services through newsletters and information events at their embassies and consulates in sending countries. In contrast, larger MTOs and their agents often advertise heavily and aggressively. Kenya Post Office Savings Bank, for example, organizes regular marketing events with Kenyan Diaspora in locations such as Minneapolis, Minnesota, and Columbus, Ohio. Smaller, regionally focused MTOs reach their client group by advertising in community papers or shops popular with the migrant community. Informal systems tend to operate by word of mouth.

Niche Innovations – In addition to fast and efficient service in areas that lack banking infrastructure, informal transfer services also offer innovative remittance methods designed to suit overseas workers' earnings patterns. In some instances this has improved service levels and led to the development of new products within the formal sector. In Egypt for example, several exchange companies now offer door-to-door delivery of money following the example of Philippine banks that successfully introduced and implemented the service to compete with unofficial market operators. Other niche market approaches can be found in Kenya and Senegal. For Kenyan migrants, U.S. based Internet services such as WatuWetu offer vouchers that can be redeemed at stores in Kenya. Similarly, Senegalese migrants in France, through groups such as Sénégal Conseils, an association in Lyon, remit funds to Senegal both in cash and in the form of goods. Through Sénégal Conseils, migrants in France can purchase goods and have them delivered to family members in Senegal.

Transactions are fairly rapid; accounts between the organization in France and the company in Senegal are reconciled perhaps two or three times a year. Those who are unable to cover the entire cost of goods immediately can pay in installments over a maximum of six months, incurring interest charges of between 10 and 50 percent. In domestic and regional markets, some transfer services have developed a niche where domestic financial systems are inefficient. In East Africa, for example, some of the courier and overland bus companies provide money transfer or transport services that many people use for private transfers, including remittances, as well as for business purposes. These cover domestic and sometimes intraregional markets but generally do not extend overseas. The next section discusses policies and regulations that influence the use of remittances and the choice of remittance channels, including formal money transfer services.

Regulatory and Policy Issues

A migrant's choices of whether and how much to remit, through what channel, and for what use are shaped by factors such as the economic and political stability or volatility of the home country, by foreign exchange and taxation policies, and by regulations and policies that affect money transfer services. Regulatory and policy contexts vary widely in African countries, but no comprehensive review has been done of the conditions that hamper or enable remittances in receiving countries. Generally, the focus of discussions on remittance-related regulation and policies has been monetary policies, particularly foreign exchange policies, and taxation. Less attention has been paid to financial and private-sector regulations and to policies that affect the availability and accessibility of financial services and products or the ease or attractiveness of investing in financial products or businesses. Equally important for their effect on the volume and channels of remittance are policies and regulations in the sending country, an area that to date has received much less attention than receiving-country policies.

Remitters' choice of channel is influenced by whether MTOs are allowed to operate in a given area, what licensing and other regulatory requirements they must meet, and who may serve as agents—both in sending and receiving countries. Recently, the international Financial Action Task Force on Money Laundering (FATF), which works with national regulators around the globe to prevent money laundering and the financing of terrorist activities, has had a noticeable effect on the financial industry, including money transfer services. FATF's work is discussed here with reference to the know-your- customer rule. Several aspects of the policy and regulatory environment in remittance-receiving and - sending countries in Africa affect migrant remittance flows—attracting, limiting, or deterring them. Those aspects include: Know-your-customer rules Financial market liberalization vs. control Licensing and regulation of money transfer services Government-led incentives for sending and investing remittances.

Know-your-Customer Requirements

Most banks will transfer money only for account holders. But opening an account— which typically requires identification and proof of residence—can be difficult for migrants, even those who have legal status. 52 new or tighter know-your-customer requirements and other regulations, adopted as part of antiterrorism and anti–money laundering initiatives, contribute to better controls, accountability, and transparency. At the same time, they have raised hurdles to using banks, both for individuals and MTOs. Know-your-customer rules have imposed new compliance require-ments on all financial service providers for client identification, verification, and record keeping. The new requirements affect providers' cost and client policies. Operationally, for example, compliance requires development of adequate or updated policies or protocols, new or adjusted systems, manuals, and staff training. Those costs are relatively more burdensome for MTOs, particularly smaller MTOs, than for banks. MTOs must finance compliance from narrow margins and ensure rollout throughout their network of agencies. The know-your-customer rule has also changed the way MTOs do business, obliging them for the first time to ensure clients' identity. The new rules have changed the way banks view MTOs as clients. Anecdotal evidence suggests that banks have become highly risk averse and are less likely to open accounts for MTOs, especially smaller firms. Some have reportedly asked MTOs to move their accounts to another bank. Because MTOs must have a link with the banking system, problems with accounts can hamper or curtail their business. Similarly, banks have tightened or increased account requirements for individual retail clients, further limiting migrants' access to banking services.

Financial Liberalisation

Generally foreign exchange controls and state-regulated financial sectors are seen as a deterrent to sending and receiving remittances. Where receiving countries enforce official foreign exchange rates or otherwise tax remittances, informal transfer channels become more attractive. In Sudan and Egypt, for example, informal channels have been a popular way of avoiding restrictive foreign exchange rules. Sudan has now introduced measures, including devaluation, to attract and channel remittances. Although devaluation was undertaken for broader economic reasons, it had the effect of making legal exchange of remittances at official rates more attractive.

In Uganda, the liberalization of the financial market—to loosen foreign exchange trade and allow foreign-denominated accounts—is said to have led to increased remittances. In a few instances, foreign exchange restrictions in sending countries can affect migrants. South African foreign exchange restrictions limit the amounts that migrants from throughout southern Africa can transfer out of the country. Remittance transfers are but one aspect of the liberalization of financial markets. Generally, however, a liberalized market will attract more remittances, and a larger share of those remittances will flow through formal channels. To what extent that happens depends in part on policies governing the licensing and regulation of money transfer services.

Licensing and Regulation of Money Transfer Services

In countries where foreign exchange trade has been liberalized, commercial banks and, in some areas, foreign exchange bureaus offer money transfer services or act as agents for an MTO. Where foreign exchange trade or remittances themselves are state controlled, the central bank or other government bank is the officially licensed channel.

Even in liberalized environments, licensing and other forms of regulation affect the range of services available for money transfer. MTOs are particularly sensitive to licensing requirements. While banks use correspondent banks or the SWIFT system for their money transfer products, MTOs must set up a network of agents and thus, unlike banks, must deal with the regulatory environment in the receiving country as well as the sending country. Rules differ from country to country and are often complex.

Where the MTO's agents are banks, the MTO may not need to register, but the partner bank must secure the approval of the central bank. In some cases, the MTO must establish itself as a legal entity before being allowed to operate in the country. Where the issue of licensing money transfer services is addressed by law or process in African countries, it is usually handled by the central bank. Because various entities provide money transfer services, different parts of the central bank are typically involved with licensing or permissions. The two key departments tend to be bank supervision and foreign trade. Banks are generally licensed to deal in foreign exchange under their banking license. This is not true, however, for most postal banks, which tend to operate under communications (as opposed to banking) statutes. Both are typically required to get approval from the supervision department of the central bank before introducing a product that involves foreign exchange. Failure to do so can lead to suspension or closure of the service. Licensing of MTOs varies by country.

In much of Africa, the agents of MTOs are licensed banks authorized by the central bank to conduct money transfer operations. In most areas, foreign exchange bureaus, too, require a license, usually granted by the central bank. But a foreign exchange trading license alone may not enable the firm to do business as an MTO. It is prudent, if not required in most cases, to seek permission of the regulator within the central bank. Most central banks, such as that of Kenya, are more inclined to permit banks than foreign exchange bureaus to operate as an MTO. South Africa prefers that banks handle money transfers. That preference was solidified by its experience with Western Union and Union African Money Transfers (UAMT), which ran afoul of foreign exchange control regulations.

On the other hand, the Bank of Uganda's foreign exchange and trade department has been more liberal in granting permission. From the author's conversations with some central bank staff, it is apparent that FATF rules and procedures have led bankers to overcompensate in order to stay "on the safe side." The result is highly conservative assessments and a preference for saying no as opposed to "let's think about how we can make it work." African regulations and legal interpretations tend to be conservative compared to those in some parts of Latin America, which allow a variety of points of sale for money transfer services, including pharmacies and other retail services. Innovation in the use of new technologies, such as transfers by mobile phone, will tend to receive a conservative assessment by regulators and are likely be limited to financial service providers, whereas much broader outreach could be achieved if nonfinancial points of sale were allowed to join the service network.

Government-led Incentive Policies

While the majority of African governments and regulators remain conservative on the question of financial services, some, recognizing the contribution of remittances to their country and people, have sought ways to facilitate them. Mali and Sudan, for example, are actively engaged in attracting remittances or in creating incentives to invest. Other schemes are offered by host countries as incentives for migrants to return home. Mali's government has tried to boost international migration by setting up a Ministry for Malians Abroad to provide information about employment abroad. In cooperation with the United Nations Development Programme (UNDP), the Malian government has set up a program for the "transfer of knowledge through expatriate nationals."

The program supports the temporary returns of Malian university professors to participate in research. With UNDP paying salaries and other costs, 133 Malian consultants have returned since the program started in 1996. Several programs have emerged from collaboration between the French and Malian governments. The Franco-Malian co-development framework, for example, inventories the skills of Malians abroad and encourages them to help support the Malian education system and small business development. The Malian Diaspora provided a fund of €2.6 million to supplement financing of local projects. For some time Sudan has granted emigrants an "incentive exchange rate," slightly higher than the official rate, to encourage them to send money home. To relieve pressures on limited foreign exchange and provide for the country's need for imports, the government initiated a "nil value" custom policy on imported goods. Under the scheme, holders of hard currency deposits remitted from abroad and retained in special accounts over six months have the right to use the funds for imports, with customs relief of up to $14,000.

Sudan's Land for Emigrants Program provided quick and easy exchange of hard currency for building plots in the Khartoum area at preferential prices. Ghanaians who have been outside the country for at least one year are allowed to bring back a wide range of goods for personal use, tax free. These include clothing, appliances (such as refrigerators), and household goods. The policy has prompted many Ghanaians to convert their remittances into goods before traveling. Once in Ghana, they sell the goods to recover their money. This practice has resulted in availability of a wide range of goods in Ghana. The International Monetary Fund (1987) estimated that 4.9

percent of total imports in 1985 went through unrequested transfer, mostly by migrants. Before 1967, Egyptian emigrants were obliged to transfer 10 percent of their income in foreign exchange. Since then, the Egyptian government has tried new and more ambitious measures to attract emigrant remittances through official channels.

Among those measures are progressive devaluation of the Egyptian pound, tax-exempt interest on special deposits of foreign exchange earnings, invitations to Egyptians living abroad to purchase foreign-currency- denominated development bonds on advantageous terms, and instant delivery of locally produced durable goods to emigrants who paid in foreign exchange. One of the Egyptian government's most successful schemes to encourage formal remittances of hard currency earned by emigrants was the special import system known as the Own Exchange Import System, which offered import permits to individuals who could provide the necessary foreign exchange from their own sources, and not from official foreign exchange pools. The main sources of foreign exchange to these importers were the savings of emigrants. The system encouraged emigrants to use their savings to finance the imports Egypt needed from abroad.

Goods financed by emigrant savings under the system represented, on average, more than two-thirds of total recorded savings sent home by emigrants. One of the effects of Egypt's liberal polices towards remittances has been that the central bank has been able to accumulate mounting reserves of foreign exchange. Thus, after liberalization, the bank had access to 18 months' worth of foreign exchange to buy imports;, before liberalization, the average reserves were less than 3 months. Compulsory schemes are still enforced in some cases. In Mozambique and Lesotho, for example, legislation compels migrants to remit 60 percent and 30 percent of their earnings, respectively. The amounts involved constitute a significant proportion of the foreign exchange earnings of both countries. Although miners (and the Chamber of Mines) oppose the system, miners' wives seem to favor it. For the same migrants, the South African miners' bank, TEBA, has developed services to facilitate voluntary remittances by mineworkers. More funds are being remitted voluntarily than through the compulsory system, suggesting that the abolition of compulsory deferred pay would not be as disastrous for these countries as is often made out.

The primary losers would not be individual households but the governments, which benefit from the interest on deferred pay. Increasingly aware of the benefits of remittances, African governments have begun to create more facilitating environments, as opposed to the early models of control. Those efforts could be complemented by improvements in financial systems and services, such as easier transfers, more service points, and opportunities to save or invest remittances. For millions of Africans, remittances fill the gap left by low or nonexistent social and welfare transfers. They thus make a developmental contribution that is very different from and indirectly complementary to public interventions.

To protect and amplify that contribution, remittances should be facilitated through incentives and a more accommodating policy environment. It is important that governments avoid the temptation of diverting remittances for other purposes or attempting to exert undue control over them. Further research and policy analysis would improve our understanding of remittances as a private and public financial flow—large, highly segmented, and consisting of many small transactions—and enable governments and their development partners to create policies that maximize the individual and social benefits of remittances.

Recommendations for Further Research

Many studies of remittances in Africa to date have been

done from the perspective of anthropologists and migration experts. While providing valuable insights, such studies, in aggregate, are dispersed, snapshot surveys of countries and sub-regions. A more integrated set of recent studies of migration, remittances, and money transfers covers West Africa, Southern Africa, and East Africa. A growing set of studies on remittances in the context of financial services reflects and responds to the recent public debate on remittances. These studies illuminate the global remittance debate but have not yet attained the levels of documentation and analysis shown in studies of remittances in Latin America and at the global level. Much more could be done, as proposed below, to collect and analyze data and translate the findings into actions by bringing together key stakeholders from policymaking and regulatory bodies, financial service providers, and Diaspora groups.

Flows – Overseas as well as domestic and intraregional flows need to be better documented and synthesized in the African context to understand their magnitude and implications, including their developmental contributions.

Financial systems – The effects of weak financial systems and various regulatory and policy environments on remittance flows and uses needs to be investigated systematically.

Financial services – Transfer service profiles, their underlying cost structures, and transaction costs are only partially understood. A much better base of knowledge is required to guide changes to policies and regulations so as to improve financial services for remittances and other purposes.

Technologies – The role of technology in the transfer of remittances needs to be explored. Communication technologies, in particular, have contributed to a quiet revolution in Africa. While still in their infancy, such technologies have already had a great effect on business and life on the continent, banking and financial services; they offer great potential to extend financial services into rural Africa and other underserved areas. How can we ensure that that potential is realized?

Migration – Because migration and remittance trends are not easily correlated, migration patterns and trends may appear to be of limited relevance. Before refocusing our attention, however, it would be wise to determine whether and how changing migration patterns affect remittances and the market for money transfer services. Such a determination will require a better understanding of the forces behind the trends in remittance flows. In particular, it will be necessary to take into account the definitions used in reporting remittances and the actual and potential effects on remittances of changes in regulations, financial structures, and service availability.

Recommendations for Policy and Regulation

The connections between financial-service policies and the volume and channels of remittances are only partially understood. To date, those connections have been explored primarily in the context of foreign exchange controls, taxation, and state monopolies in financial services. Regulations directed at money transfer operators and transfer services in both sending and receiving countries have received scant attention, despite their clear impact on the availability and viability of services. The measures promoted by the Financial Action Task Force are one source of such regulations, as are conservative regulatory perspectives that tend to limit financial services to a very narrow band of providers (primarily banks), to the exclusion of newer models of non-bank financial services and innovations in service delivery. Changes in the following areas could facilitate remittances and amplify their developmental effects by improving policy and regulatory environments.

Licensing – Current licensing regulations for money transfer services center on foreign exchange trading. For smaller money transfer operators and informal services, they often are opaque and hard to access; compliance may be unaffordable. To put ourselves in a better position to review and enhance the regulatory frameworks used in Africa, we must improve our understanding not only of African remittance markets, but also of the business models that make non-bank transfer services attractive to various client segments elsewhere in the world, and of how those models are licensed and regulated. A facilitative framework in which licensing requirements were adjusted to reflect actual needs for transparency and for managing foreign exchange exposure could greatly enhance the availability and outreach of basic financial services, including money transfers.

Regulation – In the context of transfer fees there may be room for facilitative regulatory interventions. An in-network bank transfer within South Africa costs much less than the same in- network transfer across the border to Lesotho—a situation common throughout Africa. Yet, except for foreign exchange gains and losses, the systems used and the costs incurred are the same. Could banking networks be persuaded to make their transfer fees "border blind"? A common currency simplifies the problem: in July 2003 fees dropped for Euro transfers within the European Union. The European model should be explored for markets such as West Africa, with the CFA, and for countries whose currency is pegged to the South African rand.

Ancillary financial products – Because money transfer is the pivotal service for remittances, ancillary financial services and products tend to be overlooked. This is unfortunate, because related services and products, such as savings, loans, mortgages, and other investment products could, if cross-sold with transfers, be attractive to remittance senders and receivers. Possibly the most effective step, given that the vast majority of remitters and recipients are small-time savers rather than potential investors or venture capitalists, would be to improve financial systems and services to allow for saving in connection with remittances. Saving would enhance the income smoothing effect of remittances as well as their contribution to domestic savings and capital formation. Although some governments have recognized the benefits of consolidating small remittances by allowing foreign-exchange-denominated accounts and issuing special bonds, but the capital potential of remittances does not seem to have been explored much beyond that, particularly by commercial financial and investment services.

Securitization – At the level of international financial flows, remittances have begun to make a mark. In Brazil, for example, remittance flows contribute positively to the country's credit ratings. Rutten and others have suggested that remittance flows could be securitized to provide financing for African agriculture. Similar financing deals are becoming popular in emerging markets such as Mexico, the Philippines, and Turkey. Thus treated, remittance flows may contribute to overcoming "information asymmetries in inefficient domestic financial markets and thereby improve the quality of investment in developing countries".

6

Remittances as Financial Flows

Official remittance data, published in the IMF's Balance of Payment Statistics Yearbook and in the World Bank's annual *World Development Indicators,* are an excellent starting point for analyzing remittance flows. But the accuracy of this important data is compromised by the low quality of submissions and uneven reporting at the country level. Data for African countries are particularly weak. Figures for 2000 and 2001 were available for about 60 percent of all African countries and only about one-third of the Sub- Saharan countries (16 of 49 countries).

Reported data do not always reflect private transfers through banks or other regulated channels. The data also suffer from varying levels of underreporting—notably of transfers through informal channels, which can be significant. Underreporting tends to be higher for countries with weak financial sectors or unstable political-economic situations, and for those in which significant migration occurs within the service distance of alternative or informal remittance channels.

For Sudan, Choucri estimated that 85 percent of all remittances went unrecorded. Kenya reports no data at all, but Kenyans apparently received approximately $420 million in 2002. Some flows reported as remittances belong in other categories. Uganda, currently in the process of improving its data collection, has been reporting residual foreign exchange transactions as remittances. Data presented in this study are based on the source used in the respective studies quoted. Where figures and graphs refer to Ratha, they are based on a data set for 1970 to 2001 kindly shared by Dilip Ratha of the World Bank.

This set is based on IMF balance of payments data on workers' remittances, migrant transfers, and employee compensation. Remittances are unlike other private financial transfers—they "do not constitute financial flows in the strict sense". The two reasons are that (i) remittances are classified as current transfers in current accounts, unlike other financial flows, which are recorded in the capital or financial accounts of the balance of payments; and (ii) remittances are transfers between nationals rather than a capital import from nonresidents or non-nationals which would give rise to a change in the assets and liabilities of residents vis-à-vis nonresidents.

The Cross-Strait Economic Exchange

Trade Relations between Taiwan and China

Taiwan's Mainland Affairs Council (MAC) of the Executive Yuan estimates that Taiwan's exports to China are equal to transit trade plus the difference between Taiwan's exports to Hong Kong and Hong Kong's imports from Taiwan. This estimate should be better than the figures from customs services of Taiwan and China because the Taiwan and China figures do not take different types of Taiwan exports to China into account and thus underestimate the total amount. Based on the MAC's estimates, Taiwan's indirect trade with China via Hong Kong was $25.8 billion in 1999 and $46.3 billion in 2003, increasing by 79.5% in four years. In addition, Taiwan has enjoyed a continuous and large trade surplus with China. In 1999, Taiwan ran a trade surplus of $16.8 billion, with

$21.3 billion of exports to, and $4.5 billion of imports from, China. In 2003, Taiwan ran a trade surplus of $24.4 billion, with $35.4 billion of exports to, and $11 billion of imports from, China. Since 1993 China has become Taiwan's third largest trading partner, after the United States and Japan. In addition, since 1993 China has also become Taiwan's second largest export market, following the United States. In 2002, for the first time, China became Taiwan's largest export market. According to the MAC's estimate, in 2002, Taiwan's exports to China (excluding Hong Kong), the United States, and Japan were $29.4 billion, $26.7 billion, and $12 billion, respectively.

In comparison, between 1990 and 1999 Taiwan was China's fourth largest trading partner, following Japan, the United States, and Hong Kong. Between 2000 and 2003 Taiwan was China's fifth largest trading partner, following Japan, the United States, Hong Kong, and Korea. In 2003, China's trade with Japan, the United States, Hong Kong, Korea, and Taiwan was $133.6 billion, $126.3 billion, $87.4 billion, $63.2 billion, and $58.4 billion, respectively. In addition, since 1993 Taiwan has become China's second largest supplier (Japan has been its largest supplier). In 2003, China's imports from Japan and Taiwan were $74.2 billion and $49.4 billion, respectively.

Financial Relations between Taiwan and China

According to Taiwan's official figures, in 1991 Taiwan's outward foreign direct investment (FDI) into China was only $17 million. Since 1992, however, China has become the largest recipient of Taiwan's outward investment. By the end of 1999, Taiwan's cumulative FDI in China was 14.5 billion; by the end of 2003, Taiwan's cumulative FDI in China was as high as $34.3 billion, or 47 percent of total Taiwan's outward FDI. Parenthetically, the 2003 figure included make-up registration of Taiwan's previously unregistered investments to China. According to Taiwan official statistics, there were 28 thousand cases of make-up registration between 2001 and 2004. Nevertheless, Taiwan's official figures considerably underestimate the extent of Taiwan's "real" investment in China. For instance, Perng Fai-nan, governor of Taiwan's Central Bank, estimated that by the end of 2002 the real figure of Taiwan's cumulative investment in China was about $66.8 billion. As a result, China's official data on Taiwan's investment in China seems more accurate because it is mandatory for Taiwanese businesspeople to register their investment with the Chinese government. By the end of 1999, Taiwan's realized FDI in China was 23.9 billion; as of June 2004, Taiwan's realized FDI in China was $38.4 billion, or 7.2 percent of total realized FDI received by China. Taiwan was the fourth largest source of FDI in China, next to Hong Kong (43.7 percent), the United States (8.7 percent), and Japan (8.3 percent).

However, Chinese figures might also underestimate Taiwan's "real" investment in China because many Taiwan businesspeople began in the mid-1990s to invest in China through their holding companies in third tax-exempt countries, such as the Virgin Islands and the Cayman Islands (British Central America, BCA). Taiwan's investment in BCA increased from $370 million in 1995 to $1.36 billion in 1999 with the share of Taiwan's total outward investment doubling from 15 to 30 percent. By August 2004, Taiwan's cumulative investment in BCA was $15.2 billion and its share to Taiwan's total outward FDI was 19.1 percent.

By comparison, the Virgin Islands' outward investment to China increased from $304 million in 1995 to $2.7 billion in 1999, with the share of China's total FDI growing from 0.8 percent to 6.6 percent. By June 2004, the Virgin Islands was the fifth largest investor in China, with cumulative realized FDI of $34 billion or 6.4 percent of China's total FDI. Regarding other capital flows between Taiwan and China, the Taiwanese government began to compile statistics on individual remittances to China (including household remittance, donation, and other transfer payments, but excluding travel expenditures) on 21 May 1990, and on both Taiwan business remittances to China and remittances from China to Taiwan on 29 July 1993. In 1999, Taiwan remitted a cumulative $4.5 billion to China and China remitted a cumulative $1.3 billion to Taiwan. As of August 2004, Taiwan had remitted a cumulative $22 billion to China and China had remitted a cumulative $19.4 billion to Taiwan. Nevertheless, the Taiwanese government's figures hardly tell the truth of capital flows across the Taiwan Strait. For example, Taiwan's Central Bank estimated in late 2000 that Taiwan's total capital flow to China was around $70 billion, of which $40-50 billion was Taiwan's FDI in China. That is, in 2000 Taiwan might have remitted as much as $20-30 billion non-FDI capital flow to China, including portfolio flows to China.

Taiwan's Policy of Cross-Strait Economic Relations

Strategically speaking, the Chen Shuibian administration's policy of cross-Strait economic relations serves two goals: constructing its normal relationship with China as well as developing Taiwan's economy.

In his White Paper on China policy unveiled on November 15, 1999, Democratic Progressive Party (DPP) presidential candidate Chen Shui-bian stressed the need to establish normal relationship between Taiwan and China, while the normalization of cross-Strait ties should begin with economic and trade relations. He suggested that developing cooperative economic and trade relations between Taiwan and China should be based upon three principles: balance between national security and economic interest, a comprehensive strategy of economic security and development by replacing passive policy with active management, and negotiation with China over cross-Strait economic issues.

Specifically, Chen Shui-bian suggested the principle of proportionate mutual benefit by opening the Kaohsiung and Keelung harbors to Chinese vessels in exchange for the opening of ports at Guangzhou, Dalian, Shanghai, Qingdao and Tianjin in China. In addition, he proposed a "one-way direct flight" formula, under which all air services between Taiwan and China would be operated by Taiwan airlines, with the profits shared equally by the two sides. Furthermore, he suggested strengthening review measures of Chinese investment in Taiwan's telecommunications, power, mass media, financial, securities and semiconductor sectors. Finally, he advocated that both sides sign investment protection agreements in the short term and allow for each side to set up trade representative offices in the medium term.

After Chen Shui-bian was elected president in March 2000, the most salient feature of Taiwan's cross-Strait economic policy is the so-called "integration theory." On December 31, 2000, President Chen pronounced that the integration of bilateral economies, trade, and culture across the Taiwan Strait should be a starting point for gradually building faith and confidence in each other. This, he suggested, could be the basis for a new framework of permanent peace and political integration.

President Chen explained the "integration theory" on many occasions over the next three years. For instance, on May 10, 2002, President Chen reiterated that the normalization of cross-Strait relations must begin with the normalization of economic and trade relations. He emphasized that the first step toward political integration across the Taiwan Strait was economic and cultural integration. On January 1, 2003, President Chen urged both sides to strive towards building a framework of interaction for peace and stability. Particularly, he stressed consultation and promotion of direct transportation links, as well as exchange on other relevant economic issues, which could constitute a first step forward and set the stage for further economic and cultural interaction.

Since the second half of 2003, Taiwan has indicated an increased commitment to the negotiation of direct transportation links. On August 13, President Chen pledged to resume direct links with China by the end of 2004. Two days later, the Taiwanese government issued a policy paper called "The Assessment of the Impact of Direct Cross-Strait Transportation." The assessment stressed that the effects of cross-Strait direct transportation links would be extensive and far-reaching; there would be advantages and disadvantages. The assessment concluded that both parties should sit down and negotiate on the direct transportation links as soon as possible in order to maximize advantages and minimize disadvantages for Taiwan.

On October 9, 2003, Taiwan's parliament, the Legislative Yuan, passed the revisions to the Statute Governing the Relations between the People of the Taiwan Area and the Mainland Area. According to the revisions, the Taiwanese government must draft bylaws concerning the opening of direct cross-Strait transportation links within 18 months. More importantly, government agencies will be able to entrust, on their behalf, private organizations to engage in cross-Strait negotiation. That is, Taiwan has agreed to China's preferences for the negotiation channel through private organizations over direct transportation links. With respect to Taiwan's outward investment to China, the Chen Shuibian administration discarded the long held "no haste, be patient" policy and adopted a new policy of "proactive liberalization with effective management" after the consensus reached in the Economic Development Advisory Conference (EDAC) on August 26, 2001.

Key conclusions reached during the meeting include:

1. "Taiwan first," "global management," "mutual benefits," and "risk control management" are the

pivotal principles regarding trade and commercial activities across the Taiwan Strait;
2. Adopt a "proactive liberalization with effective management" policy to replace the previous "no haste, be patient" policy regarding China-bound investment;
3. Set up flexible mechanisms to monitor movements of capital between the two sides;
4. Introduce Chinese capital to Taiwan's property and real estate market at the first stage, the manufacturing sector at the second stage, and the financial market at the third stage.
5. Establish the three links (direct trade, postal, and transportation links between Taiwan and China);
6. Gradually expand Chinese imports to Taiwan;
7. Under the principle of national security, actively open up the local tourist market to Chinese visitors.

The following will list the opening measures of the cross-Strait economic policy by the first Chen Shui-bian administration between mid-2000 and mid-2004.

Mini Three Links

On January 1, 2001, the Chen Shui-bian administration opened up the "mini three links," which legalized trade and travel between Taiwan's offshore islands, Quemoy (Kinmen) and Matzu, and adjacent ports in China. Thereafter, Taiwan has been gradually expanding bilateral flows of commodities, people, ships and financial exchange. In the beginning, China disagreed that Taiwan liberalized mini three links without negotiation with China and thus did not cooperate with Taiwan. Nevertheless, the Chinese government gradually adopted a cooperative attitude toward these measures after January 4, 2001.

As a result, cross-Strait exchange through the mini three links increased exponentially over the last four years. Based on Taiwan's statistics, the number of Taiwan's ships to China increased from 137 in 2001 to 1,221 in 2004; the number of Taiwan's people to China increased from 11,729 in 2001 to 202,371 in 2004. In addition, the number of China's ships to Taiwan increased from 45 in 2001 to 1,808 in 2004; the number of China's people to Taiwan increased from 1,041 in 2001 to 12,409 in 2004.

Table 6.1: Mini Three Links between Taiwan and China

Period	2001	2002	2003	2004	Total
Taiwan's Ships to China	137	435	776	1,221	2,569
Taiwan's People to China	11,729	28,087	81,759	202,371	323,946
China's Ships to Taiwan	45	158	567	1,808	2,578
China's People to Taiwan	1,041	1,358	3,760	12,409	18,568

Liberalising Chinese imports to Taiwan

Taiwan has gradually but surely come to relax its regulation on China's exports to Taiwan after 2000. For December 2000 only 53.9 percent of trade commodities were permitted as imports from China to Taiwan whereas this figure jumped to 77.5 percent by September 2003 and 78.2 percent by October 2004.

Liberalising Taiwan's Investment to China

After the EDAC, the Taiwanese government relaxed restrictions on Taiwanese investment in China's high-tech industry, except for items like wafer and upstream petrochemical products. It also did away with the investment ceiling of US$50 million. Instead, it established a review commission with clear standards on investment projects of over US$20 million and Taiwanese investing an amount lower than US$200,000 may register by declaration procedures. Finally, it allowed Taiwanese enterprises to directly engage in China's investment.

Opening Up Chinese Investment to Taiwan

Taiwan has put forward a three stage schedule that allows for China's investment in Taiwan: Taiwan has first allowed China's capital for investment in the real estate sector for the first stage on August 8, 2002. In addition, Taiwan plans to open up to Chinese investment in some service industries and the manufacturing industry for the second stage, and in the capital market for the third stage.

Expanding Offshore Transshipment Center

The Taiwanese government continued its support for the offshore transshipment center of Kaohsiung harbor after 2000 and further announced the Cross-Strait Sea Freight Facilitation Measures on May 7, 2004.

The Facilitation Measures made appropriate adjustments to the function of the Offshore Transshipment Center to enable more convenient and faster transportation of cargo across the Strait. In addition, the government expanded the applica-tion of the Facilitation Measures from Kaohsiung harbor to Taichung harbor and Keelung harbor. The amount of offshore transshipment increased from 365,879 cargos in 1999 to 674,775 cargos in 2004.

Table 6.2: The Operation of the Offshore Transshipment Center of Kaohsiung Port

Period	*Unloading*	*Loading*	*Total Loading/Uploading Operation*	*Growth rate*
1998	151,872	120,893	272,765	n.a.
1999	204,047	161,832	365,879	34.1%
2000	227,682	204,986	432,668	18.3%
2001	270,318	237,924	508,242	17.5%
2002	282,123	292,328	574,451	13.0%
2003	312,159	318,179	630,338	9.7%
2004	343,469	331,306	674,775	7.1%

Facilitating Air Links

Taiwan and China reached agreements on chartered passenger flights during the lunar new-year holidays in both 2003 and 2005. For 2003, it was operated by Taiwan's airlines, two routes between Taipei and Kaohsiung on the Taiwan side and Shanghai on the China side, and a stopover in Hong Kong. For 2005, it was operated by Taiwan and China airlines, multiple airports between Taiwan and China, and nonstop between Taiwan and China. The arrangement negotiation will be elaborated in detail in the section below.

In addition, the Taiwanese government announced the policy on Cross-Strait Air Freight Facilitation Measures on September 10, 2003. It promoted one-way (Taiwanese carriers operate the flights first) "restricted" and "indirect" cargo chartered flights to solve the urgent demand of Taiwan businesspeople for freight transportation. On January 2004, President Chen announced that Taiwan would expand the current uni-directional cargo chartered flights into bi-directional chartered flights through bilateral negotiation.

Facilitating Financial Transaction

After July 2001, Taiwan allowed offshore banking units (OBUs) of Taiwanese banks to engage in direct trading with Chinese financial institutions. Between July 2001 and August 2004, financial transaction across the Strait through OBUs amounted to $110.4 billion.

Allowing Taiwan's Financial Sectors to Establish Branches in China

Since 2001, Taiwan has gradually allowed Taiwan's banks, securities firms and insurance companies to set up branch offices or subsidiaries in China. As of mid-2004, Taiwan's Ministry of Finance has approved 17 securities firms, 15 family insurance companies, and 10 banks to set up offices in China. Furthermore, on April 19, 2004, Taiwan allowed Taiwan's insurance companies to invest in Chinese local companies. On March 3, 2005, Taiwan allowed overseas subsidiaries of Taiwan's financial holding companies to establish representative offices in China.

Opening Chinese Tourists to Taiwan

Since January 1, 2001, Taiwan allowed 600 and 80 Chinese people to visit Kinmen and Matsu for sightseeing everyday, respectively. However, by mid-2004, there were only 165 and 283 Chinese people traveling to Kinmen and Matsu as tourists due to China's restriction on its people. By the end of September 2004, the Chinese government began to allow people from Fujian Province to traveling to Kinmen and Matsu for sightseeing. In addition, since January 1, 2002, Taiwan allowed category-3 Chinese people, which refer to those residing abroad, to visit Taiwan for sightseeing. The second-phase relaxation was implemented on May 10, 2002, which allowed Chinese people who have resided abroad for at least four years and who have acquired a work permit at his place of residence abroad, and their spouse and direct relatives to visit Taiwan for sightseeing.

This relaxation also automatically applied to the residents of Hong Kong and Macao and Chinese people who have been approved to go abroad for sightseeing or for business trips. From the start of the trial implementation to the end of October 2004, the number of Chinese people visiting Taiwan for sightseeing amounted to 29,599.

Expanding Chinese Businesspeople

Since January 2002, Taiwan has significantly simplified and relaxed measures for applications of businesspeople and technical professionals from China to Taiwan. In particular, the total period of stay for a Chinese technical specialist applying to come to Taiwan to participate in technical research was extended from three years to six years. Moreover, in November 2004, Taiwan further relaxed the restrictions of Chinese people coming to Taiwan to engage in commercial activities and thus promote normal business exchanges between Taiwan and China.

China's Policy of Cross-Strait Economic Relations

Before mid-2000, China insisted that Taiwan accept the one-China principle before the two sides could discuss the three links. Nevertheless, after August 2000, Chinese Vice Premier Qian Qichen began to emphasize that establishing the "three links" did not mean that the two sides needed to resolve political issues first. As long as the links were regarded as the internal affairs of one country, he stressed, this issue could be solved through private-to-private, industry-to-industry, and company-to-company channels. Qian added that neither side could display flags on its ships involved in cross-Strait exchanges because flags are symbols of sovereignty.

In July 2002, Qian Qichen further clarified that the three links could be implemented as soon as possible without referring to the political meaning of the one-China principle, as long as they were considered the internal affairs of one country. In this way, Beijing de-emphasized the political significance of the three links, and the one-China principle was no longer the prerequisite for the negotiation of the three links. Nevertheless, China's proposal was quickly rejected by Taiwan. President Chen argued that the phrasing "internal affairs of one country" was equivalent to "one China," which localized and marginalized Taiwan. As a result, Qian put forward a new statement in October 2002, defining cross-Strait air and sea links as "cross-Strait routes."

On December 17, 2003, China issued a policy paper to reiterate its flexible position on the negotiation of the three links. The paper said that the three links was purely an economic matter and political differences should be shelved. It defined the three links as cross-Strait affairs and internal affairs of "Chinese people" on both sides of the Strait. It reiterated that negotiation concerning the three links was not political negotiations and might be carried out through non-governmental trade organizations beyond the political implications of one China. After Taiwan's March 2004 presidential election, however, Beijing issued a statement on May 17, stating that the three links would be established as long as Taiwan recognizes the one-China principle. This statement created some speculation that China had been changing its previous flexible political position on the three links.

On May 24, Beijing clarified that China still treated the three links as an economic issue. As long as regarding direct links as internal affairs of one country, Beijing hoped that both sides would not politicize it and would continue promoting economic exchanges. Nevertheless, Beijing mentioned "internal affairs of one country" instead of "cross-Strait routes" referring to direct links. On June 30, requested by Taipei, Beijing further reassured its previous political position made by former Vice Premier Qian Qichen in October 2002. Without the precondition of the one-China principle, negotiation on the three links is still Beijing's priority on cross-Strait relations.

Chinese scholars and officials in the Taiwan affairs system predominantly believed that Taiwan needed the three links more than China did. They thought Taiwan would benefit more from the links, whereas China's need for them was not urgent. In addition, Beijing believed that President Chen's advocacy for the links was only pre-election posturing and he did not really want them enacted. As a result, they argued that the three links would not succeed in the short run. Since China believed that Taiwan needed the three links more, and the probability of success in the short term was not significant, why has China been actively promoting the idea? Why did China adopt a more flexible approach to rescind the one-China principle as the prerequisite for negotiation of the three links, and define cross-Strait air and sea links as "cross-Strait routes"? In general, there are four reasons why China actively promotes the three links. First, Chinese leaders hope for a great historical achievement—instituting the links, a proposal that has been put forward since 1979—in order to help consolidate their status within the Party. Second, China believes that the three links are favorable steps toward both unification and prevention of Taiwan's continual moves toward independence. Beijing expects that closer economic exchanges will create more favorable public opinion toward unification in Taiwan because both sides will have common economic interests.

Third, the three links would help China solve its present economic predicament and continue its economic development. In the early 2000s, notwithstanding its outstanding economic growth rates, China's internal economic, social, and political problems continued to be severe, such as ailing financial system, poor-performed state-owned economy, stagnated agricultural and rural development, increasing income and regional inequality, and serious political corruption. After joining the WTO at the end of 2001, China has faced even more thorny economic problems. The only way for China to solve or control internal problems is to keep the economy effectively growing at 7-8 percent annually to provide sufficient employment opportunities.

For instance, in 2003, when economic growth rate was 9.1 percent, the net total of urban jobs increased by 8.59 million. In 2004, the Chinese government aimed at keeping the urban registered unemployment rate below 4.7 percent by creating 9 million net-additional urban jobs. That is, the Chinese government had to maintain at least 9 percent of economic growth rate in 2004. For instance, during internal meetings in Beijing in 2002, Premier Zhu Rongji did not mention any policy achievements, emphasizing that China still had enormous problems to be solved. He had a clear picture of China's overall situation, which led him to be less optimistic than previously. At a press conference in March 2002, Premier Zhu even argued that if the Chinese government had not adopted a proactive fiscal policy and prudent monetary policy between 1998 and 2002, "China's economy would probably have collapsed." Fourth, Beijing maintains that the three links can promote the stability and development of cross-Strait relations and thus allow China to concentrate on its economic development.

In July 2002, explaining cross-Strait relations to a visiting delegation of the Mountain Alliance, a political group from Taiwan, Vice Premier Qian pointed out that there were still many difficulties facing China; he cited peace and stability as the most important matters. To sum up, for Chinese leaders, promotion of the three links brings little risk, has a high probability of success, is a relatively-easy-to-accomplish policy achievement on the Taiwan Strait issue, and thus elevates their status within the Party. As a result, Chinese leaders would continue to place the priority of their Taiwan policy on promoting the three links.

Cross-Strait Chartered Flights Arrangement

In late October 2002, Taiwanese legislators proposed lunar new-year chartered flights between Taiwan and China to both governments. In response, China's spokesman for the Taiwan Affairs Office (TAO) of the State Council said that China would consider the application of chartered flights based on the actual situation with a hope that airlines of both sides could participate in the business. On November 12, Taiwanese Premier Yu Shyi-kun said that the opening of cross-Strait direct air links, such as point-to-point chartered flight services, was technically feasible anytime and only required negotiations.

MAC Vice Chairman Chen Ming-tong said that Taiwan welcomed cross-Strait negotiations and was ready to begin talks anytime on the chartered flights arrangement with China. Without bilateral official negotiations, Chen said, Taiwan would only allow its airlines to file applications with the Chinese government to obtain permission for indirect chartered flights between Taiwan and China by stopover in Hong Kong or Macao during lunar new-year holidays in early 2003.

However, China requested Taiwan negotiate with China through authorized private organizations on the details of chartered flights as well as reach an agreement that the arrangement should be reciprocal two-way flights the next year. In response, Taiwan emphasized that Taiwan was ready to send representatives of the Strait Exchange Foundation (SEF) to negotiate with their counterparts of the Association of Relations Across the Taiwan Strait (ARATS). But China refused to resume SEF-ARATS dialogues. Without Taiwan's authorization of private organizations to negotiate with China, on January 7, 2003, China finally approved the first indirect chartered flights by six Taiwanese airlines to China.

Nevertheless, China's TAO Director Chen Yunlin stressed that China reserved its right to have reciprocal flights from China to Taiwan the next time. In mid-November 2003, Beijing announced that its position on the 2004 new-year chartered flights was "direct, nonstop and reciprocal." In response, Taipei said that official negotiations were necessary if Chinese air carriers wanted to operate chartered flights between Taiwan and China during lunar new-year holidays. Nevertheless, Beijing insisted that both sides authorize airline companies to negotiate with each other. Without Taiwan's agreement on the negotiation model and reciprocal flight arrangements from China to Taiwan, China even proposed to allow Taiwanese airlines to operate direct chartered flights to China in 2004 as long as Taiwan agreed to allow two-way chartered flights in 2005. At the end, Taiwan did not agree upon China's proposal and thus there were no chartered flights across the Taiwan

Strait during the 2004 lunar new-year holidays. In early October 2004, Taiwan sharply changed its policy position toward China with respect to the 2005 chartered flights arrangement. Premier Yu instructed the MAC to actively promote the chartered flights arrangement based on the following principles — "bilateral, reciprocal, and non-stop" with a flexible negotiation approach.

In fact, Taiwan agreed upon all China's previous conditions on the arrangement. However, China added one more political condition on the chartered flights arrangement that Taiwan had to obey the principle of internal affairs of one country and China accused that Taiwan did not follow the principle. Furthermore, Beijing asked Taipei to authorize a private organization to negotiate the chartered flights arrangement. In turn, Taipei reiterated its previous position and welcome China to authorize appropriate persons to negotiate with Taiwan. On November 10, President Chen proposed a concrete negotiation model to China that both sides across the Taiwan Strait should follow the Taiwan-Hong Kong aviation right model to settle passenger and cargo chartered flights.

The model meant that, without any precondition, Taiwan authorized a private association with official participation to negotiate with Hong Kong's counterpart on Taiwan-Hong Kong aviation right in 2002. However, China's ARATS pointed out that functional talk across the Strait had to insist on the one-China principle. In addition, China's TAO accused that President Chen's statement "China is not our country, but an enemy" created tensions and thus China would not like to negotiate with Taiwan on the chartered flights. Finally, China defined chartered flights as internal affairs of one country. Generally speaking, China was very passive and not supportive regarding the chartered flights negotiation until the end of 2004. Suddenly, on January 2, 2005, Beijing changed its policy position. In an interview by the Xinhua News Agency, the TAO spokesman emphasized that China would work hard to promote the launching of chartered flights across the Taiwan Strait during the lunar new-year holidays. Beijing suggested that airlines across the Strait communicate directly over technical and business details and make arrangements. In the interview, the TAO spokesman neither mentioned the one-China principle as a precondition of the talk, nor defined the chartered flights arrangement as internal affairs of one country. On January 4, Taipei immediately authori-zed the Taipei Air Transportation Association (TATA) to conduct talks on the chartered flights arrangement with Beijing. Three days later, the TATA president met in Macau with Pu Zhaozhou, a senior official of the General Administration of Civil Aviation of China and executive director of the China Civil Aviation Association. Nevertheless, China ruled out the participation of Taiwan's MAC officials and SEF people in the chartered flights negotiation, but was acceptable to other Taiwanese officials.

On January 15, within just two hours, both sides reached agreement on the chartered flight issue based on the two-way, reciprocal, and non-stop principle by Taiwan's Chang Kuo-cheng, director of Civil Aeronautic Administration, and China's Pu Zhaozhou. Forty-eight flights would connect Taipei and Kaohsiung on the Taiwan side with Beijing, Shanghai, and Guangzhou on the China side from January 29 to February 20, 2005. Negotiation over the chartered flights serves a very good example for both sides to gradually work out a feasible negotiation model on bilateral economic issues. In the very beginning, Taipei wanted to exploit the negotiation on cross-Strait chartered flights arrangement as leverage to force Beijing to accept the resumption of SEF-ARATS dialogues.

Despite wanting to reach an agreement on bilateral reciprocal flights arrangement, Beijing only accepted negotiation by "private" organizations authorized by both sides other than the SEF and the ARATS. In early 2003,

China conceded to accept Taiwan's unilateral chartered flights to China and hoped Taiwan would accept reciprocity of chartered flights from China to Taiwan the following year. However, Taiwan did not accept China's proposal and thus China declined to offer one more trial of chartered flights arrangement for 2004 lunar new-year holidays.

In late 2004, Taiwan accepted China's previous conditions on the chartered flight arrangements and a flexible negotiation model with official participation from both sides. Then, China set up two extra political conditions for the negotiation: the one-China principle and internal affairs of one country. At the end, Taipei did not concede and Beijing pragmatically accepted Taipei's proposal. Both sides swiftly reached the agreement on the chartered flights arrangement for 2005 lunar new-year holidays. Particularly, both sides gradually realized that additional political conditions for the negotiation on chartered flights arrangement would break down the bilateral agreement and so both sides adopted a very pragmatic approach to resolve the issue.

China's Sanctions against Taiwan's Businesspeople

On March 10, 2000, Chen Shui-bian revealed his list of advisors for national policies, including Stan Shih, chairman of the Acer Group; Shi Wen-lung, chairman of the Chi Mei Group; Chang Yung-fa, chairman of the Evergreen Group; and Ying Qi, president of the Continental Engineering Corporation. Zhang Zhiqun, director of Shanghai Taiwan Affairs Office, soon summoned representatives of these companies to Shanghai, and expressed China's concerns about their support for Chen Shui-bian.

One month later, although reassuring Taiwan-invested enterprises (TIEs) in China that China would continue to protect their legitimate interests in China, Li Bingcai, TAO deputy director, said, "Very particular individual important

Taiwan businesspeople openly clamor for 'Taiwan independence' and advocate the 'Lee Teng-hui' line, which preaches the break up of the motherland. Meanwhile, they scrabble for profits by engaging in business and economic operations on the Mainland. Such a situation will not be allowed to continue." Li Bincai's remarks incited anxiety among TIEs and Beijing tried to play down the anxiety of TIEs. On April 24, ARATS Vice Chairman Tang Shubei emphasized that for the majority of TIEs, Beijing welcomed and encouraged them to invest in China and protected their important interests.

However, Tang pointed out, China had some opinions on only "very particular individual" TIEs, who publicly supported Taiwan independence. On May 7, one month from his previous remarks, Li Bincai reassured TIEs that China would continue to obey "Jiang's eight-point proposal" and effectively protect all legitimate interests of TIEs. He also clarified that Beijing was concerned only with "very particular individual" TIEs, who publicly supported Taiwan independence. On September 23, Li Bincai reassured TIEs that cross-Strait political divergence should not interfere with economic exchange and cooperation. He promised that China put TIEs in a very important position and would protect various interests of TIEs under any circumstance.

In early March, 2001, Chi Mei Group Chairman Shi Wen-lung's controversial comments about Taiwanese comfort women serving Japanese military persons during the World War II were published in a comic book, *Taiwan Discourse,* by Japanese cartoonist Yohinori Kobayachi. As a result, on March 10, the Chi Mei petrochemical plant in Zhenjiang, Jiangsu Province, was reportedly forced to shut down under pressure from Beijing. In addition, China launched several rounds of tax probes at Chi Mei's Zhenjiang plant, which were widely seen as Beijing's retaliation for Shi's comments. Nevertheless, on the same day, both the Chi Mei Group and Chinese authorities denied reports that the Chi Mei's plant in Zhenjiang had closed. In addition, the TAO issued a statement that China would protect the legitimate rights of Taiwanese investors in China. The next day, a TAO spokesman reiterated China's opposition to anyone making money in China while at the same time advocating independence in Taiwan. However, he also said that China would protect the rights of Taiwanese companies in China, but would also take relevant measures against anyone who broke the law. Although Shi Wen-lung did not explicitly support President Chen's re-election campaign in 2003-2004, a TAO spokesman stated after the 2004 election that China did not welcome the "green Taiwanese businesspeople." He clarified that "we do not welcome those Taiwan businessmen who earn money from the mainland and support Taiwan independence when they return to Taiwan."

In editorial comments of the *Renmin Ribao* [People's Daily], China called Shi Wen-lung a "Big-shot for Taiwan independence." China accused that Shi was President Chen's major financial provider behind the scenes. By mid-2004, the Chi Mei group was the world's largest manufacturer of important plastic material ABS and China was its major market. It has established a petrochemical complex and invested US$170 million in Zhenjiang of Jiangsu Province since 1996. After the completion of the expansion project in Zhenjiang, the total investment would reach US$600 million and production capability would exceed the group's Taiwan facilities. In addition, the Chi Mei group planned to invest more in high-tech information industry in China.

In short, the Chi Mei group had a very high stake in its investment interest in China. As a matter of fact, the Chinese government has moderately sanctioned the Chi Mei group for Shi's Taiwan independence stance by constantly probing tax issues and harassing its cooperative companies in both upstream and downstream companies.

Consequently, the Chi Mei group faced significant pressure to drop its political stance. Finally, on March 26, 2005, right after China's passage of the anti-secession law (ASL) toward Taiwan, Shi Wen-lung released a retirement statement indicating that he felt "comfortable" with the ASL. He further elaborated that Taiwan independence would only push Taiwan into war and bring disaster to the people.

He said in his statement that his ancestors came from China's southern Fujian Province and believed that "both Taiwan and the mainland belong to one China." Particularly, his statement was very significant because it coincided with the day that Taiwan's one-million people demonstration against China's ASL. Shi Wen-lung's case has created a strong impact on TIEs' political stance with respect to cross-Strait relations, since Shi was regarded as an obstinate supporter for Taiwan independence in the past. For instance, following the "Shi Shock," the Acer Group's Chairman Stan Shih declined to accept President Chen's invitation as his advisor. He said, "I have kept politically neutral and refrained from choosing sides all along." The declared excuse by Shih was to "avoid misunderstanding from the other side of the Taiwan Strait."

Parenthetically, the Evergreen Group's Chairman Chang Yung-fa quit the position as President Chen's advisor in May 2002. In essence, China's tactics was mainly economic inducement, not economic sanctions. Economic sanctions involve the threat or act by a sender to disrupt customary economic exchange with the target in order to punish the target or force change in the target's policies. Economic inducements involve commercial concessions, technology transfers, and other economic carrots that are extended by a sender in exchange for political compliance on the part of a target. "Economic inducements" are also called "positive sanctions." Generally speaking, despite punishing green Taiwan businesspeople by probing tax issues or other administration harassment from time to time, China mainly relied on its potential market and investment opportunities to induce TIEs to comply with China's political stance.

During the first term of the Chen Shuibian administration, there were five salient features of cross-Strait economic relations. First, Taiwan has been adopting an increasingly opening approach on its economic relations with China in terms of two-way mobility of commodities, capital, people, and other facilitation arrangement. Particularly, with respect to Taiwan's outward investment to China, Taiwan replaced the "no haste, be patient" policy with a "proactive liberalization with effective management" policy. Second, both Taiwan and China attached strategic significance on bilateral economic relations, particularly direct links. From Taipei's perspective, economic integration should be a starting point of cross-Strait normalization and the basis for a new framework of permanent peace and political integration. Particularly, negotiation over direct links and chartered flights arrangement should be the first step.

From Beijing's perspective, economic integration are favorable steps toward both unification and prevention of Taiwan's continual move toward independence. Third, both sides across the Strait had divergent short-term political motives advocating bilateral economic exchanges, but finally had to compromise. Taipei would like to utilize negotiations over direct links and other economic arrangement to resume SEF-ARATS dialogues and thus stabilize cross-Strait relations. By contrast, Beijing would like to achieve its political goals by imposing political conditions on these negotiations. Nevertheless, both sides stepped back after the other's strong resistance. At the end, Beijing could no longer impose political conditions on the negotiations over economic issues while Taipei had to accept a flexible negotiation model with official participation. Fourth, Beijing has successfully imposed moderate economic sanctions and inducements against TIEs over the past four years. Beijing has imposed sanctions very carefully against very particular individual TIEs to control the collateral damage. In the future, TIEs will keep a low profile in terms of their political stance on cross-Strait relations. Particularly, TIEs will not explicitly support Taiwan independence or pro-Taiwan independence political parties in Taiwan. Finally, the progress of cross-Strait economic negotiation was influenced, but at most delayed, by political agendas on both sides. For instance, before January 2005, China's response to Taiwan's proposal to negotiate on chartered flights arrangement was extremely cold and suddenly changed after Taiwan's legislative election of December 2004.

Currently, after China enacted the ASL on March 14, 2005, Taiwan has yet to respond to China's invitation to negotiate on both passenger and cargo chartered flights, which Taiwan has been advocating since late 2003. Nevertheless, Taiwan has neither rejected China's invitation nor changed its "proactive liberalization with effective management" policy. That is, Taiwan reserves its decision to resume dialogue on economic issues after the disruptive impact by the ASL. As a matter of fact, since mid-2004, the MAC has proposed a long list of economic issues to negotiate with China: currency clearance, investment protection, financial supervision, avoidance of double taxation, product importation, protection of intellectual property rights, judicial assistance, commercial arbitration, fisheries dispute arbitration, personal security, chartered flights and direct transportation links, tourism, repatriation of illegal migrants, joint crime prevention, marine pollution, and fisheries labor negotiations.

Similarly, China has recently proposed several economic issues to negotiate with Taiwan. In early March 2005, Chinese President Hu Jintao responded to Taiwanese President Chen's proposal that both sides could gradually develop cross-Strait passenger chartered flights during festivals into a regular practice as well as negotiate the issue of cross-Strait cargo chartered flights through private civil aviation organizations. Ten days later, Chinese Premier Wen Jiabao proposed negotiations with Taiwan over passenger chartered flights, Taiwan's agricultural exports to China, and China's fishery workers to Taiwan. By the end of April, the Chinese government has sent two invitation letters through an authorized private organization to the Taiwanese government seeking a quick resumption of talks on cross-Strait cargo and holiday chartered flights arrangements.

Despite current cross-Strait stalemates over the ASL, based on the experience of cross-Strait interactions over the past four years, it is highly possible that dialogue on chartered flights will resume after a certain period, as the negative impact of the ASL subsides. In turn, the negotiation might serve well as a trigger for the further development of cross-Strait relations in the next stage, particularly for direct links negotiations. To sum up, the evolution of cross-Strait economic relations will be self-sustained in a positive direction, even spilling over to the political arena of cross-Strait relations during the second Chen Shuibian administration.

7

Variety of Transnational Religious Networks

Scholars in North America have become more aware that some migrants (migrant workers, immigrants and to some extent refugees) are increasingly organizing their lives transnationally.

The revolution in communications and transportation technologies has enabled migrants to maintain strong connections with and to get involved in their homelands, and indeed with a variety of sites in different countries. Governments of the countries in which migrants originate are engaging with their migrant communities abroad, often through increasingly active consulates in receiving countries that facilitate dual citizenship, remittance and investment flows, and political involvement "back home."

There are various types of "transnational" practices, including social, economic, political, religious, and cultural. Even where the transnational activities of migrants do not have an explicit political dimension, they often have important political effects in their home countries, in Canada, and in transnational relationships. The share of emigrants and associated co-ethnics or co-nationals who are active in multiple forms of transnationalism at any point in time is often minor. However, many people are active in a small number of activities or active sporadically. Moreover, the frequency, intensity, scope and durability of transnational activities change over time. While engagement in transnationalism is complex and variable, interventions by states, corporations, NGOs and migrant organizations are institutionalizing these linkages and networks. Institutionaliza-ztion takes various forms, including hometown, regional, national or ethnic associations, remittance companies, dual citizenship legislation, extraterritorial migrant outreach programmes, reconfigured cross-border religious networks, and special worker programmes. Their presence heightens the significance of transnationalism, because these institutions are not dependent on the active participation of specific individuals, but rather, have an institutional life of their own. The political effects of the transnational activities of migrants and related cross-border advocacy groups and networks deserve particular attention in Canada. This is due to our high levels of immigration, active migrant work programmes, and the sheer diversity of our immigrant population, unmatched anywhere in the world.

In effect the transnational political activities of migrants resident in Canada constitute an important though often overlooked informal dimension of Canadian external relations, one with multiple effects on Canadian foreign policy that challenge its state-to-state emphasis. Migrant transnationalism also highlights the way that Canadian foreign policy goals and priorities are influenced by other largely "domestic" policies, including those guiding immigration, employment, and social services. Thus, migrant transnationalism points to the need for foreign policy to take into consideration diverse Canadian policy-making processes.

In an effort to reflect the realities of transnationalism and its implications, academic disciplines are developing new subfields that examine relevant changes in areas such as the conceptualization and practice of citizenship, of the state and the limits of its regulatory activities, of state-to-state international relations, and of state-emigrant relations. "Transnational studies" and "Diaspora studies" are examples of new subfields from anthropology and sociology. In political science, jobs are now advertised for people with expertise in "the politics of Diasporas" or "transnational politics." Immigration studies are shifting from their past emphasis on the incorporation of immigrants into Canadian society to also assessing the importance of the transnational relationships of migrants for their livelihoods, human security, and civic involvement.

Area-studies scholars, meanwhile, are finding that their research can longer be bound by old geographic boundaries such as "Asia" or "Latin America." They are "following" migrants and their transnational activities across borders to engage with Asian and Latin American communities in Canada and other countries around the world. Despite the importance of migrant transnationalism for Canada, academics here have only recently begun to study this phenomenon—Canadians are in this respect behind scholarship in the United States and Europe. The Canadian government, moreover, seems less aware of the importance of these activities than governments abroad, especially governments of sending countries such as Mexico or the Philippines, who have explicitly made transnationalism a part of their foreign policy concerns. In part to help address this lack of knowledge in Canada, the York Centre for Asian Research (YCAR) and the Centre for Research on Latin America and the Caribbean (CERLAC), both at York University, held a joint workshop on March 7 and 8, 2003.

The workshop brought together scholars of Asia and Latin America, academics who study immigration, NGO and immigrant organization representatives, and policy-makers. The goals were to begin to map out the transnational political involvements of migrants in Canada and to identify their implications for Canadian foreign policy as well as for future research and organizing. The workshop documented many examples of transnational connections or homeland ties maintained by various groups from countries in Asia and Latin America, including Indonesia, Hong Kong, India, Sri Lanka, Malaysia, Cambodia, the Philippines, Peru, El Salvador, Colombia, Brazil, Chile and Mexico.

Many of these states have policies that encourage nationals and their descendants to maintain social and economic ties to their homelands. However, some have or have had conflictual relations with at least some overseas or Diaspora groups (e.g. Tamils, Guatemalans, Chileans). Presenters also discussed the activities of various kinds of NGOs active in cross-border advocacy networks and/or lobbying the Canadian government around specific issues (e.g. the FTAA and migrant workers rights). This report summarizes the key policy findings of the workshop. It also aims to address what several speakers identified as a lack of policy coherence between the Canadian Department of Foreign Affairs and International Trade (DFAIT) and other federal, provincial, and municipal ministries, departments, and agencies. The report (1) outlines some of the key concepts used by scholars who study transnationalism, and provides a summary of the key research findings in Canada and elsewhere; (2) elaborates on the implications for foreign policy; and (3) suggests some directions for future policy and policy-relevant research. A summary of foreign policy implications is provided above.

This section introduces the key concepts which have emerged from the study of transnationalism and Diaspora and summarizes their key policy relevant findings and current research questions. It draws from both the academic literature and examples discussed in the workshop. Migrant transnationalism refers to the process whereby social actors who have migrated maintain active ties with their homelands, or across national borders through participation in religious, social, cultural, economic, and political networks and processes. "Transnational social spaces," "social formations," "social fields," and "communities" are phrases used to describe various scales of transnational practices, institutions and identities created through these activities. Some scholars refer to the social actors whose lives stretch across borders as transmigrants. Research on migrant transnationalism in various contexts outside Canada has produced a number of important findings, although more research is needed to assess their generalizability.

These include the following:

- Migrants often maintain contact with people and institutions in their countries or regions of origin, and new communication and transportation technologies have increased the frequency and intensity of these contacts.
- Migrant transnationalism is not new. On the contrary, there have been many cases of political and other forms of transnationalism since at least the nineteenth century. What is new is the way scholars conceptualize and study the phenomena and, perhaps, their scope, intensity, and frequency.
- Transnational activities may take various forms, including: o social (regular contact with relatives and friends back home, travel for family occasions, etc.); o cultural (e.g. celebrating ethnic, religious or national holidays associated with the home country); o religious (e.g. maintaining religious identities and practices associated with specific leaders or institutions based in the home country or region, economic support for faith-based projects and organizations); o economic (family remittances, collective remittances, investment, owning a home or property "back home"); o political (voting, raising funds for parties or social movements, lobbying the host government regarding homeland issues).

- Individuals may engage in some or all of the above types of practices. The frequency, intensity, and scope of participation vary. There may be regular patterns or types of transnational engagement associated with particular national origin or ethnic groups.
- Evidence of widespread and strong transnational ties have led some scholars to question the empirical and theoretical relevance of nation-bound categories such as citizenship, immigrant, membership, allegiance, and even nation-state. They argue instead for re-framing these categories and related processes (e.g. nation- building, class, and identity) from a transnational perspective.
- Macro-level factors play an important role in shaping transnational practices. These include political opportunities and economic conditions "at home" and in the host country, immigrant selection policies, foreign exchange rates, and international trade agreements.
- Home state policies and conditions help to shape transnational activities. Although some states ignore or reject their emigrants, many more have policies and programs aimed at fostering a sense of national belonging on the part of emigrants and their descendents. These include dual citizenship and absentee voting laws, outreach programmes for emigrants, return migrant and emigrant protection programmes, rules governing money transfers, and programmes to attract emigrant or Diaspora investment. Migrant-sending states can be categorized as follows depending on the policies aimed at their overseas populations: states that ignore or reject emigrants; policies that strengthen social ties and homeland national identity while trying to keep emigrants outside the home country; policies that encourage migrant return and re-settlement; and mixed policies with elements of both.

- The policies of the receiving state also matter: host-country immigration, refugee, citizenship, rights protection and labour market/employment policies are particularly important. State policies set parameters for migrant transnationalism and cross-border advocacy by shaping who comes to Canada and their economic and social opportunities while resident here. Settlement services shape the "warmth of the welcome" and the social inclusion or exclusion that results.
- Migrants and other non-state actors are increasingly important players in cross- border advocacy and public diplomacy. These include not only NGOs, but also immigrant groups and networks. For example, the workshop included representatives from a Canadian-Indonesian group, Canadians Concerned about Ethnic Violence in Indonesia (CCEVI), which is active in countering ethnic-based discrimination and violence in Indonesia and is working with both Chinese and indigenous people in Indonesia. Other examples abound.
- Research in North America and Europe suggests that negative racialization, racism, and discrimination sometimes contributes to transnationalism, as these experiences lead people to maintain a home country arena where they enjoy more prestige and social mobility.
- Migrant experiences of social exclusion or inclusion may have contradictory effects with respect to motivating transnational activities. Social inclusion refers to the ability of migrants fully to participate in the civic life of host countries, such as through employment rights, political participation, access to social services, rights to form associations, and freedom from discrimination. For example, the lack of recognition of the employment credentials of middle-class professional migrants pushes some of them to

maintain residence in Canada while seeking employment abroad.

- The relationship between experiences of social exclusion/inclusion and transnationalism may be mediated by demographic patterns (e.g. the migration of families versus non-family individuals) as well as macro-level economic and political processes.
- Social and economic status shapes transnational activities. Wealthy migrants are more likely to engage in entrepreneurial and political transnationalism. Poorer and middle strata migrants are more likely to focus on family-level social transnationalism and remittance sending.
- Gender shapes migration and transnationalism. Men may be more active in political transnationalism. Women may be more active in remittance-sending and social transnationalism. Workshop presentations also suggested that the gendered nature of some Canadian temporary worker programmes influences patterns of migrant transnationalism. For instance, migrant workers involved in the sex trade in Canada, the majority of whom are women, experience particularly intense social exclusion and the weakest rights protections amongst migrant workers, which hampers their ability to organize locally or transnationally to alleviate their insecurity.
- Immigrant incorporation, which is not a linear or uniform process, can take place alongside transnational activity. Newcomers can settle and become involved in the social, cultural and political life of their countries of settlement while maintaining or in some cases renewing ties to their places of origin.
- Some transnational activity may contribute to incorporation. Research indicates that advocating and lobbying in favour of a homeland-oriented agenda may have the inadvertent effect of contributing to political incorporation in the host country.

These points outline areas of agreement among scholars of transnationalism. However, there is less consensus on other issues. These include: (1) what shapes who will and who will not maintain these ties within a particular ethno-national origin group (what determines who is more likely to be a transmigrant, as opposed to an immigrant); (2) the extent to which migrant transnationalism enhances migrant political autonomy, social justice goals, or the bargaining position of migrant groups vis-à-vis their homeland government; (3) the long-term impacts of transnationalism on homeland political transformation, democratization, and the social well-being of migrants and non-migrants; (4) the relationship between various forms of transnationalism and the mode of immigrant incorporation; and (5) questions about the durability of transnational practices and institutions over time and across generations. In spite of these and other questions, scholars agree that the study of immigrant incorporation should also consider the nature and scope of homeland ties.

Although the field of Diaspora studies is older, interest in the area has surged at the same time that transnational studies emerged as a field of study. There is still disagreement whether the term Diaspora should be applied narrowly to individuals and communities that have experienced forced migration and to exile communities, or more broadly to any overseas populations. The relationship between Diaspora and transnationalism is often muddy, but some scholars argue convincingly that Diasporas represent one form of transnational community or social formation.

Key Actors in Canadian Transnationalism

Various collectivities, organizations and institutional actors mediate transnational activities. This section discusses policy based on four categories of actors or institutions that mediate transnationalism.

Canadian State-led Transnationalism

The Canadian government, through various programmes that recruit temporary workers in specific sectors (agriculture, domestic workers, nurses), lays the basis for some transnational social fields and ongoing ties. Workers from several countries, including the Philippines, Jamaica and other Caribbean countries, as well as Mexico, come to Canada through these programmes.

The duration of their stay varies, as does their access to social services and coverage by labour legislation. While the programmes that bring them are highly regulated, there are loopholes and contradictions that contribute to workers' social exclusion. For example, agricultural workers from Mexico and the Caribbean are vulnerable because of their dependency on their employers for future participation in these programmes, and policies that prevent or hinder employment-based associations.

This does not mean that all employers are abusive; it does mean that these workers lack the protection of labour and other laws enjoyed by other Canadian residents. These and other cases point to the importance of implementing commitments to protecting the social and employment rights of all migrants (including those agreed to through the Free Trade Area of the Americas (FTAA) Agreement process, discussed later). This in turns points to the need for greater articulation of foreign and trade policy on one hand, and domestic policies on the other.

Canadian immigration policy and federal and provincial employment regulations and institutions contain contradictory elements that shape and sometimes encourage transnationalism. For example, highly educated professional workers from Hong Kong (and other countries) enter Canada as landed immigrants, but are often unable to find adequate employment. They may leave family members here while returning home for employment. This form of instrumental labour market transnationalism might be reduced if policy coherence in the area of credential recognition could be promoted.

"Home" State-led Transnationalism

Not all states have the capacity to or interest in encouraging their emigrants to maintain ties. However, a number of "sending" states with emigrant populations in Canada are actively engaged in reaching out to their overseas populations, raising questions about the response of Canadian authorities. Participants mentioned a number of countries (including the Philippines, India, Peru, Mexico, Jamaica, El Salvador) and provinces (Kerala and Gujarat in India) that have ministries or offices for migrants. These government offices work to maintain remittance flows, encourage investment, and maintain emigrants' sense of homeland belonging. Some of these states allow and/or encourage double nationality and citizenship, while others do not.

Whether or not they support political citizenship on the part of their migrants, they strive to maintain the homeland ties of the latter. In the process of reaching out to their emigrants and their descendants, sending states and their political authorities are extra-territorializing the scope of their consular activity and redefining sovereignty. Consular staff and foreign-service bureaucrats are taking an increasingly proactive stance, increasing the scope of "protection" and encouraging migrant organizing. At the same time, political candidates, party representatives, religious leaders, and others are travelling to meet with their "constituents" abroad.

Migrant- led Transnationalism

Migrant-led transnationalism has widely divergent forms, objectives, and political implications, as indicated by the cases discussed. On the one hand are cases where transnationalism might contradict Canadian foreign policy objectives. For example, some Indians in Canada support religious movements associated with communal violence in India. Others invest in development projects that lead to population displacement and human rights violations in India. Transmigrants provide funding for projects like the Narmada dam, substituting for funds from the World Bank and other agencies that have withdrawn from these projects due their impact on population displacement and on the environment. On the other hand, there are many cases in which transmigrant activities reinforce foreign policy objectives.

For example, CCEVI has expanded beyond its original focus on helping ethnic Chinese victims of ethnic violence in Indonesia to also lobby the Canadian government regarding ethnic violence aimed at Indonesians who are not ethnically Chinese. They have also become involved in development projects which assist such groups. Group leaders are professionals who volunteer their time. This case seems to mirror that of Greek North Americans, who became increasingly incorporated into Canadian and American institutions as they lobbied these governments in relation to homeland politics. Diversity is also evident within specific ethnic or national communities. For example, some Tamil organizations in Canada have been important players in the Tamil nationalist movement in Sri Lanka, and Canadian media has focused on the spill over of crime and violence into Canada from that country. Meanwhile, most Tamils, particularly those with children in Canada, are incorporating into Canadian labour markets and institutions.

Some Indian migrant organizations active in Canada are working to counter the influence of transnational religious-based movements associated with communal violence, and to publicize the experiences of Islamic communities in India who have been targets of violence.

One speaker representing a community organization argued that South Asians in Canada engage in homeland politics because they experience racism and other forms of social and economic exclusion here. In contrast, she argued that immigrant politics are the domain of youth and the second generation, people who do not have active ties to their homeland. These examples point to considerable variation in the activities of transmigrants and the ways that they might enhance or undermine Canadian foreign policy.

Activities that are contradictory to the values underlying Canadian foreign policy range well beyond the 'visible' security threats of migrants with links to cross-border terrorism or crime. They extend, for example, to the kinds of transnational investments made by Canadian residents. At the same time, the CCEVI case is representative of many groups and activities making a direct and positive impact on government efforts to promote Canadian values centred on human rights and human security abroad. The cases of CCEVI, Tamils, and even non-resident Indians (NRIs) suggest that foreign-born Canadian immigrants and citizens may engage in both incorporative and transnational activities at the same time. They also suggest that the relationship between racialization and exclusion on one hand, and transnationalism on the other, deserves further investigation.

Cross-border Advocacy and NGOs

There are many cases of faith-based, labour, and other NGOs lobbying various government agencies (CIC, DFAIT, HRDC) on issues that affect the lives of transmigrants, such as the FTAA, human rights, and immigration, refugee, and asylum policies. Cross-border and transnational coalitions such as these have been important to the work and success of these organizations. The increasingly transnational and coalition-based aspects of social justice campaigns are consistent with the Canadian government's publicly stated commitment to democratically accountable multilateralism, new multilateralism, and public diplomacy. Such networks and coalitions deserve financial and other support, for they play an important role in the (re)negotiation of Canadian foreign and other policies and in promoting Canadian values and interests abroad.

Elaboration of Foreign Policy Implications

Complexity

Homeland ties, cross-border advocacy, state outreach toward emigrant populations, and other examples of political transnational activity are complex processes that defy simple classification or generalization. Workshop presentations pointed to diverse and at times contradictory objectives and motivations behind transnational activity, making it difficult to evaluate the costs and benefits for different actors. This in itself is a useful conclusion, one that suggests a need for careful investigation of political and other forms of transnationalism at various levels, among a range of groups, in order to analyze how specific activities may be advantageous to some foreign policy aims and not others, and whether and how this might change over time.

These investigations may allow Canadian policy-makers and the public to view transnational networks and activities with diminishing suspicion, and to move away from classifying them as either good or bad. Policy makers should refrain from any single approach to these practices, as some are consistent with and enhance foreign policy goals such as democratization, improved human security, and international development, while others may contradict them.

Foreign policy could go further to identify and, if appropriate, support those activities which support foreign policy goals, while being careful about inadvertently supporting activities which are not. The case of NRIs investing in a dam that the World Bank had rejected as environmentally unsound is a useful example. These investors may gain status and political leverage in relation to the Indian government. However, their efforts undermine the goals of local (Indian) environmental and indigenous NGOs, as well as the World Bank. This case underscores the complexity of the issue, particularly when compared to CCEVI's efforts to advocate on behalf of victims of ethnic violence in Indonesia.

A Need for Research that can Inform Policy

The sheer diversity and extent of transnational practices points to a need for more research and exchanges among scholars and with policy-makers so as to enable a more informed foreign policy. Relatively little is known about migrant transnationalism and cross-border networks in Canada, while research on these phenomena in the United States and Europe has a longer history. Fortunately, several efforts are underway to document and analyze patterns of migrant transnationalism in this country.

Workshop participants from the United States, Malaysia, and Canada outlined some of the kinds of data and research questions that could be pursued in Canada, and which could inform the making of foreign as well as development and immigration policy. Some specific research needs include:

a. Prevalence, use, and political impacts of remittances. Remittances constitute one of the most common forms of transnational activity. Although they involve monetary flows, remittances are based on family and other socially defined commitments. They may also have important political dimensions, particularly when they account for large shares of the foreign exchange earnings of particular countries and contribute to the survival of significant numbers of households and communities. Many state-Diaspora outreach programmes are directly or indirectly aimed at maintaining the flow of remittances and improving the image and legitimacy of the home country among the emigrant population. One of the presenters described the Peruvian government's efforts to develop consultative bodies of emigrants to evaluate consular services. The presenter suggested that the underlying agenda includes increasing the legitimacy of the Peruvian government among emigrants (who can vote in Peruvian elections) and maintaining remittance flows. The Peruvian government was modelling these consultative bodies on the Mexican model. Last year Mexico initiated a new process involving a body of delegates selected by the government to provide consultation on a number of issues, including political rights in Mexico, among Mexicans in the United States.

Although this model is new and, as yet, unproven, it is already being copied by other remittance-dependent governments in the region. The government of Taiwan has recently moved to make its consulates and embassies more accountable to overseas Taiwan citizens, reflecting both democratization in Taiwan and the political and economic influence of emigrants, who have long had reserved seats in the Legislative Yuan. Canada lacks a comprehensive or systematic database on Canadian-based remittance flows. The IMF publishes data on remittances, but there is no information on the sources, only totals received by country. While there are significant methodological challenges involved in any effort to measure remittance flows, and deepen our understanding of various forms of remittances, Canadian policy would benefit from having better data. In addition to supporting data collection, Canadians policy-makers and the public need in-depth analyses of the uses, meanings and politics surrounding remittances.

After all, most family remittances fund household and medical expenses. If there is money left over, it goes to education, housing, and major life-cycle events. Collective remittances often pay for local development projects (including roads, schools, and clinics) and disaster relief. Only in a minority of cases are they used for less desirable ends. Understanding the variety of uses to which they are put and the institutions that mediate their transfer and use could reduce suspicion regarding fundraising for overseas projects and foreign investment by Canadians with homeland ties.

b. How the Canadian context shapes transnationalism. Research on migrant transnational activities and cross-border networks based in Canada can illuminate the role of the context of reception in shaping the form and implications of transnationalism. At this point there are a number of case studies of the influence of context of reception in the United States, Britain, Europe. However, the Canadian government's immigrant and refugee selection and multiculturalism policies create a somewhat different context of reception. As noted below, we need to learn more about the extent to which racism and other rights-limiting practices contribute to transnationalism, and whether national-origin or ethnic groups present in Canada and elsewhere engage in different forms of transnationalism because of the Canadian context.

c. Complexity and variation. Over and over again workshop discussions demonstrated that there are many types of migrant transnational practices, and many kinds of related transnational associations, organizations, and networks. There is a need both for mapping this complexity, and for more specialized workshops and research around specific forms of transnationalism and of transnationalism among particular groups. To this end, future workshops are being planned on transnational religious networks (at York University) and transnationalism among Chinese immigrants (at the University of Toronto with York University support).

(d) Racism, social exclusion and transnationalism: Research on transnationalism elsewhere indicates that racism and social exclusion can contribute to transnationalism. However, the evidence is inconclusive. Work on this question in the Canadian context would contribute to Canadian policy as well as academic discussions. However, it is important to emphasize that the findings of such research should not be used to challenge the legitimacy of migrant transnationalism.

Security

It is important not to assume that migrant transnationalism is dangerous or a security threat to Canadians, or a sign that immigrant communities are not committed to civic life in Canada. Rather, migrant transnationalism often goes hand-in-hand with civic involvement in Canadian society and support for democracy, human rights, and social justice both in Canada and in home countries. Moreover, transnational livelihood strategies are crucial to improving human security in both sending and receiving countries. Remittances are particularly central to development in low-income regions and to the security of individuals and families. Therefore, in many cases, transnationalism is a direct response to insecurity and can be understood as a migrant-led way of improving human security.

Broadening the Scope of Human Security

The Canadian government's current approach to human security emphasizes the security of people abroad, especially in conflict zones. Workshop presentations pointed to the need for policy- makers to expand the scope of human security to include livelihood security, security regardless of geographic location (in Canada and abroad), and the reduction of a broad spectrum of risks, including disease, safety, shelter, civil rights protection, as well as protection from both systemic and physical violence. This would help further to link security and rights, based on the logic that the better one's access to a bundle of rights, and the greater the quality and array of rights in the bundle, the greater the security one will experience.

This approach is also consistent with the Canadian government's commitment to act on the Summit Action Plans on the protection of the human rights of migrants, including migrant workers and their families. The Canadian government should move ahead on the commitment in the Action Plans to establish an inter-American programme within the Organization of American States (OAS) for the promotion and protection of the rights of migrants. More broadly, it should demonstrate its commitment to the rights of migrant workers by immediately signing and ratifying the International Convention on the Protection of the Rights of All Migrant Workers and Members of Their Families. Notably, this convention is one of several recent international agreements that recognizes a right to some forms of transnational association for migrants and other groups. In the current context, the threat of terrorism has highlighted state security concerns, subordinating human security.

One of the consequences has been to raise suspicion of the homeland ties of migrants, particularly ties with economic, political or religious dimensions. A broader approach to human security would recognize that maintaining contact with individuals and organizations in a real or putative homeland is a legitimate activity that frequently aims to enhance human security and human rights for those involved. The assumption of guilt based on links to violent or criminal activity should only be made after due analysis.

Security and Canadian Values

Identifying and working with transnational migrant organizations and cross-border advocacy networks whose work is consistent with Canadian foreign policy and values could contribute to promoting a good image of Canada and Canadians, both overseas and here in Canada. It is consistent with Canada's international leadership in promoting peacekeeping, people-to-people dialogue, and partnerships with NGOs and other non-state actors to foster sustainable development, prosperity, and social justice.

Public Diplomacy

The transnational activities and communications of migrants and related cross-border advocacy networks often constitute a form of public diplomacy that shapes the image of Canada abroad and influences the ability of Canadian policy-makers to promote Canadian values and interests abroad. Some transnational activities on specific issues constitute a kind of informal Canadian foreign policy. Policy-makers concerned with the kinds of information people abroad receive about Canada, or who are also involved with the same issues engaged in by Canadian immigrant organizations, should pay attention to how this public diplomacy affects their work. They should encourage and assist those groups whose activities enhance Canadian foreign policy objectives and that promote an expanded definition of human security, including in multilateral fora.

The goals of these actors may not always be consistent with Canadian policies. Nevertheless, Canadian policy needs to engage with these actors and networks, rather than ignoring them. For example, it remains an urgent priority to work with Muslim groups in Canada with overseas connections. Rather than branding them uniformly as terrorists or worthy of suspicion, the Canadian government should work with these groups to foster dialogue and build bridges that will reduce intolerance and promote peace, human security, and human rights.

The Canadian government could do more to take advantage of the expertise, connections, and resources of transnational migrant and relevant cross-border advocacy networks in areas such as development and environmental advocacy and projects, human rights promotion, and faith-based organizing.

Citizenship, Rights and Marginalization

The Canadian government should exercise leadership in the human security agenda at home and in multilateral fora by broadening the rights of migrants in Canada and other countries, regardless of nationality or citizenship and despite the transnationality of their lives. As noted above, an expanded approach to security can focus attention on the ways that migrant transnational practices and cross-border advocacy may enhance the security of individuals and families who directly experience risk or vulnerability with respect to human rights or other rights and freedoms, or who advocate to reduce such risks on behalf of others.

Examples of the former would include people who cannot find adequate employment in Canada and who therefore maintain strong economic ties to their homeland (e.g. some temporary workers, some immigrants from Hong Kong); individuals with immediate family members abroad who cannot bring them to Canada for economic, immigration, or other reasons; or people who experience racism, blocked occupational mobility, or other forms of social exclusion in Canada and, therefore, seek support and security through transnational links.

A wide range ot examples of the latter were discussed at the workshop; they include cross-border advocacy around the FTAA (e.g. for human rights, labour protection, and environmental security), CCEVI's work on behalf of ethnic Chinese and indigenous groups in Indonesia, and Tamil organizations. In examining how transnationalism may be a response to insecurity and social and economic marginalization, violations of the following rights are particularly important: (i) Freedom from racism, sexism, and other forms of discrimination; freedom from oppression and persecution; (ii) Freedom of association and of participation; (iii)Social rights (including to health, education, and safety); (iv)Cultural rights (freedom of religious expression; the right to construct places of worship, to ethnic identity, and to cultural survival); (v) Civil rights (the right to equity, equality before the law and equal protection of the law, to organize unions and to other labour rights and protection); (vi) Political (the right to vote, to representation, and to hold public authorities accountable); and (vii) Local political rights (the right to a voice in municipal affairs regardless of citizenship or nationality)

Workshop presenters who discussed temporary workers, special worker programmes, and cross-border organizing from a variety of perspectives concurred that vulnerability associated with the denial of rights (whether of migrants or of their close relatives living at home) often leads workers to engage in transnational activities of various sorts. In some cases it may also prompt homeland states to lobby on behalf of overseas populations, although in others these people may be completely unprotected and lack advocates. Finally, in some cases the rights of migrants have been used by host countries as form of political leverage in their relations with sending countries. A recent example is the way that the situation of Mexican migrants in the United States was at issue in the politics of the UN Security Council vote on using force in Iraq. Holding migrant rights hostage to international relations curtails human security.

Policy Coherence

a. The relationship between social exclusion/inclusion and transnationalism: As indicated above, migrant transnationalism does not preclude incorporation into Canadian society. Although further research is needed, Canadian cases discussed at the workshop confirm findings from other countries that the incorporation of immigrants into Canadian society and their engagement in transnational activities (whether political or economic, in these cases) should not be automatically seen in zero-sum terms. Migrant transnationalism also does not preclude a commitment to Canadian values, institutions, and society. For example, CCEVI's ability to lobby the Canadian government is enhanced by members' professional and settled resident status, just as the NRI's economic success in Canada allows them to invest, in Canada and "at home."

b. Other policy linkages: We have also discussed above how transnationalism among migrant communities points to the need for efforts to ensure policy coherence over a wide range of policy areas, not only with domestic policies but also immigration and international development policies. The kinds of information about Canada conveyed abroad (e.g. by migrants to overseas relatives), and the way that transnational political practices take shape, are directly affected by what are often seen as "domestic" policies and experiences such as employment rights, access to social services such as education and health, freedom of association, and freedom from cultural or radicalized discrimination. Thus, the foreign policy community would benefit from attention to how Canadian government overseas development policies and economic and political relations with particular countries may be undermined by municipal, provincial and federal policies that affect migrants, and vice versa. More research is needed on these complex linkages.

The contemporary era is marked by globalization and the changing roles of and relations between capital, states, NGOs, and labour. It is one in which state policies often lag behind the lived experience of many people. In a world marked by the movement of people, goods, capital, ideas, and images, states sometimes treat "their" people on the basis of concepts—like territorially bounded notions of the nation-state and identity—that are fast becoming outmoded. Other states, particularly those dependent on migrant remittances, are changing the way they treat "their" people living abroad. "Host" states tend to react with greater suspicion, branding people who retain active ties to homelands as disloyal, un-patriotic (to their country of adoption), or worse—as terrorists or criminals.

The workshop pointed to the need to move away from nearly automatic suspicion of migrant transnationalism towards a more informed and nuanced understanding of its complexity and diversity, grounded in Canada-specific research. The workshop identified the ways in which many forms of migrant transnationalism support Canadian foreign policy goals, especially the promotion of human rights and human security. Canadian foreign policy and international development policy can be enhanced by (1) drawing on and supporting detailed comparative and case studies on transnational activities; (2) supporting the systematization of data collection and analyses of remittances; and (3) building bridges with organizations involved in activities that are consistent with Canadian policy goals and values.

Acceptance of people's transnational identities, practices, and values can enhance the prosperity of Canadians at home and abroad by valuing transnational ties. It can also enhance security at home and abroad by not requiring people to chose one allegiance, or a single loyalty. Acceptance of transnationality will also enhance human security to the extent that it brings enhanced rights for migrants in Canada, despite their transnationality. This rests on a modified conception of human security, one that links security to human rights and broader rights and freedoms. The workshop pointed to the need for more comprehensive understanding of transnationalism among Canadian migrants, the ways that transnationalism enhances or contradicts Canadian foreign policy objectives, and the factors that promote and shape lives that extend across borders. Because government policies influence and sometimes encourage transnationalism, policy-relevant research can also point to ways in which policy could engage with transnationalism in ways that enhance foreign policy objectives. Another need identified was that of greater policy coherence between branches of DFAIT and other ministries dealing with immigrants (CIC, HRDC) and development issues (CIDA), as well as relevant provincial and federal departments and agencies. At the federal level, greater communication and inter-departmental planning would enhance key future steps advocated by participants, including remittance data collection and analysis, the reconceptualization of security, policy coherence, and better-informed foreign policy that takes into account transnational ties.

Religion and Education Policy

The British North America Act of 1867, which established the Canadian confederation, assigned education to provincial jurisdiction. The BNA Act, however, also gave legal protection to the established educational rights of religious minorities. In the new Canadian federation, Protestants were the religious minority in Quebec and Catholics the religious minority elsewhere. Quebec continued to organize its public education into Catholic and Protestant systems. Ontario, the other populous partner in confederation, maintained "public" and "separate" (Catholic) school systems at the elementary level. Religious minority rights were equivocal in provinces which entered Canada after 1867. The legislation that brought Manitoba into Canada in 1870 established parallel confessional schools.

In 1890, the Manitoba government, in one act of a complex English/French, Protestant/Catholic, federal/provincial struggle, withdrew public funding for Catholic schools. The 1896 compromise resolution which was negotiated between the C anadian and Manitoba governments gave only limited rights to Catholics within Manitoba public schools. British Columbia, which entered Canada in 1871, established a public school system the following year. In 1905, the new provinces of Saskatchewan and Alberta followed the Ontario model.

Provincial public school systems vested considerable autonomy in local school boards. A close alliance between religion and schools, and particularly between Protestant Christianity and public schools, was taken for granted. Protestant clergymen of various denominations were often among local educational leaders. While specific denominations established Sunday schools for their own children, they expected public schools to continue to have a non-denominational Christian character. In some local jurisdictions, Christian denominational schools were part of the public system.

Religious affiliation was also characteristic of Canadian private schools. In those provinces which did not establish publicly-funded Catholic schools, Catholic education took place in private schools. Schools founded before free public education, usually under some kind of religious sponsorship, remained as elite institutions. Religious communities, Jews among them, set up their own schools. Often these schools initially supplemented public instruction but later became privately-financed alternatives to public education.

Jewish Immigration, Religion and Public Education

The turn of the century immigration of Jews brought a new religious group into Canada in substantial numbers. In both Quebec and Ontario, public opinion was widely anti-Semitic and discrimination was normal. Both provinces, however, had to make some arrangement for the education of Jewish children. In Quebec, Jewish students were reluctantly admitted to the Protestant schools. As Jewish students increased to almost 45 percent of enrolment in the Montreal Protestant schools in 1916, this awkward relationship turned into a continuing resentment on both sides. A campaign in the 1920s to establish a Jewish school system as a third publicly supported confessional system came close to implementation but failed (Rome, 1975, 1977). The substantial group of Montreal Jews interested in intensive Jewish education turned their energies to developing Jewish schools which met after public school hours, often for ten hours of classes a week. These schools, representing a range of Jewish ideological movements, were financed by tuition and fund-raising. In Ontario, particularly in Toronto, which became by far the largest Jewish community in the province, the situation was somewhat different.

Ontario public schools in the early decades of this century were characterized by a Protestant orientation. Opening exercises included readings from Scripture and the Lord's Prayer. Local boards of education welcomed classes given by Protestant clergy before or after school hours. The assumption of superiority of Christian (particularly, Protestant) civilization pervaded the teaching of literature, history and the arts. Jewish children were exposed to Protestantism not only in the schools, but also through missionary work in Jewish immigrant neighborhoods.

The active mobilization against missionaries and the manifest prejudices of the larger society minimized the effects of these religious practices on Jewish children. The ideological ferment within the community likely played an even larger role. The issue of the day was not one of whether to stay in the Jewish community or to leave, but whether to identify with the Orthodox who supported Zionism, the Orthodox who opposed Zionism, the religiously liberal, the secular Zionists, or one or another group of socialists. As the Jewish community grew, afternoon schools and congregational schools representing this range of choices were established. Until the 1950s the Ontario Jewish leadership, even in the large community of Toronto, expected that Jewish children would receive their education in public schools.

Smaller numbers of Jewish immigrants settled in the Maritimes, the prairie provinces, and British Columbia. Early in the twentieth century, Jewish day schools in Canada were established in Alberta, where some distinctive ethno-religious groups, including those recently arrived from Europe, were highly self-conscious about their uniqueness. After World War II, public education became more complex, professionalized, and secular. In the mid-1960s, as Quebec's "quiet revolution" was moving public institutions in the direction of secularization, Jews received the right to sit on the Protestant school board. In Ontario, social trends and legislation diverged. Since the turn of the twentieth century, church membership, regular worship, after school religious instruction, and Sunday school attendance have declined.

The Depression depleted church budgets, leading to reductions in programs and building maintenance. In response, an Ontario government sympathetic to mainstream Protestantism in 1944 mandated two and a half hours per week of religious instruction in public school classes, with dissenting students permitted to exempt themselves from the class. This regulation, which was valued particularly in rural parts of the province with homogeneous, fundamentalist populations, was on the books until 1990.

The impact of this regulation on the public school experience of Jewish children is indicated by two studies. A study of socialization in the early 1950s in an emerging wealthy suburb of Toronto shared by Christians and Jews noted the subordination of the quest for "salvation" to the use of religion as a support to the personal quest for "happiness," success, peace of mind and mental health. The public schools in this jurisdiction took special care not to espouse a particular religion, but to teach that religion "embodies vague recommendations against aggression, and in favor of love and sympathy".

Religious instruction was more traditionally Protestant in North York - the suburban destination of most Jews moving from downtown Toronto. In 1970, as a consequence of Jewish resistance to religious instruction in public schools, North York received an exemption from the provincial regulation. In 1990, religious instruction in Ontario public schools was held to violate the 1982 incorporation of the Charter of Rights and Freedoms into the Canadian Constitution. By then, enthusiasm for Protestant teaching in the urban school boards of Ontario was no longer present.

For several decades, school boards in metropolitan areas had been responding to their changing clientele by focusing on educational philosophies based on cultivating students' abilities to choose values for themselves, and were promoting a non-judgmental ethic by giving attention to toleration, multiculturalism, and anti-racism. This change of attitude was not found in all parts of rural Ontario, leading to an appeal to the Ontario courts to allow a Mennonite school to continue its affiliation as an alternative school within a public board. This case is discussed after reviewing the changing relationship of private schools with Canadian provincial governments and the form that this question took in Ontario as first a political and then a judicial issue.

Public Financing of Independent Schools

The 1960s onward saw private schools brought into a different relationship with many provincial governments. Established private schools, joined by such denominational groups as Dutch Calvinists, who had immigrated in the postwar period and established private "Christian" schools, lobbied for financial assistance. This broader coalition preferred using the more inclusive language of "independent" schools to the elitist connotations of "private" schools. Limited government support was extended to private schools in Alberta, Manitoba, Quebec and British Columbia in the 1960s and 1970s. By the late 1990s, 4.8

percent of Canadian students attended an independent school, compared to 2.5 percent in 1971.

The trend toward private schools was also found in Canadian Jewish education. By the time Montreal Jews received rights in the Protestant school board, the downtown afternoon schools founded by the immigrant generation had become suburban Jewish day schools. The government of Quebec brought these schools into the framework of its financial support for private schools, subsidizing a considerable proportion of the cost of the "secular studies" curriculum of Jewish day schools. Most Jewish education in Montreal now takes place in day schools. In Manitoba, Alberta, and British Columbia, Jewish day schools were also receiving public funding of some kind by the 1970s.

Ontario continued to exclude any alternatives to the public and separate schools from public funding. By the 1960s Ontario had the largest Jewish population of any province. As in Montreal, the Jewish afternoon schools of the early twentieth century had moved to the suburbs and become day schools. New day schools representing a range of ideologies - including Zionist, Conservative, Reform, and various shades of Orthodoxy - were organized in Toronto. Jewish day schools were established in Ottawa, London and Hamilton. In 1962 the director of the Toronto Board of Jewish Education noted the rapid increase in Jewish day school enrolment - from a modest 337 students in 1950 to 1,765 in 1962. Foreseeing continuing expansion, he argued that Jewish schools should turn to the provincial government for assistance. Groups of Jewish parents organized to work for this objective. In the early 1970s, following the decision of the Quebec government to extend public support to Jewish day schools, discussions were held which led to a proposal to bring one or more Jewish day schools into association with the North York public system. This proposal foundered on the issue of control over admissions.

The issue was revived following the 1984 decision of the government of Ontario to extend public financing for Catholic education beyond elementary school to high school. The Ontario Jewish Association for Equity in Education (OJAEE) was created by the Ontario region of Canadian Jewish Congress as a new body to lobby for government funding of Jewish day schools. The Ontario government appointed Bernard Shapiro, former head of the Ontario Institute for Studies in Education (the graduate level institution established to support educational research), to report on the funding of independent schools. Shapiro's report noted the inequity of public funding for only the Catholic alternative to public schools.

It recommended a form of associate status which would provide government assistance for independent schools within the public system. Despite Shapiro's subsequent appointment as Deputy Minister of Education (the senior civil service position in the ministry), there was no political will to act on this recommendation. The extension of full financing to Ontario Separate Schools was challenged in the Ontario courts on the grounds that giving public support to one religiously based school system discriminated against other religious groups. The court case was based on the guarantee of equal rights under the Charter of Rights and Freedoms, which was incorporated into the Canadian Constitution in 1982. The Ontario Court of Appeals held by a 3-2 decision in 1986 that Ontario's legislation was constitutional and that establishing a right of private schools to public financing would require a constitutional amendment.

The Ontario court decision was appealed to the Supreme Court of Canada, which ruled by a 7-0 decision in 1987 that the full funding of Catholic schools was constitutional. The court held that the right to publicly supported Catholic schools was part of the historic compromise which led to Confederation and that the provisions of the Charter of Rights and Freedoms do not override this original constitutional arrangement. The Supreme Court, however, did not refer to funding arrangements for other religious groups, apparently leaving the issue of their rights unresolved.

With no progress on the political track, in 1991 the OJAEE, in association with the Ontario Alliance of Christian Schools, sought to have the courts impose, in accordance with the Charter of Rights and Freedoms, public funding for non-Catholic religious schools. The court case was known as the Adler case, after the name of one of the parents. In 1992 Justice William Anderson ruled that the parents' rights under the Charter were being violated. However, he concluded that charter rights are subject to limits and that in this case "the impairment is within reasonable limits".

The appeal of this ruling to the Ontario Court of Appeal was unanimously rejected in 1994, with the judges ruling that Charter rights were not violated. The appeal proceeded to the Supreme Court of Canada. In 1996, seven of nine judges of the Supreme Court ruled that although the Canadian Constitution Act guarantees the funding of Roman Catholic schools in Ontario, the province is not thereby required to fund other religiously based schools. The court also noted "there is nothing in law to prevent Ontario from extending public funding to independent religious schools". The Ontario Separate School Trustees' Association issued a press release after the failure of the appeal to the Supreme Court. The president of the association said, "I want to repeat the long-held belief of our association that funding should be available for all properly accredited independent religious schools operating in the province. We have said before that, in striving to achieve justice for ourselves, we do not deem it proper to stand mute in the face of the just needs of others". While the case brought by the Ontario Jewish Association for

Equity in Education and the Ontario Alliance of Christian Schools was working its way through the courts, another religious coalition was in the courts pursuing a different tactic. The Multi-faith Coalition for Equity in Education, with representatives from Evangelical Christian, Hindu, Moslem, and Sikh communities, was formed to advance a court challenge which would, had their argument been successful, have permitted local school boards to give religious schools associate status, thus getting around the 1990 court decision that appeared to prohibit religious instruction in public schools. The composition of this coalition reflects the immigration from Asia and the Middle East that has come to Ontario in significant numbers from the 1970s on. Since the mid-1970s, Asia and Africa have become important sources of immigration to Canada, multiplying the Canadian adherents of the Moslem, Buddhist, Hindu, and Sikh religions.

In the ten-year period from 1981 to 1991, the number of Moslems, Hindus, Buddhists, and Sikhs in Canada increased 2½ times, from 287,500 to 720,000. In 1991, Ontario was the home of over half of the adherents of these religions, about 368,000, accounting for about 3.7 percent of the province's population. These increases were matched by a large increase in those reporting no religion, the stability of the Jewish percentage of the Ontario population (at about 1.75 percent), stability in the Catholic population, a falling off of the numbers identifying with mainline Protestant denominations and a growth in the number of more conservative sectarian Protestants. The greater Toronto area has been the most common destination for new immigrants. This metropolitan area is now not only multi-ethnic and multi-racial but increasingly multi-religious.

The Multi-faith Coalition for Equity in Education used as its test case the affiliation of a Mennonite Christian school as an alternative school within a rural school district. The affiliation had taken place with the support of the local community in 1977, but it was jeopardized by the strong stand taken on secularism by the 1990 court ruling against religious instruction in Ontario schools. Again the argument for equity with Catholic schools was rejected, as was the argument, used in the United States, that "secular humanism" replaces religion in public schools and is itself a form of religion. The Ontario District Court in 1994 and the Ontario Court of Appeals in 1997 ruled against arrangements which would incorporate religiously identified schools as alternative schools inside public boards.

Education Reform in Ontario

The Conservative government elected in 1995 based its platform on lowering taxes by cutting government spending. Education reform has been one of the main activities of the current Conservative provincial government. It reduced its expenditures on public education by $400 million, reduced school boards from 168 to 66, cut the salaries of trustees up to 90 percent, and moved the power to set education tax rates from the local to provincial level. By moving control of funding to the provincial level, the government substantially removed the power of school boards to decide whether to spend more or less per capita than other boards. The City of Toronto Board of Education, for example, had made significant investments in programs beyond provincial requirements.

On the other hand, the Catholic school boards, in order to maintain their clientele, had kept their level of school taxation lower than public schools. The government's changes in education financing and structure met significant opposition. School boards objected to consolidation. Teachers went on a lengthy strike across the province, with the support of parents going much more heavily to the educators than to the government. The government, nevertheless, did not change its proposals and the reforms proceeded. In July 1998, opponents of these reforms had success in the courts. An Ontario court held that the legislation removing the power to set education taxes from the Catholic school boards violated the Canadian Constitution. The Catholic school boards were willing to give up this power in exchange for an increase in per capita funding to the same level as public schools.

The court held, however, that the Catholic boards could not constitutionally agree to such a bargain. The government announced that it intended to appeal this decision and would continue in the meantime to operate under the new rules. The court's objection to the education reforms did not highlight the changing balance between Catholic and public schools, but this is also relevant. In 1901, the population of Ontario was almost 80 percent Protestant and just over 20 percent Catholic. By 1951, the population reporting their religion as Catholic on the census was over one third that of those reporting themselves as Protestant.

In 1991, the numbers were even closer, with 4.4 million of Ontario's 10 million people reporting themselves as Protestant and 3.5 million reporting themselves as Catholic. In the four years from 1993 to 1997, enrolment in public schools decreased while enrolment in separate schools increased, with corresponding decreases and increases in spending. Public schools in 1997 accounted for over 1,300,000 pupils and separate schools for almost 575,000. The Conservative government elected in 1995 has strong support in religiously conservative areas of rural Ontario, but it chose not to introduce religious issues into its controversial first-term education reforms. Each of the last three provincial elections produced a turnover in governing parties - from the Conservatives to the Liberals to the New Democrats and then back to the Conservatives. If the present government is successful in winning a second term, it may turn again to education reform and at that time address a new policy on support for religious teaching with public support.

The controversial changes already legislated are not likely to be the end of the Ontario government's educational reform agenda. The government is rumored to be considering further changes in the structure of education to be introduced after the next election. It could eliminate school boards entirely, replacing them with other admini-strative structures. In tandem with this change, or as a separate initiative, charter schools could be permitted. In charter schools, groups of parents with a common educational outlook form school councils. They may supplement public funding with their own resources, and they are able to significantly influence hiring and curriculum. Charter schools appeal in a pragmatic way to parents who want special curriculum emphases for their children - in the arts, in physical education, in the "basics," or in special education.

This type of school structure is seen by conservatives as an attractive alternative to centralized public school boards, which are seen as too expensive (too many administrators and "frills") and too often liberal in educational ideology. In contrast, opponents see charter schools as opening the door to a two-tier system in which those able to pay extra and invest time receive better public schools than those less advantaged. With respect to its policy on independent schools, the election platform on which the current provincial premier ran promised "to examine the inclusion of denominational and other private schools" in the public system. In 1998, the province listed over 600 private schools. Over two-thirds have some kind of religious affiliation.

The list also includes 78 Montessori schools, 7 Waldorf schools, 28 First Nations (native North American) schools and assorted private learning centers, academies, and special population institutions which do not list a religious affiliation. The government lists 35 Jewish and 17 Islamic schools. The other hundreds of identifiable religious schools are Christian. Some of these are remaining elite private schools. Almost a hundred are identified in the list as Amish or Mennonite. A small number are identified as Seventh Day Adventist (11), Canadian Reformed (7), or Baptist (9). However, most of the identifiably Christian schools put the word "Christian" in their names. Many of these are identified with the Ontario Alliance of Christian Schools. Another group is part of the network of Evangelical Christian schools.

Ontario could follow the lead of Alberta, British Columbia, Manitoba, and Quebec by extending financial support to independent schools. Alternatively, it could set in place a system, like a voucher system, in which a basic educational grant would follow each student into any school which meets provincial standards. In formulating its policy towards religious education, the government also has to consider whether it can somehow incorporate religious teachings within the public school structure. It could include denominational religious education within a charter school framework. A document prepared in 1993 by the Multi-faith Coalition for Equity in Education, which gives some details of various ways that public funding might be extended to teaching religion, is discussed below.

After the Supreme Court of Canada in 1996 rejected the argument to extend funding to non-Catholic religious schools on the basis of equity, the various groups with the same goal of receiving public support for their schools joined into the Working Group on Educational Equality. In August 1997 the executive assistant to the Minister of Education and the parliamentary assistant to the minister held a meeting with the Working Group. The representatives of the government announced that the government had "philosophically accepted" funding for religious day schools. According to Manuel Prutschi of Canadian Jewish Congress, the government intends to let the public catch its breath from the recent significant changes in education before implementing its promise to fund independent schools. The provincial government of Alberta, which has an outlook similar to the one presently in power in Ontario and has been in power longer, has moved further in the direction of provincial aid to independent schools.

Enrolment in independent schools in Alberta increased by 50 percent in the decade from 1985/6 to 1995/6. In 1998, in response to recommendations of its Private Schools Funding Task Force, the Alberta government announced that it was increasing its grants to independent schools by about one-third. Recipients were henceforth required, in addition to continuing to follow provincial curriculum guidelines, to appoint principals with teaching certificates and to establish parent councils if they were not already in place. The Alberta government also insisted on a formal policy that "all private schools must not offer programs that in theory or in practice will promote or foster doctrines of racial or ethnic superiority or persecution, religious intolerance or persecution, social change through violent action, or disobedience of laws".

The Alberta experience also provides a precedent for a charter schools program, which the province introduced in 1994. The implementation has been controversial, with problems of governance - internal divisions, conflicts over administration, budgetary issues - the main focus of complaints. The largest charter school has been closed. Others have had charters renewed with conditions or been incorporated into school boards as alternative schools, with a lower degree of autonomy. In 1997/8, the province listed eleven chartered schools. In 1998/9, there will be nine charter schools in operation.

Model for Religious Education

The debate over education and religion is to some extent parallel to the debate over multiculturalism and education. Multicultural policy has been part of Canadian politics since 1971, and part of Ontario politics since shortly thereafter.

Since that time, federal and provincial governments have spoken of the diversity of cultures in Canada as one of its strengths and have sponsored programs based on the dual goals of the preservation of cultural diversity and civic integration. The almost thirty-year Canadian experience with multiculturalism provides a perspective on proposed policies on religious diversity in education.

Specific proposals for educational policy on religious diversity are in some ways similar to those for educational policy on cultural diversity, but they are in some ways different. Multicultural policy has been implemented in education in various ways. Public school curriculum has been rewritten to be more inclusive. Sometimes inclusive multicultural education involves teachers making sure that the mix of students in the class learn about each others' "culture" and become more tolerant of value judgments based on cultures other than their own. Multicultural education often involves a focus on racism, both historic and contemporary. Multiculturalism also has implications for staffing policy, as diversity of staff is adopted as a system goal.

One of the most visible implementations of multiculturalism has been the establishment of what were originally called "heritage language" classes, which now go under the heading of "international language" classes. A group of parents may request that a local school establish a class of up to 2½ hours a week to teach a language which is neither English nor French. The program also includes "Black cultural studies."

A parent committee, in consultation with the board of education, hires the teachers. These classes have been held in after-school hours, on weekends, or sometimes for half an hour a day during regular school hours. The most dramatic proposal to implement multiculturalism in education was the proposal for a Black school with substantial control by a local school council over curriculum and staffing. No level of govern-ment agreed to investigate this proposal.

Multicultural policy has been carefully distinguished from policy regarding religion. This distinction has been easier to make in principle than in practice. In the area of heritage/international languages, for example, Greek classes have been taught on weekends in Greek Orthodox churches; sometimes Hebrew has been taught in coordination with synagogue schools. The shift in immigration patterns from the early 1970s to the late 1990s has also blurred the distinction between cultural and religious diversity. Up to the early 1970s, the main source countries of migrants to Canada were European. The languages and cultures of immigrants from Europe may have been different from mainstream Canadians, but their religion, to the extent they practiced, was one or another form of Christianity.

As noted above, Asia and Africa have become important sources of immigration to Canada, multiplying the Canadian adherents of the Moslem, Buddhist, Hindu, and Sikh religions, creating a society which is not only multi-ethnic and multi-racial but increasingly multi-religious. The experience with multicultural education does not offer guidance on two important issues. First, cultural diversity is a somewhat different phenomenon from religious diversity. Cultural diversity can be brought into schools in a framework based on the civic ideals of toleration and the everyday practical relativism of the modern culture. Ideas about the coexistence of multiple cultures, the blending of cultures, or cultural change can be invoked to reduce the threat of "identity politics" dividing students into hostile camps. In contrast, religions usually present themselves to their adherents as the "only" or "best" source of truth; religious movements often stand in opposition to each other; and they often resist the idea that their beliefs and practices have somehow changed. How can a policy of religious diversity respond to these positions? Concern about raising these kinds of issues appears to have been a reason that multicultural policy kept its official distance from religion. Can different absolute truths be taught without teaching hostility, on the one hand, or insincerity, on the other? Should schools give equal time to all the religious traditions represented in the student body? Can students share each others' religion in the same spirit that they can be taught to share and appreciate each others' "culture"?

Second, while non-Catholic religious minorities have worked to establish their own alternative schools, only a few proponents of multicultural education promote separate schools for different cultural groups. Ontario does have a publicly supported system of French language schools available to its approximately 350,000 francophone. The legitimacy for these schools does not come from multicultural policy but from bilingual policy.

French language schools are seen as a significant contribution to Canadian national unity and a recognition of entrenched constitutional rights. Otherwise, private schools based on cultural differences are limited. In contrast, minority religions include enthusiastic proponents of alternative education who have been successful in establishing independent schools by raising financial resources on their own. How is a policy on religious diversity in education to respond to the existence of these schools and the desire to establish new ones?

Religion and Education Policy

During the period in which both the teaching of Protestant religion and aid to independent schools were controversial, the provincial government passed the question of religious education over to various study commissions. The Royal Commission on Learning was one of the addresses for submissions on these issues. Two briefs submitted in 1993 and 1994 to the Royal Commission on

Learning presented, in the first case, an alternative strategy for religious education and, in the second case, more details about how incorporating parallel religious teachings into a publicly supported system might work. The 1993 brief was received from the Ecumenical Study Commission on Public Education. The Ecumenical Study Commission on Public Education was formed in 1969 in response to the recommendations of a previous public inquiry on religion in the public schools.

An official coalition of the Anglican, Baptist, Lutheran, Presbyterian, Roman Catholic, and United Churches, it was historically favorable to maintaining some degree of Christian teaching in public schools. The submission of the Ecumenical Study Commission noted the existence of "different kinds of separate schools," but devoted its recommendations to "multifaith education about religion in inclusive public schools." It distinguished its approach to religious education from "religious instruction, religious indoctrination and proselytism." It proposed developing a comparative religion curriculum which would stress tolerance of differences, "the identification of values and principles shared by different religions," and "respect for religion [as] a fundamental dimension of human experience."

The Ontario Multi-faith Coalition for Equity in Education, which later became one of the partners in the Working Group on Educational Equality, submitted a contrasting brief a few months later. The Ontario Multi-faith Coalition for Equity in Education described itself as comprised of "member groups representing four religious communities in Canada - Christian, Hindu, Islamic and Sikh." It listed among its members the President of the Islamic Society of North America, the Secretary of the Ontario Council of Sikhs, the past president of the Canadian Council of Hindus, the past president of the Hindu Federation of Canada, the Chair of the Coalition for Religious Freedom in Education and the treasurer of the ISNA Islamic

School. The submission identified three principles to "equip students for responsible citizenship."

1. Religion is integral to education.
2. The primary responsibility for the education of children lies with parents.
3. Public education must provide choice and equity.

The proposal to implement these principles called for the establishment of two educational initiatives. The first initiative is similar in structure to the international languages program which takes place within the framework of multiculturalism in Ontario schools. A group of parents would be entitled to petition a school to establish a program which would respond to the particular faith and values of the parent group. These opt-in programs would be part of the regular school program, not extra cost options. The recommendations on staffing the opt-in classes did differ from present arrangements for staffing international language classes. International language instructors are often not certified teachers, as the pool available for such part-time instruction is limited. The opt-in proposal calls for classes to be "under the supervision of a certified teacher" and adds that "parents, elders and other qualified adult volunteers from the community involved would be encouraged to participate."

The second educational initiative recommended is the establishment of "religious and values based schools." These could be newly established within existing public school buildings or they could be existing private schools given associate status with the public system. In the first option, "religious and values based schools" would fit into a charter schools model. In the second option, Ontario would follow the lead of the four other provinces which give support to independent schools. The Ontario Multi-faith Coalition explicitly pointed to the Shapiro report as a starting point for this initiative.

In its proposals on school governance, the Ontario Multi-faith Coalition proposed school councils. Its brief made references to a similar idea in Quebec. It did not refer to the concept of charter schools or to the arrangement in Alberta, although it is a similar proposal. The brief recommended school councils in which parents would be the majority but which would also include representations from "senior students, teachers and support staff, as well as from community interests." School councils would not be mandatory, but would develop ad hoc from grass roots initiatives. School board nominations for principal would be subject to the agreement of the school council. Councils would begin with an advisory role in expenditures of the school budget. The Coalition brief supported "a move towards school based budgeting and management."

Globalisation, Transnational Religion and a Dilemma

Read within the Canadian context, the proposal for parallel state-supported multifaith education uses rhetoric which is familiar to any student of Canadian multiculturalism. However, it is difficult to see the arguments for multifaith education outside of the changing context of the relationship between non-Christian religions and public education in a variety of jurisdictions. Changes in patterns of international trade, population movements, and communications are associated with a different understanding of cultural distinctions within local political jurisdictions. In the period of the rise of nation-states, deviant cultural groups could at best expect to be considered minority groups - that is, groups whose members fell outside of the standard cultural ideal for the nation but who were entitled to citizenship rights, often with the expectation that their descendants would assimilate into the dominant culture of the nation. In the contemporary period, deviant cultural groups are coming to be thought of more as Diasporas which maintain a continuing transnational tie with each other and with a homeland.

The understanding of the world as a global society with multiple Diasporas coexisting within national boundaries reinforces the transnational character of religion. The major religious movements - Judaism, Christianity, Islam, Buddhism, Hinduism -historically have been both transnational in ideology and also significantly affected by pre-modern conditions of local isolation. Only in the modern period of intense nationalism did religious denominations give primary attention to becoming national churches which defined their field of activity first of all within the political boundaries of the nation-state. It is no surprise that one aspect of globalization is the emergence of a latent transnational identity within religious groups. Religious communities not only speak to concerns about meaning in life at the level of humanity as a whole, they also provide transnational networks of trust and mutual assistance in an insecure, risky society.

Aid to independent schools was initiated in Canada in the 1960s and 1970s, a period in which Canadian nationalism was unusually strong. At that time, providing government aid to the schools of Canada's Protestant minorities and to Canada's Jews could readily be seen as extending more equitable treatment to those without constitutional rights while not endangering the integrationist agenda of the Canadian provinces. The independent school movement of the 1990s looks somewhat different. It has moved in the direction of promoting local institutions which focus on identification with transnational religious movements rather than identification with Canada. These considerations put the Jews of Ontario in what may seem to some to be a very interesting dilemma.

On the one hand, the arguments about equity and financial stress are compelling. Public funding of Ontario Catholic schools - one religious alternative to public schools - and not others is widely perceived as simply inequitable. The inequity imposes financial penalties on parents who send their children to the hundreds of independent schools based in other religious traditions. Parents of students in Jewish day schools pay twice for education - once to the public system and once to the schools their children attend. Elementary fees are in the area of $7,500 per year per student. Secondary tuition is higher. The privately borne school costs also impose a financial burden on the Jewish federations of Ontario. The Toronto federation, the largest, devotes about $7 million dollars from the annual United Jewish Appeal fund-raising campaign to subsidies to day school parents.

Jews do have a stake in having the public schools receive resources that would promote their quality. Since many Jewish students begin in the public system and most students move from Jewish day schools to public schools, Jewish students in Ontario spend more time in public school classes than in private Jewish schools. Nevertheless, within the Jewish community the present arrangement is generally considered inequitable. On the other hand, modern Jews have turned to the ideal of a nondenominational civil society as protection against centuries of prejudice, discrimination, and violence.

Civil society has been more than a framework to establish a minimum consensus on human rights among a divided population. In the views of its philosophers, civil society also stands for a moral order in which the necessity to tolerate differences is turned into a virtue. Civil societies have promoted what have been called "civil religions." A civil religion teaches that the population is bound together into a community by common transcendent values. These values express the ideals on which the community is based and set the standards for relationships between citizens. Each civil religion has its own peculiarities. Civil religions which celebrate democracy teach that the virtues of tolerance, civic brotherhood, and respect for individual differences belong in each citizen's private life as much as they do in formal public norms. The moral dimension of civil society is taught in various places, but a central location has been the public school. Public school education is not only public in the sense that it is publicly financed. It is also public in the sense that part of its mandate is the reproduction of the public itself - the preparation of the next generation to act as citizens.

If students are removed from the public school to state-supported schools which teach the priority of particular value systems over those of civil society, can the moral dimension of civil society be maintained? If the moral dimension of civility declines, can the formal structures of civil society be maintained? The views of Gary Duthler, the executive director of the Association of Independent Schools and Colleges in Alberta (AISCA), and one of five members on the Alberta government's Private Schools Funding Task Force may be useful on this issue.

As noted above, according to the new relationship between independent schools and the Alberta government, AISCA bylaws were to be changed to state that "all private schools must not offer programs that in theory or in practice will promote or foster doctrines of racial or ethnic superiority or persecution, religious intolerance or persecution, social change through violent action, or disobedience of laws." Duthler commented, "The wording is pretty careful. It says 'racial and ethnic superiority or persecution,' so they cannot teach that a white person is better than a black person. But it says 'religious intolerance or persecution,' so they will still be able to teach religion, and even say that one world view, such as Christianity, Judaism or Islam, is superior to the other". The reader can decide whether this is a careful balancing of the dual obligations of faith and citizenship or the first step down a slippery slope. For over two thousand years, Theravada Buddhist beliefs and teachings have influenced Cambodian social norms and systems of social stratification. Over ninety percent of Cambodians are ethnic Khmer Buddhists. In rural villages, the Buddhist wat (temple) was the primary institution outside of the family, and played a key role in disseminating information from outside the village. Theravada Buddhism inspired Cambodian national and cultural identities and gave broad guidance regarding standards of conformity for men, women, and children. Traditional Khmer society consisted of three main status groups: urban royalty and government officials who lived in small towns and urban areas; rural based peasants; and Buddhist monks.

By the mid-twentieth century, however, two separate Buddhist systems, affiliated with rural and urban locales, were identified. The urban, referred to as Thommayuth, was first introduced in 1864 from Thailand and represented an aristocratic approach to Buddhism. It emphasized Western ideals and education, strict adherence to the vinaya (rules of monastic discipline), as well as classical Khmer culture. Mohanikay, the original rural, village-based practice of Buddhism, remained entrenched in traditional behaviour and folkways, and supported a conservative, rather than reform, approach. Mohanikay was present in every village, town, and city, effectively integrating the entire country with some sixty-five thousand Cambodian monks residing in over three thousand temples.

Between 1970 and 1975, when Cambodia was under the pro-American government of Lon Nol, more than one-third of the wats were destroyed by American bombing and communist retaliation. During the four years under the Khmer Rouge (communist Cambodians), the entire Cambodian religious and cultural system, famous for its tranquillity and temperate lifestyle, was brutally dismantled and ravaged: few temples were left, most Khmer sutras and Buddhist commentaries were destroyed, and all monks either killed or defrocked. Over twenty-five thousand monks were executed or died from numerous hardships, many of them senior monks with religious knowledge (ceremonial training and meditational insights) who were responsible for providing ritual healing therapies. During the Vietnamese occupation (1980-1993), most de/rocked monks were not allowed to resume monastic life.

Ordination was restricted to men fifty years or older, thus creating a severe shortage of monks to perform ritual services, teach Pali chants and suttas, and rebuild pagodas. In the late 1980s, when younger men were again able to be ordained, many senior monks had already died, taking with them years of experience and historical knowledge of Khmer Buddhism.

Despite the extreme shortage of monks and teachers, Cambodians in both Cambodia and the Diaspora continue to strive to re-create religious and cultural traditions, and to redefine their significance as crucial icons of national and individual identity.

Impact of the Khmer Rouge

For over thirty years, the Cambodian people experienced unrelenting war, violence, and catastrophic stress. The massive five year American military bombing campaign in Cambodia (beginning in the late 1960s) and the fall of Saigon to Vietnamese communists gave rise to four years (1975-1979) of genocide against the Cambodian people by Khmer Rouge under the leadership of Pol Pot. The extremist rule of the Khmer Rouge enforced a countrywide administration based on acknowledged force, intimidation, murder, and torture.

The evacuations and abandonment of cities, the forced rural labour, and the purges of class enemies were based on Maoist methods learned by Khmer Rouge leaders during the Chinese Cultural Revolution. Many of the Khmer Rouge soldiers who entered the capital city, Phnom Penh, on 17 April 1975 were young (twelve-sixteen years old), uneducated, rural children orphaned by American bombing campaigns. Few had ever been to a city, and all were indoctrinated into extreme communist ideology. Within three days of the Khmer Rouge occupation, all inhabitants of Phnom Penh were forced to evacuate; those who resisted or questioned were instantly shot (ibid.). Roads leading to rural areas were clogged with over two million evacuees. For weeks no food, shelter, or water were provided; there were only orders to keep moving away from the city. Khmer people who are now resettled in Canada speak of how men, women, children, and even hospital patients were forced at gunpoint to leave Phnom Penh and other cities. Several recall how family members were separated or died of exhaustion and illness along the roadside during this time. As simultaneous evacuations occurred in every major city and town in Cambodia, the schools, hospitals, banks, post offices, libraries, and temples were systematically plundered and destroyed by Khmer Rouge cadres.

Individuals associated with these institutions were either immediately shot or imprisoned and executed. The Khmer Rouge hastily established rural work communes across Cambodia to accommodate the millions of displaced people. Every Cambodian man, woman, and child was affected by the forced evacuation of Cambodia's cities and towns. The evacuation resulted in horrific living conditions in rural slave labour camps, mass killings and executions, starvation, rampant disease, family separation, and complete social disintegration. Former government officials, soldiers, merchants, educated and professional people, classical dancers, members of the royal family, artists, Buddhist monks, and anyone perceived as being influenced by the West (for example, speaking French or wearing glasses) were targeted by the Khmer Rouge for immediate execution. Almost two million Cambodians, one quarter of the population, died during this time.

Cambodians now in Canada who survived the communist Khmer Rouge regime recall their hard labour in fields, working long hours without rest, the lack of food and sanitation, being under constant surveillance, and witnessing murders and numerous other acts of brutality. They speak of watching their children and parents die of starvation, family members being shot and beaten, countless acts of petty cruelty and suffering, and feeling unceasing indignity, despair, fear, and terror. In the words of one Cambodian-Canadian woman, "those who survived were leftovers from the dead."

Canadian Resettlement

Following the fall of the Khmer Rouge in 1979, hundreds of thousands fled to Thailand and Vietnam. Approximately three hundred thousand Cambodians eventually resettled in several Western countries (the United States, France, Britain, Australia, and New Zealand), with Canada becoming home to over twenty thousand (ibid.). Most Cambodians who entered Canada arrived as refugees during the early 1980s. The few before that time were diplomats, business people, and students, most of whom resided in Quebec. These Khmer were granted permanent resident status when Cambodia became internationally isolated after 1975. Several others outside Cambodia also came to Canada during this time as United Nations High Commission on Refugees (UNHCR) convention refugees. Both groups were subsequently able to sponsor surviving family members and friends from Thai refugee camps.

After 1979, the majority of Cambodians came to Canada as "designated class refugees" through federal government and private sponsorship programmes. Their accomplishments in resettlement, their gradual re-creation of Cambodian culture and community ties, and their successful attempts to rebuild shattered lives are a testament to the strength and tenacity of the Khmer spirit. From 1980 to 1992, Canadian resettlement opportunities were provided for 18,602 Cambodians. Fewer than five of these Cambodians were

Buddhist monks, most of whom continued on to the United States to join the large Cambodian temples there. Immigration totals do not include the small numbers of Cambodians who arrived prior to 1980, nor do they include children subsequently born in Canada.

Further, Canadian immigration statistics do not account for the approximately one thousand Khmer Kampuchea Krom (individuals who identify themselves as ethnic Khmer but were born in Vietnam and are, therefore, listed as Vietnamese refugees), or for those Cambodians who claimed they were Vietnamese in Thai refugee camps in order to improve their resettlement chances in Canada. Figures for the 1991 census show considerably fewer Cambodians (14,440) than the immigration data for the twelve year period between 1980 and 1992. Recent 2003 census data reports less than 22,000 Cambodians in Canada, despite over twenty years of family sponsorship and natural increase. The under-representation of census data stems from various factors: language difficulties prevent many Cambodians from completing census forms, and some remain suspicious about divulging personal information or are reluctant to reveal the number of Cambodian families living in one household. In 1990, only 214 Cambodian persons entered Canada, and in subsequent years annual numbers have not increased substantially, reflecting continuing difficulty in sponsoring family members. Fifty-five percent of Cambodian refugees accepted by Canada were government sponsored, and 45 percent were privately sponsored, with approximately equal numbers of males and females in both categories.

Most private sponsorship was through Christian congregations under the "Master Agreement" mandate of three main groups: the Christian Reform Church, Catholic Immigrant Aid, and the Mennonite Church. Except for Quebec, the majority of Cambodians who resettled in Canada were rural people, with little education or knowledge of urban life. Approximately 84 percent of Cambodian refugees admitted into Canada reported receiving little or no primary education in Cambodia, 3 percent completed primary school, 2 percent stated they finished high school and had some post-secondary education. Ninety-two percent could not speak either of Canada's official languages.

Outside of Quebec, there were few Khmer translators in 1980 who could provide interpretive services or arrange orientation and support activities for Cambodian refugees. Government and social service programmes were limited, overextended, and oriented toward the considerably larger Sino and ethnic Vietnamese groups. Since the total number of Cambodians in Canada comprised a very small portion of the Indochinese refugees, Cambodians were frequently assumed to be "Vietnamese Boat People," and their special needs (as survivors of genocide) were not adequately understood. The virtual absence of an intellectual elite among Cambodian refugees in Ontario meant that there was little advocacy or cultural brokering on their behalf. Neither government nor private sponsors had the experience or the resources to effectively recognize and address the background and psychological requirements of Cambodian refugees, especially highly vulnerable individuals such as widows and orphans.

The lack of culturally appropriate services affected Cambodians at both personal and community levels. Since 1981, a Cambodian association in Toronto (funded by provincial and federal government grants) provided basic settlement services to Khmer newcomers. Until the mid-1990s, the Toronto association was separate from the large Khmer Buddhist and cultural community groups, unlike Montreal where a close cooperation always existed between the Communaute Khmere du Canada and the Pagode Khmer du Canada (Khmer Buddhist temple). By the year 2000, little government funding (either provincial or federal) was available for Cambodian programs in Ontario, although a few agencies, such as the Carlington Community Health Centre and the Somerset West Community Health Centre in Ottawa, the Jane-Finch Family and Community Centre in Toronto, and the London Cross-Culture Learner Centre, continue to provide assistance and counselling to Cambodians in need.

Cambodian community sources estimate the number of Cambodians living in Ontario to be ten thousand, half of whom are in Toronto. The rest reside in Ottawa, Kingston, Hamilton, London, St. Thomas, and Windsor. Montreal has the largest concentration of Cambodians, with estimates ranging from eight- to ten-thousand. According to 2001 census data, British Columbia, Alberta, and Manitoba have fewer than one thousand Cambodians each. Until 2003, most Toronto-area Cambodians lived in the high-density, newcomer neighbourhoods of the Jane-Finch and Jane-Sheppard areas. Despite their high community concentration, few individuals with leadership and organizational skills could be found to help establish and maintain a Cambodian community centre or related mutual aid associations.

This reflects the absence of Cambodian teachers, administrators, medical doctors, military professionals, traditional healers, and monks in Ontario. Further, due to past conditions of distrust, miscommunication, and power conflicts, networks beyond family and friends remain weak. The continuing legacy of the Khmer Rouge keeps Cambodians suspicious and critical of those aspiring to, or already in, positions of authority. Political representatives from Cambodian partisan groups continuously visit overseas communities to garner funds and support, but their activities exacerbate painful memories among older Cambodians in Ontario and further alienate the younger generation. Cambodian refugees have not only lost families (immediate or extended), homes, possessions, social identity, and status, but also a sense of trust in one another—what Giddens refers to as "ontological security". This lack of trust is difficult to overcome and hinders the development of what Coleman refers to as a community's "social capital," those social structures which make it possible to achieve particular goals and replicate familiar structural relations between people to generate networks of obligations, expectations, and trustworthiness. Social capital is an "asset created by trust, solidarity, and social cohesion embedded in the individuals of a community," yet is most absent among Cambodians, the majority of whom experienced massive mistrust, fear, and broken relationships. The lack of social capital and limited social networks not only impact a community's economic and institutional development, but also result in low levels of defence when their collective interest is threatened.

An absence of social capital has existed throughout Cambodian resettlement in Ontario, and is especially evident in the lack of culturally appropriate services and programs for their social and health care needs and in their limited cultural activities, advocacy for sponsorship issues, and effective strategies to resolve youth difficulties or deal with neighbourhood hostility.

Given the dimension of psychological trauma experienced by Cambodian refugees, the enormous challenges they faced in adapting to Canada, and the overwhelming need to re-establish family networks, not enough time or energy has been available to rebuild their community networks and social capital. Several successful initiatives are, however, becoming increasingly evident: the recent expansion of Buddhist temples in Maple (north of Toronto), Hamilton, London, and Windsor; large numbers of Cambodians purchasing homes in new neighbourhoods north of Toronto; greater participation of Khmer youth in higher education; considerable stability in marriages; the appearance of several Cambodian dance troupes (especially in Ottawa);

and annual gatherings such as the Cambodian picnic in Long Sault Provincial Park in Ontario where upwards of ten thousand Cambodians come from Montreal, Ottawa, Toronto, and elsewhere in Canada and the United States.

Despite educational and linguistic barriers, Cambodians remain employed in the work force. Clusters of individuals tend to work at particular organizations, such as Apsopulse (electronic assembly work) in Ottawa, high-tech factories in Kanata, Cuddy Foods in London, car assembly plants in Kitchener, factories in Hamilton, and manufacturers in Newmarket. Clothing factories employed skilled tailors, and also offered home-sewing contracts. Several Cambodian women have home-based flower arranging or sewing businesses in addition to their regular employment. Some operate a small store or a booth at local markets. Some men make extra money playing popular music in Cambodian bands, and there is much demand for those few Cambodians having traditional classical music skills at weddings and religious celebrations. Few Cambodians are self-employed, and those who are tend to be Chinese Cambodians who have small, family-run specialty stores (groceries, currency exchange, flowers) or food franchises (Subway Sandwiches, Coffee Time Donuts).

One Cambodian owned business, Angkor Marble Import and Export, is a large organization with numerous employees. There are only one or two restaurants identified as Cambodian in Ontario, although several Cambodians own restaurants featuring Thai and Vietnamese food. Among the younger generation born and raised in Ontario, two separate employment patterns emerge. Those who left school early (at age sixteen), either to marry or due to family pressures or a lack of support and interest, tend to find employment where other friends or family work, such as in local factories. Those who remained in school, completing college or university, are more likely to work in offices or in skilled professions (for example, social work, nursing, engineering, computer science). Despite the similar class background amongst the parents' generation, subtle but distinct class distinctions based on education and professional skills are now appearing among these younger Cambodians. Most Cambodians prioritize work. The income generated is often used to finance return visits to the homeland or to send remittance payments to support dependant family members remaining in Cambodia, either of which can require thousands of dollars in gifts and donations per year or per visit. The older generation, particularly, tends to favour sending remittances to rebuild religious and cultural institutions in Cambodia. The recent success of temple fundraising in Ontario further demonstrates the overwhelming importance among Canadian Cambodians to support and rebuild religious institutions in home villages and regions.

Religious Identities among the Cambodians

The majority of Cambodians in Ontario are ethnic Khmer who identify themselves as Theravada Buddhist, with a small number converted to Christianity. Large community gatherings generally occur on Buddhist holidays: the Cambodian New Year (April); the Pcum Bin festival honouring the ancestors (September); the Kathin festival to present gifts to monks (late October); and Visak Bocie, the celebration of the birth, death, and enlightenment of the Buddha (May).

Of the many Buddhist communities in Toronto, Cambodian refugees have experienced the greatest difficulty re-creating Buddhist practice and traditions. These difficulties reflect the absence of strong social networks and relationships from which cultural and religious bonds can be reaffirmed and re-established (that is, social capital), and the continued consequences of extensive physical and mental health debilitation caused by the Khmer Rouge genocide. In Toronto, Hamilton, and London, three distinct religious identities are evident among Cambodians

(Buddhists from Cambodia, Kampuchea Krom, and Christian Cambodian), each with its own type of transnational connections and degree of social cohesiveness. Buddhist Khmer from Cambodia retain limited transnational linkages, most revolving extensive personal relations with family and friends, mediated cultural forms of music and dance, support for religious reconstruction, and dependence on a severely limited supply of Cambodian monks offering religious leadership. In contrast, Kampuchea Krom, who are ethnic Khmer from Vietnam, exhibit extensive transnational networks and linkages and have merged political, economic, family, religious, and cultural facets into a successful nationalist discourse that is effectively articulated.

In Vietnam, Kampuchea Krom are religious and ethnic minorities clinging tenaciously to the identity and practices of Theravada Buddhism. The distinct language and expression of Theravada Buddhism (especially in contrast to Vietnamese Mahayana Buddhism) provides the foundation of their ethnic-based nationalism and their strategy of resistance to the overt Vietnamese assimilation efforts. Although Kampuchean Krom support from lay leaders and monks has been crucial for the expansion of Cambodian Buddhist temples in Ontario, most of their transnational networks have been established apart from the larger Cambodian community. Kampuchean Krom transnational activities include mutual aid associations, professional advocacy and interest groups, unique religious organizations, and effective political mobilization in both Vietnam and globally.

The small numbers of Khmer from Cambodia who converted to Christianity (in the refugee camps or through sponsorship) also have significant transnational connections. Conversion-based linkages and networks tend to be through highly organized, very active Christian involvements in Cambodia, usually American-based Evangelical groups offering a variety of support systems to new Christians throughout the world. Through this support, numerous Khmer Christians from Ontario and the United States have returned to Cambodia to "seed" churches and initiate educational and healthcare programs. Transnational faith connections provide all three groups with meaningful frameworks through which people contribute time, effort, and support. The networks and linkages enhance social cohesion within local Canadian communities and in the homeland communities.

Cambodian Buddhists

The struggle to establish and maintain Cambodian Buddhist temples has been exacerbated by the chronic shortage of Buddhist monks from Cambodia. Until November 1996, the Ottawa Cambodian Buddhist temple had the only permanent monk in Ontario. The Toronto temple (Cambodian war) did not have a resident Cambodian monk, although several elderly nuns would go daily to attend to the shrine and recite prayers. One or two learned lay men (achaa) were also available to perform some rituals and religious services. An elderly Kampuchea Krom monk associated with the temple in Montreal resided there intermittently between 1983-1995. To provide Buddhist ceremonies, the Toronto temple relied on inviting guest monks from Cambodian communities in Montreal and the United States, or requesting the services of Theravada monks from the Laotian community. In April 1995, the Toronto Cambodian Buddhist community purchased a large house in Maple, just north of the Toronto city boundary.

This has became a monastic institution, permanently housing a monk who arrived from Cambodia in 1996 (originally there were three, but two disrobed soon after arrival); Khmer Buddhist monks who can stay only as long as their visitor visas allow (reflecting continued sponsorship difficulties); temporary ordained monks; and Duan chee who live there short-term to cook, clean, and do temple maintenance. For many Khmer, Buddhism remains the primary expression of the Cambodian way of life. Much of the traditional Cambodian culture still practised in Canada is through family and life rituals (weddings, blessings, funerals), traditional cuisine, language, and behaviour patterns (gender roles, age/status hierarchy) influenced by Buddhist beliefs and practices. Community gatherings are geared toward the ceremonial cycle of celebrations and commemorations, beginning with New Year festivities in April.

All provide opportunities to wear Khmer clothing and participate in traditional music and dances. Traditional leadership roles are maintained through the activities of the monks and achaas who provide temple services and rituals, and through men's participation in temple organization and administration, financial accounting, fund-raising, and monastic sponsorship attempts. Achaas and monks are actively involved in numerous aspects of Cambodian community life, facilitating funerals, memorials, exorcisms, blessings, healings, merit-making, and life transition events (such as weddings). The chronic shortage of monks, however, severely restricts these activities. The continuing lack of social and economic capital among Cambodians combined with bureaucratic indifference makes sponsorship a very difficult process.

To alleviate the shortage of ritual specialists, temple leaders invite monks from Cambodia to visit for a year and then apply to extend their visa. To this end, connections with temples in Cambodia and elsewhere are diligently maintained. Conversely, temples in Cambodia continually solicit donations to rebuild temples and train monks, most of whom are newly ordained. Canadian Khmer bring large sums of money with them when they visit Cambodia, primarily to help their families, but also to re-establish temples in the home village or to become recognized as a patron in the building of a new temple. Any kind of support for Buddhist temples and monks is recognized as meritorious and enhances social status and prestige in both Cambodia and Canada.

The transnational role of religion is also connected to that of the performing arts such as music and dance, both of which are crucial to the negotiation and expression of socio-cultural identity in Cambodia and the Diaspora. Classical music and dance remain an integral part of Buddhist ceremonies and life-cycle rituals, distinct from the non-religious popular forms evident at large community dances and informal parties among family and friends. Cambodian religious, music, and dance traditions are actively retained within the community; their symbolic and institutional power provide strong historical and cultural links to Cambodia. Most Cambodians listen to classical and popular Khmer music in their homes, and many own hundreds of videos featuring a wide variety of dances and songs. Music and dance performances are especially elaborate during New Year's celebrations, at traditional Cambodian weddings, or as an enhanced feature during social events, such as fashion shows.

The influence of global transportation, mass-media, and communication networks is especially crucial for the re-creation and redefinition of Khmer music and dance in the Diaspora communities. Since few experienced teachers survived the Khmer Rouge, many dance and music instructors are self-taught from videos, compact disks (CD's), and the occasional travelling troupe of performers. In addition to classical and popular music and dance being transmitted via cassettes, videos, CD's, digital video disks (DVD's), Karaoke, and the internet, religious teachings from respected monks and laymen in Cambodia are increasingly available in these forms. Transnational identities and connections between Cambodian Canadians and Cambodia are nurtured as they are shared among family and friends in the Diaspora. The establishment of three new Cambodian Buddhist temples in Hamilton, London, and Windsor was primarily accomplished through the organization and commitment of Kampuchea Krom monks and lay people. Despite their significant involvement, the label of not being "really Khmer" has frequently been directed toward the Kampuchea Krom. In this regard they readily acknowledge their liminal status in Cambodian communities. Because Kampuchea Krom have lived for generations in Vietnam and most speak Vietnamese as a second language, their identities as Khmer are different from the ethnic Khmer who were born and raised in Cambodia. Much of the suspicion directed toward Kampuchea Krom is rooted in the centuries old aggression and mistrust between Cambodia and Vietnam.

Since 11 September 2001, religion's potential for causing conflict has received far more attention than its ability to contribute to cooperation and reconciliation. At the same time, however, there has been an increase in the number of initiatives to promote interreligious dialogue, both locally and between religious leaders at the global level. The Middle East has been a major focus area of such efforts, with dialogue initiatives often aimed at reducing tension between religious communities at the national level, as well as building trust and understanding internationally. Some European states have made interfaith dialogue an integral part of their foreign policies, with delegations of religious leaders being sent to visit each other, international conferences held, and local initiatives supported.

This policy brief discusses the use of interreligious dialogue in two central Middle Eastern countries: Syria and Lebanon. It provides a general assessment of local, transnational and international attempts to engage religion for the purposes of building trust and reducing tension, and examines the sustainability of existing cross-border religious networks between Syria and Lebanon in the wake of the assassination of former Lebanese Prime Minister Rafiq al-Hariri. Finally, the brief evaluates the international community's engagement with Syrian and Lebanese religious leaders, before presenting a number of policy recommendations. The findings and recommendations contained in the brief are based on two case studies conducted by Frida Nome of the International Peace Research Institute, Oslo (PRIO), with funding from the Norwegian Ministry of Foreign Affairs.

Religious Dialogue in Syria and Lebanon

Syria is a religiously diverse country, with a large Sunni Muslim majority and minorities made up of Christians, Alawis, Druze, Ismailis and others. In order to meet the challenges posed by this multiplicity of religious loyalties, the Syrian government – which is headed by an Alawi president – has opted to create a 'supra-religion' based on the idea that the Arab nation is a cultural unifier for Syria. The government aims to unite all Syrian citizens by focusing on their common Arab identity and down- playing competing affiliations, such as tribe and religion. The official discourse concerning religious diversity in Syria is dominated by depictions of harmonious co-existence.

This 'language of harmony' is reflected both in popular speech and in local interreligious dialogue initiatives. A number of different institutions and individuals work to promote interreligious dialogue in Syria. The most profiled of these involve leaders with high clerical status, who are able to initiate meetings between patriarchs, muftis, shaykhs and other high- ranking religious leaders. Such initiatives are either supported or sanctioned by the government, and they largely focus on dialogue between Christian denominations and Sunni Islam. They are often more concerned with international issues than with home affairs, and are clearly visible in the international dialogue arena, with representatives and delegates regularly attending conferences abroad. The same limited number of clerics and institutions also constitute the 'receiving' end for dialogue activities within Syria: it is they who welcome most of the international delegations of religious leaders that visit Syria. The Syrian government also supports the Iran-based taqrib conference, which aims at rapprochement between different Islamic formations – and particularly between Sunni and Shia Islam.

In addition to this, there are a number of less visible dialogue initiatives within local communities, promoted by enthusiastic resource persons within different religious formations. Some of these are opposed to the government's approach to a national 'supra-religion', working instead to explore the differences and problems that exist between various religious groups, as well as their similarities and possibilities for harmonious co-existence. Religious Dialogue in Lebanon Focuses on Tackling Internal Sectarian Unrest Lebanon's political system is organized along religious (so-called sectarian) lines, with these divisions dominating both official and popular discourse. Each of the country's religious formations has affiliations with a range of interest groups, clerical orders, religio-political organizations and political parties. Lebanon has a long history of political unrest and civil war, with individuals' sectarian affiliation often (but not always) indicating their political stance in the various conflicts.

Religious leaders play an important role within the Lebanese system, and many have considerable influence both on parliamentarians belonging to their own faith group and on the country's political parties, as well as within their respective communities of believers. The higher-ranking religious leaders within most of the officially recognized religious establishments are engaged from time to time in formal dialogue efforts aimed at reducing sectarian unrest within the country. As a general rule, interfaith work directly addresses the volatile relationships between Lebanon's religious groups. It facilitates meetings to encourage and enable better understanding between

Christians and Muslims; between Sunnis, Shias and Druze; and between a variety of Christian denominations.

Transnational Networks of Co-Religionists

Aggravated Bilateral Relations Between Syria and Lebanon Have Affected Cross-Border Contact Between Co-Religionists. Most religious communities in Syria and Lebanon have loyalties that extend beyond the borders of their own states, across which they form networks with members of their own faith in different countries. Consequently, transnational religion functions as an additional and alternative meaning system to the political entities of the states. Many religious leaders in Lebanon focus on the family and kinship ties that exist between Syrians and Lebanese in explaining the special relationship between these two countries in particular. They report of being engaged in a variety of activities with co-religionists across the border, such as clerical cross-border visits, institutional meetings, educational collaboration and pilgrimage. Some of these transnational religious networks are formally structured in terms of organizations and establishments – such as patriarchates, educational institutions and annual conventions – while others are spontaneous and based on personal relationships.

The states of Syria and Lebanon also have a history of close collaboration in matters of economics, security, and domestic and foreign policies. How- ever, the assassination of former Lebanese prime minister Rafiq al-Hariri on 14 February 2005 represents a turning point in the relationship between the two states, as it caused a breakdown in the bilateral symbiosis, along with the voicing of enmities between different population groups. The subsequent withdrawal from Lebanon of 14,000 Syrian troops was followed by the departure of thousands of Syrian workers and a drop in the flow of people and goods across the border the everyday contact between the peoples of both states, as well as the long-established cross-border religious networks. Although formally structured transnational activities seem to have been more susceptible to the changes in bilateral relations between Syria and Lebanon than informal networks, they nevertheless have the greatest potential to secure continued cooperation across the state borders. Informal religious networks are largely maintained by individual actors, and thus defended solely by those individuals themselves. Formal networks of religious actors have more organized support, and also much more to lose if ties are broken. For this reason, they often have members who are dedicated to working to sustain cross-border contact.

Religious Networks as Alternative Channels in Bilateral Conflicts

Religion provides people with transcendent authority – a capacity that gives religious leaders the ability to speak on behalf of something larger than the state. It also gives a moral strength that may be used, or misused, to transform potential conflict situations. In the context discussed above, efforts to prevent further animosity between Syrian and Lebanese citizens may be the most relevant contribution for religious actors. Additionally, religious cross-border networks provide alternative meaning systems and contact channels that can be used when bilateral relations are unstable.

Many religious leaders in Lebanon identify religious education as one of the most important ways of fostering good relations with co-religionists in neighbouring countries. Through studying in inter- national environments, people get to meet fellow students, scholars and clerics from their own faith residing in the different countries of the region and become part of a knowledge-based transnational community. Professors and delegates travel across state borders to teach; students of theology matriculate at seminaries abroad; younger students attend religious schools abroad; and some students learn directly from spiritual leaders. For Christian groups, it is primarily institutes of theological learning that bring students from different countries together. For Sunni and Shia Muslims, learning centres such as Islamic universities and faculties, as well as traditional Islamic seminaries, create comparable transnational environments for students of Islam.

International Community's Engagement with Religion

Religion is an important factor in the lives of most Syrians and Lebanese, as well as in the state politics of their respective countries. Therefore, actors involved in policymaking towards or within these two states need to be clear about the possibilities offered by engagement with different parts of the religious establishment. With whom to engage and what methods to use obviously depend on the objectives of the engagement.

Diversify Dialogue Partners

The international community's engagement with religion in Syria and Lebanon largely focuses on contact and collaboration with a limited number of high-profile religious leaders. Clerics with high standing may have considerable outreach within their respective communities and may therefore be influential opinion-makers. Many of these leaders, however, have close ties to governmental institutions and power-holders. This may indicate that their views represent particular political strands, or even the government itself.

The close links to power enjoyed by prominent religious leaders may increase their influence when it comes to political decision making, but may similarly reduce their influence on public opinion. The international community's focus on engagement with such a limited group of religious leaders entails a lack of diversity. Many of the religious leaders involved in international dialogue conferences are already members of national dialogue initiatives, some of which are initiated or funded by the states concerned. The same individuals are involved repeatedly in different activities, and few new faces are added to the international dialogue arena over time.

This lack of diversity excludes a great number of potential dialogue and cooperation partners. As it, in effect, basically supports initiatives sanctioned by governments, it may concurrently undermine the work being carried out within local communities by religious leaders with lower ranking within religious hierarchies. The international community's strong focus on a limited number of religious leaders has furthermore led to the neglect of other influential segments of the religious environment. Much could be gained, for instance, from engaging the theological institutions where future religious leaders are educated.

Recommendations

Engage in dialogue with lower-ranking religious leaders in addition to the top segment of clerics. Reaching out to preachers, prayer leaders and shaykhs of local religious communities would increase the 'contact surface' and enable wider outreach. Many lower-ranking religious leaders and preachers are highly influential within their communities. Include religious leaders who are not fully 'qualified' in terms of religious dialogue discourse. Some of the religious leaders who regularly participate in dialogue conferences seem almost too well versed in dialogue, and often talk in a prescribed dialogue discourse, such as the 'language of harmony'. Include theologians who educate future religious leaders of the region, as well as their students.

Finding Alternative Dialogue Partners

Contact and cooperation with religious actors in the Middle East is often 'delegated' to clerical delegations. Religion plays an important role in many sectors of society, and religious institutions engage large numbers of people with a variety of approaches to their own religion. Religious establishments offer a number of different activities for their members – such as women's groups, scouts, students groups and other special-interest groups. Sectors outside the religious establishment of the West, therefore, could also be encouraged to engage in a broader dialogue arena through these channels. Recommendations Allow/ encourage special-interest groups and other civil society organizations in the West to engage in dialogue and cooperation with similar groups within the religious establishments of Middle Eastern countries. Promote Academic Dialogue and Cooperation Many theological institutions in the Middle East publish their work in Arabic, while most Western institutions publish in English.

There are few meeting points between the two language groups within the written academic discourse. Further, few academic conferences manage to bring together scholars from Western and Middle Eastern countries. This has a negative impact well beyond the academic environment, as scholars are often instrumental in informing public debates, both locally and internationally. Supporting the participation of Middle Eastern scholars in international conferences and funding translation of academic work into English to encourage publication in international academic journals should be considered in this context. Western scholars could similarly be encouraged to publish in Arabic-language journals.

Recommendations

In Syria and Lebanon, religious education is most often seen as the responsibility of individual religious formations. In order to get closer to the religious establishments, as well as to avoid a one-sided focus on secular academic learning, theological institutions could be considered as cooperation partners. Student exchange with such institutes should be encouraged. External actors should engage with formal religious institutions, as well as influential individuals. Formal religious networks operating in the transnational realm have greater outreach and may be more stable than informal networks in times of conflict. These may be engaged in efforts to reduce tension between citizens of different states. There are many ways to engage with religion in Syria and Lebanon, as in the Middle East in general. The choice of methods to use and what actors to cooperate with largely depend on the objectives of the engagement.

Interfaith dialogue between religious leaders of high clerical status has its own value. It has a potential to strengthen networks and increase understanding between individual participants, as well as between their religious or national communities. The international community's engagement in interreligious dialogue within the two countries, however, is often one-dimensional. The focus is almost exclusively on high-level leaders, and many of these have strong ties to governments or parliamentary leaders. A diversification of dialogue partners, with a stronger focus on lower-ranking leaders, would enhance the potential for reaching out to a wider audience. Practical initiatives and exchange agreements with religious special-interest groups and educational institutions, such as theological learning centres, would be similarly rewarding both for Western and Syrian/Lebanese partners, because, among other things, it would strengthen the contact points for the next generation of religious leaders.

8

Indian Transnationalism

Coherent organizational structures within the movement, integrated organizing strategies to recruit new members, and autonomy from transnational networks lead to successful social movements. The theory develops through an extended comparison of a religious nationalist and a feminist movement in India. This model explains variation in success over time as it draws attention to organizational aspects of social movements. The major finding is that the success of a social movement depends on mundane community activism rather than networks of transnational activists or framing of ideas. Social movements that have clear channels of communication and cooperation among the various organizations that constitute the movement are more likely to be successful at developing a public agenda.

Movements that invest time and money in local communities are better able to recruit new supporters. Their cooperative organizational structure enables them to match new recruits with appropriate organizations and activities so as to sustain commitment through engagement. Transnational networks are most important as sources of financial aid for Southern social movements. Fundraising based on individual contributions allows organizations to remain flexible and responsive to local communities. Fundraising through institutional donors runs the risk of agenda capture by transnational networks and fragmentation within the movement as a result of competition for funds. The data are drawn from fieldwork in South Asia and the United States of America. Interviews, primary documents of social movement organizations, and participant observation techniques are used. This study provides a framework to study social movements in comparative, historical perspective and addresses the more general question of successful social transformation. The study also provides practical implications for the management of civic associations that are part of a social movement. As a comparative historian interested in race and colonialism, I sometimes find myself wondering what all the fuss is about when people advocate transnational history. Putting the definitional niceties of the term 'nation' aside for the moment and using it, in a vernacular sense, as something like 'country', both race and colonialism are inherently transnational phenomena.

Confronted with the call to transnationalise, therefore, the historian of race and colonialism might well recognise how Mark Twain must have felt on discovering that he had been speaking prose all his life. Even in internal-colonial contexts, at least one of the contending parties originally came from somewhere else, a fact that continues to demarcate the relationship. As often as not, this demarcation is inscribed in the language of race. I have argued that race is a regime of difference that has served to distinguish dominant groups from groups whom they initially encountered in colonial contexts. These contexts were inherently spatial, the groups involved having previously been geographically separate. Thus we might adapt Mary Douglas' celebrated dictum that dirt is matter out of place to human dirt, the racialised, who are constructed as fundamentally contaminatory. It would be hard to find a construct of race that has not involved concepts of spatiality and contamination, usually in association. Hence the frequency with which the racialised are spatially segregated to hygienic ends. This principle has not been particular to the modern discourse of race, which emerged in company with colonies and nations. Anti-Semitism and Islamophobia, enduring proto-forms of European racism, applied internally and externally respectively: to the Jew within, who characteristically 'wandered' – a spatial determination – from ghetto to ghetto, and to the Saracen, Turk or Mahomedan, who threatened – and thereby constituted – the borders of Christendom from without. To deal with race and colonialism is, therefore, to take transnationalism (or, before the nation state, some form of transregionalism) for granted. Again, therefore, what is all the fuss about? It seems to me that transnational history's radical potential is a matter of its address. Until relatively recently, the call to transnationalism has been largely confined to historians of the United States (this is despite the fact that its principal advocate has been an Australian, Ian Tyrrell). Transnational historians have critiqued the Anglo centric historiography in which the United States has figured as miraculously conceived from Puritan sources, pointing to the formative contributions of Native American, African, Spanish, French, Chinese, Irish and other nations.

To this extent, transnational history is a subset of United States minority history writing or, more broadly, of history from below. Self-consciously transnational histories differ from the generality of minority accounts, however, in insisting on the migrations and other global transactions that preceded and continue to underlie minority status in United States society. The nation is not axiomatic. For transnational history – and here pan-Africanism may be seen as paradigmatic – minorities have pre-United States genealogies to which space is central.

But to say that the call to transnational history has been directed to historians of the United States and not to historians of colonialism raises obvious problems. One has only to mention Native Americans or African Americans for the incoherence of the distinction to be patent. Thus the issue is not one of distinguishing between histories of colonialism on the one hand and histories of United States society on the other. It is about how and why that false distinction came to be established. What kind of exceptionalism is it that absolves United States history from – or, perhaps, enclaves it within – the global narrative of European colonialism?

In promising to dismantle that solipsistic historiography, transnational history has a radical potential that can be compared to the postcolonial project of dismantling the sovereign subject hood of the West. For this potential to be realised, however, transnational history will have to extend its purview beyond its current, unfortunately narcissistic preoccupation with White-settler societies. Accordingly, while it is refreshing that transnational history should now be establishing a foothold in Australia, whose White-settler national mythology has historical correspondences with that of the United States, we should remain mindful of the varied range of colonial social formations.

The exclusion of minority genealogies in favour of a dominant group's monopolizing of the national narrative has been a commonplace of accounts of the nation since Ernest Renan's famous 1882 lecture on the forgetting that is central to nationalism. This kind of selective amnesia would seem to be particularly congenial to settler-colonial nationalism. After all, settler colonialism strives for the elimination of the native in favour of an unmediated connection between the settlers and the land – hence the notion of building clone-like fragments of the mother country in the wilderness. In this fantasy, nobody else is involved, just settlers and the natural landscape. Such a situation is clearly conducive to solipsistic narratives. On this basis, it is not surprising that transnational history should be developing in settler societies. Yet the screening-out of other contributions may well be endemic to the nation state formation itself, rather than particular to its settler-colonial variant. This consideration suggests ways in which we might widen the scope of transnational history writing. Moreover, the very distinction between European and settler societies occludes the actual histories of European state formation (think, for instance, of Norman England, the Basques in France and Spain, or the Nazi *lebensraum* in eastern Europe). In this light, one could cite the Comte de Boulainviller, in early eighteenth century France, as a metropolitan precursor to self-consciously transnational history writing.

In a nice conflation of race and class, Boulainviller reduced French history to a contest between a 'race' of external conquerors, the Francs, and the native Gauls, the invaders becoming the ruling class by right of conquest. In classic settler-colonial style, this involved Boulainviller in basing his own class's claim to dominance on their not being native. In settling, though, and asserting their transcendent bond to the territory of France, they became so. By contrast, European authorities in franchise colonies such as British India or the Netherlands East Indies did not, in the main, come to stay. They remained as agents of the metropolitan power, their agenda being the aggrandisement rather than the cloning of the metropolis.

In such colonies, nationalist momentum came from among the ranks of the natives. They, rather than the colonisers, proclaimed an eternal bond between themselves and the land. Yet the historiography of franchise-colonial nationalisms, unlike that of settler nationalisms in dominion territories, is unproblematically transnational. There has not, for instance, been a struggle to write Indians into the history of British India to compare with the scholarly energy that had to go into finding Aborigines a place in the Australian national narrative. In this light, the core issue that transnational history problematises is the core characteristic of the nation state itself: the assertion of privileged affinities between particular groups of people and particular parcels of land. Stated in these more general terms, transnational history has no necessary confinement to settler societies in the West. I wish to argue that, by adopting a transnational approach to other situations, we can contribute to the postcolonial project that Dipesh Chakrabarty has termed the provincialising of Europe.

In what follows, I intend to revisit a topic that I have previously written about, only this time in a more self-consciously transnational manner. In a critique of Gayatri Spivak's 'Can the Subaltern Speak?', I noted that, for all their differences, Hindu nationalism and British colonialism had concurred over the exclusion of Indian Islam from the colonial encounter. In particular, they had shared the assumption – embarrassing for anti-colonial nationalists, affirming for their colonisers – that key features of Indian nationalist discourse were themselves a colonial endowment inherited from the European rationalist tradition.

Using the example of the early nineteenth century Bengali reformer Rammohun Roy, I argued that this widely-held assumption was not only misleading but could only be maintained so long as the Indian Islamic tradition was overlooked; that key rationalist premises attributed to the European enlightenment could be found already expressed in Indian Islamic discourse, where they testified to a post-Hellenistic Arabic-language inheritance which, as a result of the translation movement in al-Andalus, had also bolstered the European Renaissance. In returning to Islamic rationalism by way of India, colonising Europe was returning to its own repressed. Bringing a transcontinental Islamic inheritance together with Indian nationalism and British colonialism, the analysis was manifestly, albeit inadvertently, transnational (not to say transhistorical).

Nonetheless, al-Andalus hardly fits the nation state category, while the 'nation' of Indian nationalism was still at a very early stage of its imagining, so the discussion was also somewhat unorthodox in transnationalist terms – as, of course, was its application to a non-Western, non-settler colonial context. Moreover, the analysis sought to decentre Islamophobia, instancing the contradictory variety of Islamophobic legacies involved in the current global malaise. On all these grounds, and trying to keep repetition to a minimum, I would now like to return to the analysis with a more informed transnational awareness, in the hope of casting some light on what might be called the creole genealogy of Western imperialism.

A derivative discourse? Opening the 1933 celebrations to commemorate the centenary of Rammohun Roy's death, the great Rabindranath Tagore was unstinting:

> Rammohun Roy inaugurated the modern age in India. He was born at a time when our country, having lost its links with the inmost truths of its being, struggled under a crushing load of unreason, in abject slavery to circumstance. In social usage, in politics, in the realm of religion and art, we had entered the zone of uncreative habit, of decadent tradition, and ceased to exercise our humanity. In this dark gloom of India's degeneration Rammohun rose up, a luminous star in the firmament of India's history with prophetic purity of vision, and unconquerable heroism of soul. He shed radiance all over the land: he rescued us from the penury of self oblivion.

Tagore's panegyric is in keeping with a well-established historiographical formula that unites an otherwise diverse range of scholars, both Hindu and European. Rammohun, the 'father of modern India', is seen (whether approvingly or with resentment) as a conduit between enlightened Europe and a regressive Brahmin elite, who were awakened and vitalised by his campaign to reform Hinduism. This campaign, which Rammohun conducted in English and other languages, harmonised with the ideas of European philosophers and missionaries, in particular orientalist scholars who had devoted themselves to recovering Hinduism's pristine purity from beneath the corruptions that, in their view, had accumulated over the centuries that had elapsed since its original enunciation. In its orientalist rendering, pristine Hinduism bore a distinct resemblance to the monotheism and ethical precepts of the Christian West. Thus the price of Hindu redemption was the predicament that Partha Chatterjee has termed derivativeness. 'As inaugurator of modern India, therefore, Rammohun pioneered the embarrassing irony that the emancipatory ideology with which Indian nationalism sought to mobilise an anticolonial movement was itself a colonial endowment'. In the sectarian balance, Hindu renaissance is synonymous with Muslim decline. In claiming to have recovered Hinduism's lost glories, European Orientalists abetted a Brahminical narrative in which the intervening era of Muslim rule figured as a period of darkness and decay that separated an interrupted Hindu golden age from the present.

In colonising India, the British East India Company was also delivering it from Islam. Through an analysis of Rammohun's reformist creed, I hope to show that Indian nationalism's derivation anxiety required not only the humiliation of colonial conquest but also the suppression of Islamic discourse as conditions of its possibility. The historical process of nationalist self-fashioning entailed the discursive erasure of this fact.

Rammohun's career occupies a crucial transitional site in this regard, since the premises that were to secure his place as founder of modern India can be found already formulated in a Muslim-addressed tract written in Persian and Arabic that this Hindu figure published in 1804, over a decade before he embarked on the Anglophone career of reform on which his reputation is based, and well before he had learned enough English to have had any meaningful exposure to European ideas. The existence of this tract, the *Tuhfat-ul Muwahhiddin* ('Gift to Monotheists'), is well enough known. The problems treated in the *Tuhfat* are classical ones. Their specification and assemblage, together with the propositional protocols employed, bear the unmistakable imprints of both Judaic and Hellenistic reasoning. Contrary to Eurocentric assumptions, however, this does not entail that they were taken from European sources since, in addition to sharing in Christianity's Hebraic inheritance, the Islamic philosophical canon incorporates a Greek legacy which is as profound as that of the Pauline West. This chapter is not concerned with Rammohun's individual qualities but with the optic that his career provides into the historical terrain that he so conspicuously occupied. His significance is extrinsic. Focusing on the *Tuhfat* enables us to see not only that Indian nationalism (at least, in its Bengali origins) was structured by the exclusion of Islam, which is hardly news.

It also enables us to see the nationalist predicament of derivativeness in a reciprocal context. For the exclusion of Islam is also foundational to Western discourse – where, too, it represents a form of derivation anxiety. In seeking to provincialise Europe in this way, the intention is not to metropolise anywhere else but to underscore the inter-textuality of the major discourses involved. This chapter will briefly survey the community between Islamic and Western discourse, on which basis it will identify the Islamic character of the *Tuhfat* and illustrate the extent to which Rammohun's post-1815 anglophone reformist ideology continued its distinctive principles.

In conclusion, the chapter will consider some of the diverse ways in which the exclusion of Islam has been reproduced and maintained in the historiography of Indian nationalism. Taking salient examples from a varied range of histories – Christian-hagiographic, Hindu-nationalist, secular-liberal, Marxist, postcolonial – we shall see how, beneath their otherwise considerable differences, these accounts agree on excluding the Islamic inheritance that Rammohun Roy brought to the enunciation of Indian (proto-) nationalist discourse.

Arabic into Latin

In al-Andalus (Iberia), in the eleventh century of the

Christian era, Ibn 'Abdun warned his fellow Muslims about the activities of the translators: 'One should not sell scientific books to Jews or Christians... since they translate these scientific books, attributing authorship to their own bishops and coreligionists when they are actually Muslim works'. Since Ibn 'Abdun's time, a minority tradition of Western scholarship (including Bacon, Leibniz, Voltaire, Gibbon and Priestley) has sought to rectify the suppression of Europe's scientific, philosophical and cultural debt to the Islamic or Arab-speaking world, a debt which was incurred in al-Andalus.

The background to the Andalusian achievement can be briefly outlined. In the wake of the division of the old Roman Empire into Eastern and Western blocs that were comparatively watertight (Sicily, extending up to Naples, being an exception), a rough distribution of the cultural inheritance of classical antiquity obtained whereby, while the Eastern (Byzantine) empire maintained the scientific, philosophical, literary and cultural legacy of Greece, the Western (or 'European') empire found itself the repository of the relatively reduced inheritance of the Latin world. During the momentous century or so following Muhammad's death, Islam spread outwards from the land of its origins with an unstoppable vitality that exceeded even that of imperial Rome.

In the process, most of Byzantium and Sassanian Persia were taken over and their Greek philosophical and scientific learning (though not the poetry and literature) translated into Arabic, usually from the Syriac or other Byzantine language into which it had earlier been translated but sometimes from the original Greek. Over the next century or so, this learning was subject to the vicissitudes of survival under the aggressively militaristic regime of the Ummayyad Caliphate, but it managed to live on in the eastern outposts of the Islamic empire, particularly in exiled Nestorian centres of learning in eastern Persia, where it was augmented with scientific (especially astronomical) and mathematical knowledge emanating from India.

With the ascendancy of the 'Abassid Caliphate and the shifting of the political centre of the Islamic world to Baghdad, science and philosophy were actively encouraged and magnificent libraries assembled. The exiled legacy of ancient Greece was brought to the centre of Islamic culture, where, among other things, it was enlisted to buttress Islam's dialogic armature in response to disruptive theological problems, concerning revelation, monotheism, predestination and the like, which had arisen through contact with the different faiths of the conquered peoples. To secure key elements of the Islamic tradition which were still being transmitted orally, the 'Abassid caliphs sponsored the wholesale commitment of knowledge (including the *Quran*) to Arabic script, in the course of which project, during the eighth and ninth centuries of the Christian era, most of the Greek philosophical and scientific sources available today were translated into Arabic.

Somewhat prior to these latter developments – in the early eighth century A.D. – and on the north-western frontier of the Ummayyad empire, Visigothic Andalusia was conquered in a series of expeditionary raids carried out by combined forces of Arabs and Berbers and brought under the administrative control of Qayrawan, the regional headquarters of the African segment of the empire, situated in modern Tunisia. Though the Berbers had adopted Islam, they maintained cultural and linguistic separateness and continually agitated against the over lordship of the Arab minority. This antagonism continued into al-Andalus, so that, when the 'Abassids expelled the Ummayyad caliph 'Abd ar-Rahman and his followers from Damascus in 750 A.D. and moved the capital to Baghdad, the fugitive ar-Rahman sought allies amongst the disaffected Berbers, at first in Africa but finally and successfully in al-Andalus, where he established his family dynasty from Cordoba in 755 A.D. Despite the administrative and political dividedness of the Islamic world, a comparatively high degree of logistical cohesion was maintained.

Relegated to provincial status in the far west, the Ummayyad sultans in Cordoba displayed an attitude toward science and learning which was markedly different from that which had characterised their predecessors in the Damascus Caliphate. They patronised the importation of intellectual and scientific (especially medical) knowledge from the eastern centre and attracted a number of polyglot Jewish intellectuals from Mesopotamia and elsewhere. In its third century (i.e. during the 10th century A.D.), the Ummayyad dynasty in al-Andalus produced two rulers, 'Abd ar-Rahman III and al-Hakam II, who successively presided over a period of extraordinarily fruitful interchange and collaboration between Muslim, Jewish and Christian intellectuals, all writing in Arabic, in Cordoba, Toledo, Seville, Granada and other centres.

By this stage, whatever a scholar's religion, the language of scholarship was definitively Arabic, and Muslim faith had no necessary connection to Arab ethnicity. In following centuries, the work of translation having been effectively completed, most of the greatest developers of the Hellenic tradition (Ibn Rushd [Averroës], Ibn Sinha [Avicenna] and Ibn Maymun [Maimonides] to cite but three) took their Aristotle, their Galen and their Neoplatonism from Arabic sources and did not even know Greek. The Greek only lived in the Arabic. This was the world of learning that became available for translation into the Latin of the Western Empire as a result of conquest – or, more specifically, of the *Reconquista,* the Christian *jihad* into al-Andalus through which an emergent Europe embarked on the Crusades. It should be stressed that 'world' of learning here signifies a dynamic tradition which, far from acting as an inert or neutral transmitter, creatively and critically engaged with the Greek legacy over a long period of time, extending it, changing its emphases, reshaping it and incorporating new elements from outside.

The *Reconquista* brought about a coexistence of Latin

speaking (or, at least, writing) conquerors and Arabic speaking locals, generating a requirement for dialogue and, accordingly, for translations and translators. From the thirteenth century on, translation into Latin was increasingly done directly from the Greek. Prior to this, however, from the tenth-century translations of information concerning the astrolabe to the comprehensive alienation of knowledge that fuelled the intellectual transformation that Charles Homer Haskins termed the 'Renaissance of the twelfth century', Europe (or what was to become Europe) principally derived its scientific and philosophical advancement from its exposure to the Arabic tradition. Under different circumstances, things could have been otherwise – after all, the Greek texts had theoretically been available in western Christendom all along. As Haskins again put it, however, the Latin world '*could* have got much Greek science in this way, but for the most part it *did* not'.

Some scholars have attributed the European Renaissance and (by implication at least) the bulk of global modernity beyond it to Islamic inspiration, while others have dismissed such claims as emanating from naive enthusiasm, Islamic conviction or both. The non-committed have occupied a surprisingly narrow stretch of middle ground. Through all this, the integrity of the Islamic Other has remained robust, since almost no-one has problematised the process whereby the substantial commonalities between Islamic and Western discourse have persistently been erased in favour of a stark and mutual contrariety (a notable exception is the work of Maria Rosa Menocal). Focusing on the commonalities linking Islam and the West is at least superficially at odds with the stress on otherness that runs through Edward Said's *Orientalism*. Incommensurability does not plausibly account for the intensely specific virulence that has animated Western discourse on Islam. Islam gets under – more accurately, is already under – the skin of the West. The two have never been separate after all. Not only do we share a book, but Muslims have had the blasphemous temerity to find our Saviour deficient from within and to claim that an impostor has furnished them with the remedy. Pagans, savages or barbarians are merely ignorant; they cannot blaspheme.

Nor can they frustrate the coming of universal Christianity. They are safely Other. To appreciate the intensity of Western discourse on Islam, we should recognise it as not simply a species of undifferentiated Othering, but as a quite specific suppression of sameness. This consideration further underlines the historical contingency of the convergence between European Islamophobia and Hindu communalism, whose history is not marked by this particularity of European discourse.

Mughal to British

In the wake of the Clive's victory at Plassey in 1757 and the subsequent transfer of the Mughal right to administer and tax (*diwani*) to the East India Company in 1765, the political and economic bases to Muslims' marginalisation were spatially correlated in a general shift whereby major foci of power and learning followed the gravitation of economic activity to the British centre. The formative years of the British regime saw Muslims generally left out of the economic, political and cultural boardrooms of the colonial interchange.

As a Hindu *bhadralok* (member of the urban elite) steeped in Muslim culture, Rammohun is, therefore, a transitional figure who still evinces a confluence that would be emphatically undone in later colonial discourse. Born into a Mughal court and dying in England, Rammohun even exceeded at being transitional. In between, his career encapsulated the sea-change going on around him. After a period of youthful travelling which seems to have included some formal Islamic training at Patna, he accumulated considerable wealth through commercial dealings with

British interests and took on a number of financial and estate management posts with British employers, in particular John Digby.

In 1815, more than ten years after the publication of the *Tuhfat*, he settled in Calcutta, where he took up the tireless and multilingual public attack on corruptions and abuses for which he was to become renowned, rapidly antagonising Hindu orthodoxy by translating sacred writ into popular and even foreign languages. On the basis of his reading of the Hindu (which, for him, meant Vedantic) canon – a monotheistic, rationalist and socially reformist construction of sacred writ that strikingly resembled that of the European Orientalists – he launched a campaign to clean up Hinduism, singling out polytheism, idolatry and *sati* (burning widows alive) for particular attention.

In contrast to European critics of contemporary Hinduism, however, Rammohun was even-handed in his denunciations, applying the same standards to Christian practices as he did to Hindu or Muslim ones. In my view, the adroit switch whereby he repeatedly held British institutions accountable on their own terms represents one of the formative moments of Indian nationalism. Accordingly, while he so admired Christian teachings that he learned Greek and Hebrew in order to translate the Gospel, his resultant *Precepts of Jesus* contained only the moral and social teachings, omitting the miracles, divine incarnation and other supernatural machinations that he regarded as irrational and absurd in popular Hinduism. Consistently, rejecting the Christian Trinity and Hindu polytheism alike, he set up the first public unitarian association in the world (the Atmiya Sabha, soon to develop into the Brahmo Samaj, whose influence on the nationalist movement would be disproportionate to its numbers) to which he attracted, among others, the Scottish evangelist William Adam (who thereby became known among the European community as the second fallen Adam!). In this and many other regards, Rammohun's public career articulated the characteristically nationalist demand for Indians and Europeans to be subject to a common set of rational universal conditions.

The decade that intervened between the appearance of the *Tuhfat* and the commencement of that public career has led to the *Tuhfat*'s being seen as disconnected from Rammohun's historical mission. In consequence – and much more significantly – the genealogy of Indian nationalism is disconnected from the Indian Islamic tradition. As we shall see, however, there was no rupture between the *Tuhfat* and Rammohun's later programme. The decade in question was probably taken up with such mundane but demanding distractions as the making of money and the learning of English.

The Tuhfat

Rammohun's object in the Tuhfat is an 'enquiry into the truth and falsehood of various religions', an undertaking which has had him dubbed the founder of a characteristically post-Enlightenment enterprise, the science of comparative religions. Again and again, in impeccably rational-empiricist style, he opposes the dead weight of unreflective habit (fostered by those with a vested interest in the maintenance of traditional institutions) to the pristine endowment (intuition, reason, sensory experience) which affords humanity the ever-present possibility of true belief ('Oh God give me strong power for making distinction between habit and nature'). True belief is attainable 'without instruction and guidance from anyone simply by keen insight into, and deep observation of, the mysteries of nature'. These capacities are manifest and irrepressible, as evidenced by the fact that people everywhere and at all times acknowledge 'the existence of One Being', even though they conceptualise that Being in different ways. Despite this, however, divergent concepts of the attributes and requirements of the One Being ('an excrescent quality') engender sectarian conflict. In common with the philosophies, the Tuhfat attributes distortions of the truth to priest craft, the founders of religion being the 'first class of deceivers', who exploit the credulity of the common people by claiming miraculous or supernatural corroboration for their missions.

Once their followers have accepted illogical or impossible beliefs, the way is open for their tolerance of correspondingly baneful social practices. Pre-eminent among such illogical beliefs is idolatry, which Rammohun excoriates tirelessly. He is also concerned to discredit miracles, noting dryly that people are less gullible when it comes to concerns worldlier than religion. Where phenomena defy human understanding (as in the cases of 'many wonderful inventions of the people of Europe and the dexterity of jugglers') then intuition would prefer to attribute the failure to the limitations of our own understanding than to 'some impossible agency inconsistent with the law of nature'.

Whether in the Tuhfat or in his later works, Rammohun's writings only make consistent sense when they are read in relation to a constant set of strategic ends. Throughout his career, his sovereign end was equating monotheism with social benefit. So far as monotheism is concerned, Rammohun's problems start with the Tuhfat's founding premises. For it is either the case that acknowledgement of the One Being is universal or that illogical beliefs are producing polytheism and idolatry, but surely not both. Indeed, if it really were the case that monotheism was general, the Tuhfat would not have had a problem to address. Thus the appeal to popular sagacity which underlies the claim that monotheism is generally observable is starkly at odds with the Tuhfat's contemptuous reference to the 'Muquallids or common people following that religion [idolatry] by blind imitation'.

The point is not, of course, to critique the Tuhfat but to show that its inconsistencies are consistently motivated by Rammohun's pedagogical ends. Where they conduce to social benefit, for instance, religious beliefs that cannot be substantiated by either observation or reason are nonetheless excused the charge of illogicality. Hence irrational beliefs in souls and after-lives are to be excused in view of the restraining fear that they exercise, whereby people 'refrain from commission of illegal deeds'. On this basis, even the founders of religion need not all be deceivers (Rammohun, after all, was later to become one himself). It depends on whether or not their teachings conform to Rammohun's particular version of the truth.

This nexus in the Tuhfat's thinking – the necessary interdependence of dualistic monotheism and social welfare – lies at the heart of the difficulty that Rammohun was trying to overcome in 1804. Associated with the link between monotheism and social welfare is Rammohun's dismay at the cruelty and corruption occasioned by religious sectarianism, which anticipates the Brahmo Samaj's linking of theistic universalism with social harmony. Similarly, as noted, Rammohun's desire to refute prophecy and revelation while privileging particular canonical traditions prefigures his selective invocation of the Vedanta. The Orientalist narrative was inherently cyclical: a golden age had given way to an era of corruption from which redemption now offered itself. Given the Edenic structuring of this narrative (innocence – fall – redemption) the extent of its distribution through Western discourse is hardly surprising. By the same token, nor is it surprising that it should also structure Islamic discourse. In bringing together questions of reason, revelation, tradition and social welfare within an Edenic framework (founding truth – distortion – return to truth) the Tuhfat was conforming to a pervasive model. These Tuhfat themes continue to preoccupy Rammohun through his post-1815 writings, where they have been held to testify to a Christian and Utilitarian influence. I am not suggesting that the later Rammohun was unaffected by imported ideas – given the extraordinary historical foment in which he found himself, this would be unthinkable.

Nonetheless, a reading of the Tuhfat shows that the principles of his Anglophone ideology were already formulated before he could have been significantly exposed to such influences. In other words, Rammohun's endorsement of foreign doctrines arose from their concordance with a position that he had previously developed rather than from their novelty. Moreover, the Tuhfat treats issues and themes which had been extensively discussed in Indian Islamic disputation. Rammohun's characteristic arguments were recognisably drawn from this indigenous tradition, which had been developing in India for the better part of a millennium.

Quite apart from these considerations, the idea that he could have been familiar with English writings in 1804 is rendered implausible by John Digby's account of the timing of Rammohun's acquisition of English. By 1801, he 'could merely speak it well enough to be understood on the most common topics of discourse, but could not write it with any degree of correctness'. His sustained study of English appears to have commenced as late as 1809, when he became Digby's dewan (administrative agent) in Rangpur. Rammohun's own anonymous account clearly dates his acquisition of English as subsequent to the Tuhfat (and, incidentally, affirms the Tuhfat as a precursor to his engagement with Christianity): Rammohun Roy; who, although he was born a Brahmin not only renounced idolatry at a very early period of his life, but published at that time a treatise in Arabic and Persian against that system, and no sooner acquired a knowledge of English, than he made his desertion of idol worship known to the Christian world by his English publication.

Rammohun's association with Fort William College from 1801 to 1804, together with commercial activities that brought him into regular contact with East India Company servants, have been held to have been adequate for imparting a familiarity with Western philosophy and ethics, but his lack of an adequate command of English makes this unlikely. Moreover, Colebrooke's landmark Essay On The Vedas, from which Rammohun is alleged to have derived his later enthusiasm for the Vedanta, was not published until 1805 – i.e. after the Tuhfat – so the monotheistic and socially benign principles that he was to divine in the Vedanta were certainly not new to him. Indeed, his most intense study of Hinduism would appear to have taken place at the same time as he was mastering English – in Rangpur, after 1809, in association with Hariharananda Tirthaswami. In sum, therefore, the evidence renders any significant Western input into the Tuhfat implausible.

Previously indicated some of the major lines of transmission whereby, mutatis mutandis, the Hellenistic legacy in Islam 'was also incorporated into the Mughal theatre of Islamic civilization, where the young Rammohun, whose Brahmin father was a Mughal courtier, came to imbibe it as a central component of his polyglot education'. Of particular note is al-Shahrastani's Kitab al-milal wa'l-nihal, which was widely read in late eighteenth-century India, together with the teachings of Shah Wali-Allah of Delhi and his son Shah Abdul-Aziz. With more specific reference to Rammohun's immediate milieu, the Persian Dabistan Mazahib (conference of religions), which was inspired by religious debates that had taken place at the court of the ecumenically-inclined Mughal emperor Akbar, is significant. The Dabistan was well-known among Islamic scholars in eighteenth-century Calcutta. Maulavi Nazr Ashraf of the Sadr Diwani Adalat, whom Rammohun would have known, edited the first printed edition of the Dabistan. Francis Gladwyn had translated the first chapter into English in 1789. The rest of the work was not translated into English until 1843, ten years after Rammohun's death (Anthony Troyer, one of the translators of the 1843 edition, had known him personally).

The Dabistan is devoted to comparative discussion of religions, including Islam, Hinduism, Judaism, Christianity and others. So far as Rammohun is concerned, the most striking section occurs towards the end of the work – in the third volume – where Akbar's Ilahi [personal faith] is represented by a philosopher who engages in disputation with, among others, a Muslim, a Christian and a Brahmin. The Dabistan's philosopher thus took on adversaries almost identical to those whom Rammohun was later to engage.

Whether or not Rammohun was directly indebted to the Dabistan, however, the point at issue is the availability of an indigenous discourse rather than his personal relationship to it.

Where intertextualities are concerned, it is difficult to nail down particular influences from within a complex and evolving world tradition with any degree of confidence. It has been asserted that the major Islamic influence on the Tuhfat was the Mu'tazilite school (or heresy) which flourished in Baghdad and other centres from the eighth to the eleventh centuries of the Christian era. The Mu'tazilites championed the primacy of reason and freedom of the will, maintained the strictest interpretation of monotheism and denied the eternity of the Qur'an. They also insisted that their beliefs conduced to a just social order. The Mu'tazilites would thus seem to present a plausible precedent for Rammohun's central contentions (though his concept of social justice was at stark variance to theirs). But there is no reason why he should have lifted his ideas from one Islamic source alone. Rather, the premises and concepts which animate the Tuhfat recur throughout Islamic disputation. To illustrate the manifest general influence, it is hard to avoid arbitrariness. I happen to find greater resonance between the writings of al-Razi and the Tuhfat than I do between the Mu'tazilites and Rammohun's text, but this is not to say that this influence was necessarily formative either.

Al-Razi's attitude to knowledge was consistent with utilitarianism. He valued knowledge in proportion to its practical worth. The three means whereby he ensured the reliability of knowledge were the same as those of the Tuhfat – reason, intuition and authentic tradition. Consistently with this, al-Razi valued treatises on astronomy, logic, geometry and medicine more highly than sacred works, even than the Bible and the *Quran*.

These sentiments not only recall the Tuhfat. They also harmonise with the controversial letter on education that Rammohun was to write to Lord Amherst nearly twenty years after the Tuhfat was published. In this letter, Rammohun recalled the 'sanguine hopes' that money earmarked for an educational institution would have been 'laid out in employing European gentlemen of talents and education to instruct the natives of India in Mathematics, Natural Philosophy, Chemistry, Anatomy and other useful Sciences'. Since a traditional Hindu school had been chosen instead, one like those that already abounded in India to no social advantage, Rammohun complained that 'This seminary... can only be expected to load the minds of youth with grammatical niceties and metaphysical distinctions of no practicable use to the possessors or to society.'

These sentiments, which are clearly in accord with the views of al-Razi and others like him, also recall the split that Partha Chatterjee has shown to haunt the articulation of Indian nationalism. For Rammohun would have plenty of time for metaphysics in other contexts. But metaphysics belonged in the inner world of Indian culture and spirituality, a world that was quite separate from the outer world of material advancement that it was proper for Europeans to make available to Indians. Al-Razi was familiar with Indian science, which he employed in his medical practice. The traffic was not one-way. Further, while al-Razi himself may not have attracted widespread support, his works were extolled by al-Buruni, whose writings on India secured him continuing attention there.

The correspondences multiply. Half a millennium after al-Razi, the aforementioned Shah Abdul-Aziz exhibited a split attitude to the British which also anticipated Rammohun's. As observed, Rammohun was to treat traditional Sanskritic learning as an internal Hindu matter, demanding that the British should not involve themselves with 'useless' (in material-scientific terms) metaphysical concerns but should provide a progressive Western education.

Similarly, Shah Abdul-Aziz issued a fatwah declaring land occupied by the British to be daru'l harb (infidel territory) whilst simultaneously permitting the study of English and extolling British achievements in arts and industry. This ambivalence prefigures the division in the Indian Muslim elite, embodied in the Deoband and Aligarh schools, which corresponded to the division in Brahmo Samaj ranks that David Kopf has attributed to Rammohun's own split approach.

In short, one could go on citing correspondences indefinitely. Persistence is ultimately unnecessary, however, since the Tuhfat itself explicitly and abundantly declares its Islamic orientation. The issue is not the Tuhfat's Islamic credentials, which can hardly be doubted, but its continuity with Rammohun's anglophone campaign of reform as that was conducted in texts that he published after settling in Calcutta in 1815.

English writings

The premises that dominate Rammohun's English

writings are precisely those that had earlier dominated the Tuhfat. Still pairing monotheism and social utility, his later publications repetitively champion reason and sensory experience as grounds for discrediting institutionalised traditions and furthering his own brand of sacred writ in a manner wholly conforming to the Tuhfat's argumentation. Accordingly, while regularly citing Hindu authorities in support of his contentions, he is careful to establish that the doctrines which he associates with these authorities are both rationally sound and socially beneficial:

> I agree in the first assertion, that certain writings received by the Hindus as sacred, are the origins of the Hindu law of inheritance, but with this modification, that the writings supposed sacred are only, when consistent with sound reasoning, considered as imperative.

As in the Tuhfat, distortions of scripture are promoted by leaders of religion, who prey on the ignorance of the populace. Institutions sponsored by leaders of religion foster division and war between people, 'everlasting dissensions' are being occasioned by their conflicting interpretations of original truths. Not only do the leaders of religions remain the first class of deceivers, but the Tuhfat's positive formula for the attainment of true belief remains the same. Thus the induction from nature whereby the Tuhfat argued that God's existence was inferable by everyone is ascribed to Vyasa's position in the Vedanta, which explains 'the Supreme Being by his effects and works, without attempting to define his essence'. Accordingly, divine truth is not the preserve of any single creed. That this rules out miracles is presupposed in the selection criteria of the Precepts of Jesus and explicated in the Appeals in their defence: 'Had his doctrines of themselves made that due impression, the aid of miracles would not have been requisite, nor had recourse to.'

To substantiate his claim that all religions are monotheistic, the later Rammohun returns to the Tuhfat's empirical premise: in China, in Tartary, in Europe and in all other countries, where so many sects exist, all believe the object whom they adore to be the Author and Governor of the Universe; consequently, they must also acknowledge, according to their own faith, that this our worship is their own. Rationally unsustainable eschatologies are excused in the English writings on grounds that are familiar from the Tuhfat: The virtues of this class [i.e. peasants or villagers] however rests chiefly upon their primitive simplicity, and a strong religious feeling which leads them to expect reward or punishment for their good or bad conduct, not only in the next world, but like the ancient Jews, also in this.

Similarly, Rammohun's regard for Christian ethics, the single issue around which the allegation of Western models is strongest, is expressed in the Introduction to the Precepts of Jesus in terms which are pure Tuhfat: a notion of the existence of a supreme superintending power, the Author and Preserver of this harmonious system... and a due estimation of that law which teaches that man should do unto others as he would wish to be done by... The former of these sources of satisfaction, viz, a belief in God, prevails generally; being derived either from tradition and instruction, or from attentive survey of the wonderful skill and contrivance displayed in the works of nature... [the latter]... moral doctrines, tending evidently to the mainten-ance of the peace and harmony of mankind at large, are beyond the reach of metaphysical perversion, and intelligible alike to the learned and to the unlearned. Where Christianity is concerned, though Rammohun values the connection between religion and good works, he is not prepared to overlook offences for which he criticised other religions in the Tuhfat. Thus he condemns Christian sectarianism as well as its miracles and paradoxes. In common with Muslim theologians, he asserts that Trinitarianism is a later corruption of an originally monotheistic creed, in one place attributing the origin of Islam to this corruption. He compares the Inquisition and witch-burning to sati. In short, he holds Christianity to account on its own terms – a tactic which, as I contended above, was formative for Indian nationalism.

In this light, we need to consider why Rammohun should have chosen Christianity as a vehicle for his ideals in his English writings, especially since Islam was equally compatible with them. He testified to studying Euclid and Aristotle from Arabic sources. Moreover, not only did he dress, eat and even, it seems, marry in a Muslim manner. He commended Muslims, along with Sikhs, Christians and the Kabir Panth, as renouncers of idolatry, he characterised the idea that Christ personified the mercy of God as a Muslim concept, he acknowledged the monotheistic purity of Islam, he noted that, in contrast to the divisions within Hinduism, Muslims observed one homogeneous and harmonious social order, and, in evidence to a select committee of the British House of Commons, even suggested that there were more honest Muslim lawyers than Hindu ones.

In these connections, though, he was addressing a predominantly English audience, so Christianity was the appropriate strategic idiom for him to adopt. Furthermore, given the effective eclipse of Mughal rule, Islamic discourse was marginal to colonial power. In Muslim dress, Rammohun's universalism might have appealed to munshis, but no-one else would have noticed. Since this is precisely the fate that had befallen the Tuhfat, it is no accident that he should have started to learn English a short time after its publication. One could go on producing examples of the co·icord-ance between Rammohun's English writings and the Tuhfat but it hardly seems necessary. A difficulty in presenting this argument is that a reading of Rammohun's corpus bears it out so consistently that substantiation becomes a labouring of the obvious. Thus we turn now to the historiography, considering some salient examples of a pervasive cross-factional consensus whereby Rammohun's career has served to effect a rupture between Indian Islam and the enunciation of Indian nationalism.

Polar History Writing

Traditional histories of the emergence of Indian

nationalism conventionally counterpose Christian Europe to Hindu India, an exclusive pairing that admits a number of variations. The predominantly literary quality of the model of the Brahmannical/Christian encounter excludes the unlettered discourses of debt-bonded subalterns. It also effaces the generality of Muslims. In particular, the image of British foreigners taking over from Mughal foreigners suggests that Indian Muslims had somewhere to go back to. It does not matter where. Their effective disappearance is the practical outcome.

The same exclusion operates in a variety of historiographical guises. Some are obvious. It is only to be expected, for instance, that a Christian account should play down the consequence of Islam and emphasise that of Christianity. Sophie Dobson Collet's The Life and Letters of the Raja Rammohun Roy was a pious exercise designed to demonstrate the virtues of a colonial subject to an English readership. It remains the most widely cited secondary source on Rammohun.

Collet did not question the Tuhfat's manifestly Islamic provenance; she simply discounted its significance for Rammohun's later career. Nonetheless, as a Unitarian convert to Trinitarian Christianity, she remained able to acknowledge that it was 'indubitable that Rammohun always retained a large amount of sympathy with Islam for the sake of its cardinal doctrine of the unity of God, and that he warmly appreciated the good which had thence resulted in counteracting Hindu idolatry'.

Though a Hindu nationalist is as likely as a Christian to discount Islam, the situation is complicated by Rammohun's having a foot in two camps – how to relegate the Muslim part without jeopardising the nationalist part? This dilemma found serial realisation in the work of Romesh Chandra Majumdar, the doyen of Hindu-nationalist historians. Majumdar consistently stressed Hindu/Muslim dividedness and cast Islam as antithetical to the nationalist ('freedom') movement. In keeping with this view, Majumdar divided British domination into two phases, a benign one (the suppression of Muslim power) and an oppressive, subsequent one. From a communal perspective such as this, it would be unthinkable that a major restatement of Hindu ethics should have sprung from Islamic precedents. Thus Rammohun must have got his ideas from the West. Majumdar did not shrink from iconoclasm; this made Rammohun the first great comprador.

Yet this evaluation marked an extraordinary turnabout. Ten years earlier, in his History of the Freedom Movement in India, Majumdar had represented Rammohun as the 'first and best representative' of the new spirit of rationalism. In a manner reminiscent of European Orientalism, the earlier Majumdar had singled out Rammohun's opposition to 'medieval' forces for particular credit, medieval and Mughal being readily interchangeable. Thus Rammohun could enlist British inspiration to rouse India from a period of medieval decay without unduly compromising the Hindu nation's credentials. Despite their incongruity, Majumdar's ambivalent versions of Rammohun consistently sustained a Hindu-nationalist agenda. Since the Mughals were no less foreign than their British conquerors, the early phase of British domination could figure as the lesser of two evils in a way that did not have to compromise nationalist memory. The contrasting depictions of Rammohun do not affect this outcome. All that changes is the periodisation: the earlier depiction makes him part of the benign phase of British rule, while, in the revised version, the same actions, displaced into its oppressive phase, become compradorship. Either way, Islam is excluded from a nationalist version of the colonial duality. The exclusion of Islam does not require a religious basis, however. A secular dichotomy – especially the modern liberal assimilation of East/West to traditional/modern – is no less solidifying within its poles. David Kopf's bifurcated title, British Orientalism and the Bengal Renaissance, belies his attempts to complexify the two parties to the colonial encounter.

For, although he went to considerable lengths to show how the category 'British' split up into conservative/liberal, Orientalist/Anglicist and so on (with the bhadralok correspondingly divided into orthodox/progressive, etc.), Kopf failed to avoid the familiar dualism of penetration and response. From its title on, Kopf's subsequent book, The Brahmo Samaj and the Shaping of the Modern Indian Mind, makes even grander claims for Rammohun's legacy. This book's manifest pretension is to the reconstruction of a quantity known as 'the modern Indian mind' from the evidence of a small association of Bengali bhadralok, without regard either to the whole of Muslim society or to the rest of the Hindu population (or, for that matter, to the rest of India).

In it, Kopf returns to the European division between Orientalists and Anglicists, reaffirming Rammohun's encounter with Orientalism as the model for the rest of the century (and, presumably, for the entire 'modern Indian mind'). Kopf's Orientalist-Anglicist controversy corresponds to Majumdar's chronological division of British colonialism. The era of Orientalist predominance, of which Kopf approves, accords with Majumdar's early benign period, while the ensuing Anglicist ascendancy is for both scholars a victory for racial suprematism. Regardless of their doctrinal differences, both require a division whereby British rule has an early, relatively benevolent phase, since they use this phase to graft Europe's ideological import onto a Hindu version of indigenous tradition.

The notion of colonialism having a positive initial phase is also stamped on Indian Marxism, where it has caused any number of problems. Without embarking on a resuscitation of the Asiatic Mode of Production, we should at least recall in this connection that the Marx of the New York Daily Tribune articles saw British incursion, for all its violent rapacity, as injecting the historical germ necessary to disrupt the stagnant balance of Indian society and let loose the dynamic tensions which would eventually propel India into the capitalist era and thence on to its own socialist revolution. In conformity with this perspective (and with his Comintern line that the revolution would flow from the colonies), the pioneer Indian communist M. N. Roy contended that the iron hand of British rule provided the objective conditions for an Indian act of emancipation, while Palme Dutt maintained that the 'objectively progressive' aspect of British colonialism was its destruction of village economies that had prevented people from rising above subsistence preoccupations.

In a colonial context, one of the drawbacks of orthodox Marxism is that the category 'class' is blind to ethnic differences. The religious and colour-coded nature of colonial domination seems incidental. Thus we should not expect that an Islamic increment should significantly affect a Marxist critique of bhadralok ideology. The issue is not the etymology of comprador thinking but its conformity with colonial relations of production. In a careful analysis of the material conditions of Rammohun's thought, S. N. Mukherjee did not erect the usual barrier between the Tuhfat, to which he attached considerable importance, and the rest of Rammohun's ideas. He also allowed the possibility of looking on Rammohun as a tantric opponent of Bengali Vaishnavism and/or as 'the last prophet of the Indo-Islamic syncretic movement carrying on the tradition of Kabir, Dara Shikoh [Akbar's son] and many others'. Ultimately, however, the dual encounter – in this case, East versus West as feudal (or Asiatic) versus capitalist – was bound to eclipse such heterodox inspirations:

Rammohun's faith in individualism was inspired by Western political philosophy, more particularly by the works of Locke and Bentham, but individualism was also part and parcel of the social, religious and economic aspirations of the Bengali middle class. Moreover, the social model of Rammohun – a competitive market society – corresponds to the social reality of Bengal in the early Nineteenth Century. Rammohun was impervious to Bentham (he was not). The point is, rather, that 'individualism' is not dependant on Bentham (read Europe). It can select other notations. For instance, Maxime Rodinson argued cogently that the Neoplatonic tradition in Islam provided a model for individualistic philosophy that was as capable as its Western-Christian counterpart of subtending an emergent local capitalism. The issue is important because the one-to-one correlation between 'market society' and certain European philosophers makes individualism (among other things) impossible without European invasion. This, in turn, subordinates Indian history to the global narrative of European capitalist expansion as surely as missionary ideologues subordinated it to the coming of universal Christianity. Mukherjee's account is built on what Partha Chatterjee terms 'the condition of discursive unity':

> This condition is nothing other than the assumption that the history of Europe and the history of India are united within the same framework of universal history, the assumption that made possible the incorporation of the history of India into the history of Britain in the nineteenth century: Europe became the active subject of Indian history because Indian history was now a part of 'world history'. In substantially ruling out an Islamic contribution to the enunciation of colonial nationalism, however, Chatterjee himself might be seen to have subscribed to a global incorporation. In his influential postcolonial account, which merits more extended consideration, Chatterjee scrupulously and regularly registers Indian nationalism's dependence on the exclusion of Islam.

Yet there is a tension between this acknowledgement and the structuring of his narrative. In his account, the predicament of derivation produced a powerful dual agenda. On the one hand, Indian nationalism aspired to the technical, material and political advantages that colonialism had made available; on the other, it sought to resist the colonisers' intrusions into native life. The outcome was a division into discursive domains that resemble the public and private spheres of feminist critique. Thus outer became to inner as material to spiritual, as universal to particular, as economic to cultural and so on, a trade-off whereby nationalists' rising to the colonial bait in the domain of science, economics and statecraft was counterbalanced by an aggressive particularism, an insistence on irreducible difference in the inner-family world of Bengali language, religion and culture.

For Chatterjee, this inner domain, which gave nationalism the autonomous difference from Europe that a self-conscious and self-producing national project required, was prerequisite to the development of political nationalism, conventionally dated from the founding of the Indian National Congress in 1885. This reversal of the received order of priorities enables Chatterjee to backdate the emergence of nationalism proper to the 1860s, which saw the development of a new, self-regulating internal realm of Bengali language and culture with the confidence to exclude Europeans. Though his prioritising of nationalism's inner realm enables Chatterjee to date nationalism from the aftermath of the Great Insurrection of 1857 (which the bhadralok had failed to support), it also installs a rupture between the preceding period of reform and the nationalist movement. Nationalist self-sufficiency is distinguished from Rammohun-style reform, which sought to regulate Bengali society by enlisting the support of the colonial masters. The problem here is that Indian Islam also lies on the other side of this rupture. Thus we should consider Chatterjee's periodisation.

As observed, what interests Chatterjee is not so much the separation of nationalism's two discursive domains as their mutual effects, the ways in which each 'has not only acted in opposition to and as a limit upon the other, but, through this process of struggle, has also shaped the emergent form of the other'. This dynamic mutuality leaves behind the static pairings – traditional versus modern, status versus contract, feudal versus capitalist, etc. – that colonial discourse has made familiar. Thus subalternity is not simply a feudal throwback, and the nationalist elite are more than merely an incomplete version of the capitalist moderne.

Rather, together and singly, in their ceaseless co-formation, they are historically specific. This interpenetration of the two poles, a Saussurian procedure inherited from Ranajit Guha, performs a crucial methodological function.

It is the basis on which the Subaltern Studies group insists that Hindu–Muslim antagonism is not some atavistic residue from a superseded era but an active constituent of colonial modernity. This structuralist element, shared with the earlier Foucault, is conducive to abruptness of periodisation (Chatterjee terms his version of Foucault's episteme shift a 'narrative break'). In before-and-after mode, Chatterjee reads Mritunjay Vidyalankar's history of India, published in Bengali in 1808, to show how the inculcation of European narrative forms modernised the historical consciousness of educated Bengalis. Mritunjay's narratology, which Chatterjee memorably dubs 'entirely pre-colonial', is shown to lack the distinguishing features of the first criterion of nationalist history writing, a consciousness of the nation as historical agent and of the historian as forming part of it. Rather, the agents in Mritunjay's chronicle are gods and kings.

Moving forward half a century, Chatterjee then finds the requisite national agency, and historians identifying with it, in Bengali textbooks of the 1860s and 1870s: History was no longer the play of divine will or the fight of right against wrong; it had become merely the struggle for power. The advent of British rule was no longer a blessing of Providence. English-educated Bengalis were now speculating on the political conditions that might have made the British success possible. This is no doubt the case, but consider the following statement, which could well be the implicit referent of Chatterjee's 'blessing of Providence'. It was made by a Bengali in an appeal to the King of England in 1823, around four decades before the origin of nationalist historical consciousness as Chatterjee dates it:

Divine Providence at last, in its abundant mercy, stirred up the English nation to break the yoke of those tyrants [the

Mughals] and to receive the oppressed natives of Bengal under its protection... your dutiful subjects consequently have not viewed the English as a body of conquerors, but rather as deliverers, and look up to your Majesty not only as a Ruler, but also as a father and protector. This appeal has been taken by Majumdar to show that Rammohun, who penned it, was so anxious to celebrate the replacement of the Mughals by the British that he repudiated India's Islamic inheritance. Yet it was actually a none-too-subtle serving of what his audience wanted to hear. The excerpt is part of an indignant demand that recently introduced press regulations be withdrawn. The flattering comparison between the British and the Mughals allows the regulations to be depicted as incompatible with the qualities that had enabled the British to defeat the Mughals in the first place. As Rammohun's strategy unfolds, however, the self-same comparison produces the possibility that continued abuses of British power would be resisted violently. In stark contrast to Mritunjay's version of 'Divine Providence', therefore, Rammohun's conduces to anti-colonial agency on the part of Indians. The initially favourable comparison with the Mughals being agreeable to his English audience, Rammohun goes on to suggest a corollary whereby much less pleasant consequences would follow if they continued with the press regulations – consequences which conspicuously involved conscious historical agency, including the establishment of independence on the part of the subjected:

The greater part of Hindustan having been for several centuries subject to Muhammadan rule, the civil and religious rights of its original inhabitants were consistently trampled on, and from the habitual oppression of the conquerors, a great body of their subjects in the Southern Peninsula (Dukhin), afterwards called Marhattahs, and another body in the Western parts now styled Sikhs, were at last driven to revolt; and when the Mussulman power became feeble, they ultimately succeeded in establishing their independence. As this example shows, Rammohun himself was not above tactically acquiescing in the characterisation of the Mughals as foreigners. A more important point is the extent to which his campaigning anticipates characteristics that Chatterjee confines to the second half of the nineteenth century. Moreover, might we not be forgiven for discerning a tacit admission on Chatterjee's part that the supposedly European-derived nationalist mode of historical memory, the one that was lacking in Mritunjay, might be found (if only we were allowed to look) in Persian and Arabic?:

> This [Mritunjay's] was the form of historical memory before the modern European modes were implanted in the minds of the educated Bengali. In Mritunjay, the specific form of this memory was one that was prevalent among the Brahman literati in eighteenth-century Bengal. What, then, was the form followed by Bengali Muslim writers? The court chronicles of the Afghan or the Mughal nobility are not of concern here because these were never written in Bengali. Or consider the following:

> Another source often acknowledged in the Bengali textbooks is the series called The History of India as Told by Its Own Historians... these eight volumes comprise translated [into English] extracts from over 150 works, principally in Persian, covering a period from the ninth to the eighteenth centuries. It was a gigantic example of the privilege claimed by modern European scholarship to process the writings of a people supposedly devoid of historical consciousness and render into useful sources of history what otherwise could 'scarcely claim to rank higher than Annals'.

The problem with this, of course, is that, having excluded Persian works from our concern, Chatterjee is not in a position then to reassimilate them to the entirely pre-colonial status that he assigns to Mritunjay. Not, that is, unless 'entirely pre-colonial' is a condition of discursive unity. Chatterjee nowhere argues, let alone shows, that Indian Islamic discourse in Persian lacked historical protocols to distinguish it from Mritunjay's epistemology. The periodisation that Mritunjay's missing modernity sustains requires suppression of the counter example of Rammohun Roy, whose narratology was as nationalist, on Chatterjee's own criteria, as was his establishment of that native self-improvement organisation the Brahmo Samaj. Despite their substantial differences, therefore, these various historical approaches agree on endorsing a recalcitrant Hindu/European binarism in which the two parties are contrapuntally homogenised. Whether or not the category 'nation' is altogether appropriate to this situation, transnational history's insistence on a wider global perspective provides a basis for unravelling such homogeneities. In its connectedness to Indian Islam, the Tuhfat is strategically situated in two senses. First, it represents a moment when colonial discourse is not yet fully established (in Raymond Williams' sense) – an interregnum, somewhere between thesis and antithesis but still short of synthesis, when the discursive elements of the colonial regime are still emergent. By identifying such moments, we can more clearly see what colonial discourse is structured to screen out. Second, it marks a space beyond the penumbra of colonial influence in which (proto-) nationalist discourse could be thought. In both respects, the case of the Tuhfat raises the question of the mechanisms whereby indigenous alternatives to European models became occluded.

In its various divisions – pre-nationalist period, early benign phase, etc. – the historiography touched on above has sought to quarantine an era in which Hindu and European discourses confronted each other as antithetical monoliths. The desire to graft the imported onto the local, both conceived as pristine, reflects an essentialist preoccupation with origins. Yet when it comes to origins, a Europe so riddled with transnational supplements is itself constitutionally derivative. Islamic Neoplatonism presents Europe with a formative derivation anxiety. In confronting Muslim India, Europe was also returning to its own repressed. By inscribing this return, we can begin to provincialise Europe.

Bibliography

A.H. Armstrong, ed., Classical Mediterranean Spirituality, World Spirituality 15, New York: Crossroad, 1989.

Anderson, H. and E. Foley, Mighty Stories, Dangerous Rituals, San Francisco, CA: Jossey-Bass, 1997.

Angelika Malinar, The Bhagavadgita: Doctrines and Contexts, Cambridge: Cambridge University Press, 2008

Annemarie Schimmel, Mystical Dimensions of Islam, Chapel Hill: University of North Carolina Press, 1975.

Armstrong, Karen. Buddha. New York: Viking Penguin, 2001.

Babin, P., The New Era in Religious Communication, Minneapolis, MN: Fortress Press, 1991.

Barnstone, Willis (Ed.), The Other Bible, HarperSan Francisco, 1984.

Barrett, David V., The New Believers: Sects, Cults and Alternative Religions, Cassell & Co: London, 2001.

Bowker, John (ed.), The Oxford Dictionary of World Religions, Oxford University Press: Oxford, 1997.

Bavinck, J. H., The Church between Temple and Mosque, Grand Rapids: Eerdmans, 1966.

Bruce, S., Religion in the Modern World: from Cathedrals to Cults, Oxford: Oxford University Press, 1996.

Burnett, David, World of the Spirits: A Christian Perspective on traditional and Folk Religions, London: Monarch, 2000.

Chan, Wing-Tsit, trans. and ed. A Source Book in Chinese Philosophy. Princeton: Princeton University Press, 1963.

Chandra, Lokesh, Iconography of the Thousand Buddhas, International Academy of Indian Culture: New Delhi, 1996.

Conze, Edward (translator), Buddhist Scriptures, Penguin Books:New York, 1959 (1981).

Creel, H.G., Chinese Thought: from Confucius to Mao Tse-tung, University of Chicago Press, 1953.

Dawood, N.J., (translated with revisions) The Koran, Penguin Books: NY, 1997.

De Bary, Wm. Theodore (ed.), Sources of Indian Tradition, Columbia University Press: NY, 1958.

Dominic Goodall, ed. Hindu Scriptures with New Translations, Berkeley: University of California Press, 1996

Donald S. Lopez, Jr., ed., Religions of China in Practice, Princeton Readings in Religion, Princeton: Princeton University Press, 1996.

Donald S. Lopez, Jr., ed., Religions of India in Practice, Princeton Readings in Religion, Princeton: Princeton University Press, 1995.

Eichhoefer, Gerald W. Enduring Issues in Philosophy. San Diego: Greenhaven Press, Inc., 1995.

Gitlin, T., The Whole World is Watching, Berkeley, CA: University of California Press, 1980.

Hiebert, R. E., D. F. Ungurait and T. W. Bohn, Mass Media IV: An Introduction to Modern Communication, New York and London: Longman, 1985.

Holm, Jean and John Bowker, eds., Human Nature and Destiny, London: Printer Publishing, 1994.

Jacob Neusner, Judaism as Philosophy: The Method and Message of the Mishnah, Baltimore: Johns Hopkins, 1999.

John Renard, Seven Doors to Islam: Spirituality and the Religious Life of Muslims, Berkeley: University of California Press, 1996.

Johnston, R., Reel Spirituality: Theology and Film in Dialogue, Grand Rapids, MI: Baker Academic, 2000.

Joseph Dan, Jewish Mysticism, 4 vol., Northvale, NJ: Jason Aronson, 1998.

Krishna Sivaraman, ed., Hindu Spirituality I: Vedas through Vedanta, World Spirituality Series 6, New York: Crossroad, 1989.

Kurtz, Lester R., Gods in the Global Village, Thousand Oaks, CA: Sage, 2007.

Lyden, John. Enduring Issues in Religion. San Diego: Greenhaven Press, Inc., 1995.

Malise Ruthven, Islam: A Very Short Introduction, New York: Oxford University Press, 2000.

Melton, J. Gordon, Martin Baumann, eds. Religions of the World: A Comprehensive Encyclopedia of Beliefs and Practices. Vols. 1-4. Santa Barbara: ABC-Clio, 2002.

Mircea Eliade, ed., The Encyclopedia of Religion, 16 vol., New York: Macmillan, 1987.

Ninian Smart, Dimensions of the Sacred : An Anatomy of the World's Beliefs, Berkeley: University of California Press, 1996.

Nouwen, Henri J.M. The Road to Daybreak: A Spiritual Journey. New York: Doubleday, 1988.

O'Flaherty, Wendy Doniger (ed. and trans.), The Rig Veda: An Anthology. Penguin Books, NY, 1981.

Paul Williams, Mahayana Buddhism: The Doctrinal Foundations, New York: Routledge, 2008.

Peter H. Van Ness, ed., Spirituality and the Secular Quest, World Spirituality 22, New York: Crossroad, 1996.

Peter Harvey, An Introduction to Buddhism, New York:

Cambridge University Press, 1990.

Renou, Louis, ed. Hinduism. New York: George Braziller, 1961.

Rinpoche, Sogyal. The Tibetan Book of Living and Dying. New York: Harper Collins, 1993.

Shakir, M. H., (trans.) The Holy Qur'an, Tahrike Tarsile Qur'an, Inc: NY, 1997.

Stephen J. Laumakis, An Introduction to Buddhist Philosophy, Cambridge: Cambridge University Press, 2008

Steven Heine and Charles S. Prebish, eds., Buddhism in the Modern World: Adaptations of an Ancient Tradition, New York: Oxford University Press, 2003.

Sushil Mittal and Gene Thursby, eds., The Hindu World, New York: Routledge, 2004.

Tu Weiming and Mary Evelyn Tucker, eds., Confucian Spirituality, World Spirituality 11, New York: Herder & Herder, 2002.

Warms, Richard, James Garber and Jon McGee, eds., Sacred Realms: Essays in Religion, Belief & Society, New York: Oxford University Press, 2004.

William A. Graham, David Burrell and R.J. McCarthy, eds., Al-Ghazali's Path to Sufism: His Deliverance from Error (al-Munqidh min al-Dalal) and Five Key Texts, Louisville: Fons Vitae, 2000.

William C. Chittick, Ibn Arabi, Makers of the Muslim World, Oxford: Oneworld, 2005.

William C. Chittick, Sufism: A Short Introduction, Oxford: One World, 2000.

Xinzhong Yao, An Introduction to Confucianism, Cambridge: Cambridge University Press, 2000.

Zaehner, R.C. (translation), Hindu Scriptures, J.M. Dent and Sons: London, 1966.

Index